Pat is one of the ageing population, the silent (or not) majority, who feel they have landed in a strange parallel universe. Not just because they can never find their specs or that they humiliate their kids every time they step on the dance floor, but because their whole heritage and ancestry has been rubbished, and their forefathers branded as 'misguided souls'.

Having been raised on the premise that God was an Englishman, or at least would definitely have spoken English, she wonders who decided all this?

WHATEVER HAPPENED
TO THE ENGLISH?

DEDICATION

To my dear father, BJP, who would have been bemused,
and to those who have put up with my ranting,
Baggy, Peewee, Sweepea, Kloeby, and Grumpy.

And Lest we forget –
To 'our boys' everywhere who keep the faith against all odds.

PAT REEAT

WHATEVER HAPPENED TO THE ENGLISH

AUSTIN MACAULEY

A CIP catalogue record for this title is available from the British Library.

ISBN 978 1 84963 046 7

www.austinmacauley.com

First Published (2011)
Austin & Macauley Publishers Ltd.
25 Canada Square
Canary Wharf
London
E14 5LB

Printed & Bound in Great Britain

ACKNOWLEDGEMENTS

To Tom Fallick,
with thanks.

Contents

IS IT ME?

"It is your civilization, it is you: however, much you laugh at it, you will never be happy away from it for any length of time. The suet puddings and the red pillar-boxes have been entered into your soul. Good and evil, it is yours you belong to it, and this side of the grave you will never get away from the marks it has given you".[1]

Defining the English has now become a much more complex matter. A list of terms ranging from reserved, polite, honourable and eccentric to arrogant, racist imperialists. They traditionally drank tea, played cricket and had a stoical approach to life, everything was 'not a drama'. Our celebrities included Robin Hood, King Arthur, Henry V, and Sir Winston Churchill to name but a few characters that I need to rely on for inspiration.

There was always a sense of pride in fair play with a mustn't grumble mentality, though the attitude towards 'Johnny Foreigner' became a point of contention. Kant astutely said: "The English do not despise or dislike other nations they just ignore them." So is this an accurate description of the English of today or just a thing of the past? Does Englishness have a future? Racked with guilt and self-flagellating about their role in the history of the world, are the English just putting their heads in the sand and hoping all will turn out for the best?

I've heard it said that the nearest you will get to a traditional English village, today, is in France. It is true that a Frenchman will jump into his French car, drive to his French holiday villa and drink French wine. An Englishman will jump into his Japanese

---

[1] George Orwell, 'England My England'.

car, holiday in a Spanish villa and consume Italian wine. Obviously patriotism for the English does not extend to the market place. With most top premiership teams now being brought up by foreign businessmen and many top English premier teams having very few Englishmen playing, what is going on? When the manager of the England team struggles to speak English and so do the players, is it too late for redemption?

In economics our balance of payments for international trade comprises of us buying foreign goods, and them buying out our companies. Seems fair. So has England and the English moved to the land of the dodo?

'I thought we'd eliminated them.'

But hang on I'm being too simplistic, you can't look at the English through one social group. What about class? Class is not exclusively an English phenomenon but just a way of defining the layers and structures of society. In America it's defined by wealth. In India it is by a caste system, which the English have been blamed for re-enforcing in their occupation of India. A debatable point. No wonder you're feeling concerned. Now that the caste systems of other nations have been imported here within the immigrant communities, the Government is looking at possible legislation to rectify this. Is everything our fault? The burden of guilt worsens.

Reality TV has become a new art form thriving on social and human conflict. When Big Brother's Jade Goody ranted at Shilpa Shetty, it was 'posh totty' versus 'common cah'. When 'white trash' was faced with the classy high caste Indian Bollywood actress the situation exploded. It brought two worlds together in a class conflict, and Jade was no Eliza Doolittle. Two women who would never have entered each other's spheres of being were thrown together in a simulated cage. When Shilpa failed to understand Jade's dulcet tones, mistaking whale (well) and looking bemused at her annunciation it was enough to drive an Essex girl mad. With two other females from similar class backgrounds feeling exposed, the combination was explosive and pack mentality took over. The cool self-control of the Indian upper class actress was enough to push the situation out of control. The outcome was predictable and proved to be a great commercial success with viewing figures going through the roof. The 21st century celebs who had just wanted to take the money and run had unwittingly moved into a drama of epic proportions.

The dilemma is that drama, as a creative art, allows the audience to remain at a certain distance from the conflict, and, enables the actors to just go home. When it is meant to be 'reality' it causes questions in the House of Parliament and the entertainers can no longer walk away.

Anti-bullying campaigners commenced Bullying on a mega scale and the naive starlets got worse than a bad critical press, they got death threats. The only winners were the TV producers and the press who had managed to manipulate the public to get maximum mileage. For a programme that had become increasingly boring, controversy had saved the day. The last taboo was not race but class. Jade's death ironically made her a heroine once again, but she didn't die laughing.

The average English football hooligan is not far removed from the Elizabethan foot soldier or the mob that turned up at local executions. The historical perception of the English lower class was raucous, bawdy, prone to fisticuffs and always ready to drink until they fell over. Ring any bells? When the Blair Government extended the licensing hours, they visualised a Parisian style café pavement society, late night supper and a glass of wine. Instead, should they have been shocked, when they got young men and women, with skirts up around their bottoms, the women that is, drinking themselves into oblivion and falling over in a pile of their own vomit? They needn't have. In the 18th century the paintings and engravings of Hogarth, of streets littered with drunks and scenes of gratuitous violence could just as easily be Southend when the clubs turn out. Hogarth held a mirror up to English society and his work portrays the tragic comedy of social disorder through social stereotypes. He flayed conspicuous consumption through satire and held the gate open for the arrival of Victorian values which ultimately saved the day.

At the end of the 19th century, the Church, the Temperance Movement and Methodism had gone a long way to providing the restraint which was needed to bring society back into line. In the same way the Puritans had followed the Elizabethans and the Victorian had pulled back from the Regency period. The reality is that 20th century social development portrays the continuous erosion and decay of Victorian social values by people who KNOW they know, best. Bring on the political elite.

For any 1950s child it was easy. We were taught that Mr Churchill epitomised dogged English determination. We happily enjoyed reading Enid Blyton and didn't even realise it was full of racist, sexist and classist issues. We did not see the significance of Big Ear's desires on Noddy, or the implications of Noddy being mugged by naughty gollywogs in the dark woods. In 2009 Noddy celebrated 60 years of being a top children's favourite. But now naughty Noddy has to be censored. This is probably so people with big ears will not be offended. At school we sang English ballads, patriotic songs, sea shanties and hymns. As for the terms to explain the things we didn't like, well, political correctness would have banished a large proportion of them.

But now things are different, we have the Scottish, the Welsh and the British. How bizarre. So where do the English go? The English had always found security in their institutions. So we have Parliament, that's a very English institution. But hang on, in the past 15 years the English have had a Government packed with Scottish MPs. Yet the Scottish have got their own Parliament as have the Welsh but the English Parliament is in fact British. Are you confused yet? If the Scottish and Welsh nationalists get there way they could be looking at the break up of the union but what about English nationalism? Well they tried to stop that by calling the English colonialist racists if they celebrated their nationhood or used their flag. But the English are now starting to use their flag particularly to celebrate the England football team. Ok so that is a problem.

And what about the Church of England? Well possibly "even God has now left the Church of England".

An institution that is so unsure of itself, its role and what it believes in, that it sways to and fro on the back of political correctness and is now as soft and fluffy as the Archbishop of Canterbury's facial hair.

Well it's no use fretting and retreating to your castles. Now that's a really English phenomenon. All Englishman need their bit of land. The French were baffled when a social political commentator in the 1960s commented that 'putting the English into flats would be the demise of the nation'. It was possibly true. Whether it's the castle or the gate, the moat or the front door, all Englishmen like to feel that they can close it and retreat to their sanctuary. Well if you do see an intruder trying to get in, the advice would be to hold the door open for them. If not, you could be justifying yourself in court, m'lord, against a member of a minority group, who is socially excluded and could end up suing

19

you for damages, if they happen to fall over in the process of robbing you!

The Royal family, well that's better, the Monarch is after all the English monarch, and historically the defender of the faith. The Queen is possibly our only hope. So our entire future is reliant on a Germanic octogenarian. Well at least the Queen does epitomise dedication to duty which is a very, English quality. But if the Queen dies, will the liberal establishment demand an end to English domination of Buck House, and implement an 'A' list? Could the European Union, who after all do want to end the English monarchy, demand a vote in Brussels?

So why bother with the English anyway, when some historians tell us we're nothing but a bunch of mongrels. Well steady on now. It is true that by 1066 England was a mixture of invaders largely Germanic, but by 1066 the population had stabilised and the national character was evolving. The Act of Union pulled together the great imperial nation, which was the workshop of the world and in control of a quarter of the land mass. The British society of the Victorian era controlled an empire and the British institutions, whilst also being controlled by the Scottish and the Welsh were seen as pinnacles of the British culture. This Island was held together by a strong culture of shared identity, values and faith. Society demonstrated cohesion. The English were happy to be part of Gt Britain because they saw themselves as the major player.

In the 1960s the English seemed to be consumed into a new age of Britishness. The flag of St George was not waved at the 1966 world cup final it was the union flag. England was the leader of the union. The English saw themselves as British, for pensioners this is still a concept, which they struggle to understand and gallantly bring out their union jack thinking it symbolises England. Union jack T-shirts and bags were proudly flaunted and London was the centre piece with its successful fashion and record industry. The English did not need to prove themselves they thought it was self-evident Britain was still great and the English were driving this. They were happy for the other parts of the union to be partners. The confidence of the 1960s was justified by the World Cup glory and the high world profile of the entertainment industry. Little did the English understand that they were on the ebb before the decline, when their own lack of national identity would be used as a weapon to shoot them with.

It was during this time that the flowering of liberalism seized the opportunity to slay the conservative establishment. The English were pilloried as post colonialist aggressors who sacked the world in order to line their own pockets. The great poets of a different age and attitudes like Kipling, Rupert Brooke even Browning, were pilloried, censored and ostracised for representing a view that was too patriotic and colonialist. They came from an age which, we were told, we had to forget because we were guilty. Britain was forced to move away from its past tradition of assimilating immigrants and being proud of its own culture and history. To the new liberal elite the English, in particular, were merely majority oppressors who had to do penance. Economic and cultural liberalism had arrived and the political elite, always anti-nationalist and pro globalists took control. The English were guilty because they were a majority group. The Scottish, who had played a dominant role in empire were off the hook, they were a minority. The age where any minority is a natural victim group and any majority are automatically the aggressors, had arrived.

In the age of multi-culturism the expression of English traditional values became synonymous with racism. This policy became policed by local and national bureaucrats. They had a mission to enforce state defined virtue and to promote racial ethnic and cultural differences. They stamped out the majority values which had held the UK together. The traditional use of comic satire, which had always kept politicians and bureaucrats from taking themselves too seriously, was dying under the strain of political correctness. The cultural defence of free speech at all costs, was censored and only minority groups had a voice.

So we turn to football, and get out the flags of St George. Forget it. Rumour has it that David Blaine complained that Wayne Rooney, in the 2010 World Cup, had less action in the box than him. Any Englishman watching the likes of the English football squad mouthing pitifully to the national anthem whilst players and managers from other nations pound their heart and shed tears, wonders what will become of a nation with no anthem, no day and no future.

The England rugby players fair a little better going at it with great gusto, but what are the crowd singing? Swing slow sweet chariot, what is that about? What's wrong with, Land of Hope and Glory (oops, mentions war and Jesus). Well, on a personal level, I would vote for 'There'll always be an England'. Well possibly it could be banned under the trade descriptions act. It could be that the only time the English will look at revisiting the national song is when God Save the Queen becomes the next gay anthem.

So the British liberal victim culture is now fully embedded. The Scottish want their own identity, which the liberal socialites have always supported, but they are now worried that this may now actually happen, causing the break up of the union. So Victorian values are almost totally destroyed, the national identity which had held this island people together is all but gone. The union is now slipping into disarray and the English have been forgotten (aren't they British?). They look slightly puzzled. The New Labour Government under 'call me Tony' had created a Britain that was purely a marketing model, merely a state of mind 'cool Britannia'. They fabricated a society by marketing clichés, and a strap line, not even Churchill would have been arrogant enough to do that. They needed a homogeneous national identity that was essentially British. The English were unnecessary. They had lost their pride and identity. Britishness could morph into and embrace multi-culturism and diversity which was very much more difficult for the English. Britishness could incorporate the multicultural society which they visualised, not Englishness, which was destroyed alongside Victoriana. Ultimately, victim hood had created a state of social paralysis.

So what of the English now? The Government having created a multicultural society are now in what they call a post multicultural period, having disintegrated the traditions, faith and values that once held society together, they are now desperately trying to re-brand a new society which fits their agenda. Gordon

Brown, was worried about being a Scot in an English Parliament (he should have been more worried about the Milliboys). He assured us he was happy for us to fly the union jack and re-establish our British nationality. Well thanks Gordon. But hang on the Scots have got their own identify, their own sporrans and kilts and their own parliament. Wait a minute so have the Welsh (not so happy about the sporrans), they can have a leek (dastardly English stereotyping of a minority group). But what about the English? David Cameron kept on about society being 'badly broken' and is trying to promote the need for common core values, without knowing what they are. Yet the history of England was banned from schools, the narrative Island story was taken away from our kids and they were left with 'Topics and themes'.

Now politicians harp on about 'our country' without understanding what country they are talking about. But Michael Gove is, thank goodness, trying to look at the loss of the narrative of our history, as all kids love a good story, and has turned to a history book that was written in Victorian times 'Our Island Story'.

So what of the English now? When a nation loses its pride it loses its personality which is an expression of its culture. W Scott Fitzgerald astutely said: 'personality is only an expression of confidence''. If you lose your confidence you lose your personality. The English are on their uppers, looking continuously back and relying on a range of clichés which only identify with a state of mind not a state of reality, and looking for a future.

Well certainly more of them are leaving the country. Since 2001, 120,000 per year have been setting up little Englands in places like the hills of Spain. Well fear not, let's have a few lines from some of our celebs to make you feel better.

Come in Robin Hood (oops no data). King Arthur, no words from him but I believe he's lurking in a cave somewhere asleep to be awoken by a bell when the English need him. Well I hope he's stirring. We can have a few words from our future Henry V talking to his pal Falstaff.

"These lies are like the father that begets them; gross as a mountain, open, palpable. Why, thou clay – brained guts; thou notty – pated fool; thou whoreson obscene, greasy tallow-keech."

Now come on Henry what about Agincourt, one of our greatest victories:

"I see you stand like greyhounds in the slips, straining upon the start. The games afoot; follow your spirit: and, upon this charge, cry – God for Harry! England and St George!"

Well that's rousing but the problem is Henry V was, apparently, a man of few words and, so historians say, actually said: "Come on let's go men." But never mind, the magic of the English Bard's words were enough to rouse Englishmen at any time and were appropriately used to rouse the nation during World War II. Which brings us to another English hero, Mr Churchill.

"We shall not flag or fail. We shall go on to the end, we shall fight in France, we shall fight on the seas and oceans, we shall fight with growing confidence and growing strength in the air, we shall defend our Island, whatever the cost may be, we shall fight on the beaches, we shall fight on the landing grounds, we shall fight in the fields and in the streets, we shall fight in the hills; we shall never surrender."

Well I only know that my mother told me that when as a teenager she heard that speech she was ready to go to the garden shed, get out a king size spade ready for any unsuspecting German to pop his head around their back door. Is that spirit still alive out there somewhere? Who knows. So my task is challenging, but let's explore these problems more fully and end this beginning with a quote from another writer who also grappled with the English, J.B. Priestly.

"The problem with making English plays about English people is that English people do not want to make a scene."

THE PROBLEM

"Our ancient culture was a forest that took a thousand years to grow and less than half a century to cut down. Now that the trees are all flattened, the people who massacred them find that they are shivering in a howling wilderness that they are powerless to restore to its former shape."[2]

So the demise of an English culture, which was homogeneous for a thousand years or more has gathered pace to such an extent that England as a national entity is in question. Up until quite recently history has always given the English a sense of themselves from Agincourt (Cry God for Harry, England and St George) to the Spanish Armada, the Somme and the Blitz. Even now the attitudes of our boys in Helmann Province are probably not that different from the troops the night before Agincourt or the Somme. They are still a relatively homogeneous group from this, now so called, multicultural nation.

But under the Blair Government attitudes towards 'our boys' became confused. British soldiers were not seen as having the status they once had as saviours of the nation. They were demoralised and unsure of their role in society. The military covenant was under threat. The bond between the people of the nation and its protectors, set up by Wellington came into question and the Royal British Legion had to campaign to get this clarified. Those who had a clear role in protecting the culture and way of life of the nation were under threat because no one knew what that way of life should be, or indeed what the culture was.

---

[2] P. Hitchens, *The broken compass*.

When British Muslims in Luton gate-crashed the celebration of our troops returning home it was a wake-up call. The Brown Government called for Union Jacks to be flying from all public buildings in an attempt to re-enforce the unity that they realised they had lost, and David Cameron ranted on about our 'broken society'.

'Come on Noddy the age of innocence is over...'

Hence those of a certain age were bemused to see what their forefathers celebrated as victories now demeaned. Frightened to speak out, and unsure of their role, those traditional barrack room boys, affectionately termed Taff, Jock, and Paddy have been put in the glasshouse and 'leapfrog' is now openly encouraged. The army bases within the UK are told to remove their union flags if they are operating in Muslim areas in order to not offend in their own country. Other nations fiercely guard their borders, and the French break every rule in the EEC book and get away with it. Feel victimised? So you should.

England started as a mix of conquest and integration with Celtic culture and this fusion in the land of England gave rise to a well-developed culture. Scotland, Wales and Ireland shared many of the values but had different aspects which they cherished. The Industrial Revolution changed some of this but the culture in the much larger towns and cities was not at odds with what had gone before. There was a sturdy self-dependency and mutual help was at a local or family level. The English culture was one that had its roots in how people naturally came together.

"To express the qualities that are peculiarly England's: the unity of England, effortless and unconstrained, which accepts the unlimited supremacy of Crown in Parliament so naturally as not to be aware of it; the homogeneity of England, so profound and embracing that the counties and the regions make it a hobby to discover their differences and assert their peculiarities; the continuity of England, which has brought this unity and this homogeneity about by the slow alchemy of centuries."

I'm going to argue that three main consequences have undermined the naturally evolved English culture. These are a liberal and chaotic approach to immigration, political correctness and the political elite's destruction of the working classes. When people from different cultures are assimilated they have the potential to change the culture. Previous bouts of immigration did not do this because they were relatively small and the immigrant groups came with the intention of assimilating and embracing the English way of life. This is still true in Scotland where Asians think of themselves as Scottish first. The legacy of Empire and the

27

politically correct multiculturalism has meant that some immigrant groups have come with no such clear intention and have then been encouraged to retain their distinctive identity, even language. A policy which is divisive but difficult to now rectify.

Whilst some London schools struggle with teaching to 80 different languages, a supply of transient Australian teachers are the only thing that keeps the schools open. Well at least that's one less culture to worry about. Welfare payments are designed to be non-discriminatory. This has had implications for the rate of immigration as potential immigrants can see little risk in coming while they find a job. After the July bombings the attitude did change but is confused, even chaotic. Ruth Kelly called for an end to multiculturalism, but when the fury died down Blair just fudged the issue hoping it would go away and the English just went back to pruning their roses.

The Blair Government's response was to bring in Tessa Jowells as Minister for operas, and to set up a Ministry for Social Cohesion, whatever that is. Cameron finally raised the issue again in 2011, possibly under pressure from European leaders.

The implications for the indigenous English have been even greater with the emergence of a welfare-dependent underclass whose social mores are certainly not aspired to by immigrants and who are loathed by the political elite who created them. New Labour's Economic boom was fuelled not by a miracle but by cheap immigrant labour and cheap credit, with both bubbles obviously going to burst. Whilst our own indigenous underclass live on welfare rather than low wages, the Government seem surprised that now, with three generations of welfare dependent, that they do not belong to a society which was always driven by the protestant work ethic, and is now driven by obtaining money by any means. The idea of universal benefits is mirrored in all aspects of life and the law, and the 'Left' in politics emphasize universal human rights. When there is a multicultural society the treatment of individuals by the State may well need principles not necessary in a single culture but universal principles are not tempered by centuries of experience or formulated locally. Without an overarching narrative from shared experience there is no way of resolving conflicts between different universal principles. So now crackpot judgements come down from on high and no one dare say " bollocks".

Intellectuals from all backgrounds have a vested economic interest in all of this: jobs for lawyers, sociologists, researchers and the illusion for politicians that they are doing some good. Yet democracy itself is now in question. With English issues now being voted on by Scottish and Welsh MPs and yet many Scottish issues only being voted on by Scottish MPs in their own parliament. Where is the democracy for the English? The political figures became so keen on 'cosying up' in the middle ground that the Liberals became muddled and half moved to the left (Greens) and half to the right (economic liberals). As they decided whether to dive to the left or the right poor Ming was unable to move quickly enough in either direction and was deposed.

Politicians are generally committed to saying sorry for things they didn't do, and not for things they did do. Gordon Brown invited Maggie Thatcher to Tea at Downing Street, presumably in order to seek approval for his prudent good housekeeping, as the 'canny' Scot that he always pretended to be. David Cameron panicked as his millionaires were lured away to work for the Labour Government. So he got on his bike to ride into the sunset and was followed by his Lexus carrying his bags. Is it any wonder that voters are confused. When Nick, Dave and Gord appeared on their presidential style TV debate Gordon had his fixed sneer, looked lovingly at Nick, and agreed with most things Nick said. Nick was busy remembering the names of everyone in the audience, so he could be seen as a 'good sort' whilst Dave looked a bit lost having just been de-poshed by one of Barack Obama's aides.

All this was very disconcerting for TV voters who were presented with a very confident Nick who seemed 'very nice'. Unfortunately for Nick, the following day the tabloids exposed some of his policies and he lost some of his charm. The problem is that Nick was seen as the anti-politician vote, probably because not many knew who he was. Well things got even more confusing as politics became a bit of a soap opera with the Nick, Dave and

Gordon X factor show. So the TV viewers decided to get out and vote but of course then many of them weren't actually allowed in to vote, and when they did get in there was not a sign of Nick, Dave or Gord on the ballot papers. Very confusing.

So politics is now about personality not policy. Hence single issue Campaigning is the new politics and the language of marketing pervades all areas, and slogans are the new truths. Ah let's have a slogan to change the world. Red Ken and his team did this very effectively years ago with London Transport. They changed it to 'Transport for London'. Well how more significant that sounds. The Royal Mail became 'Consignor' and then decided to change it back again. I suppose if you can't change what you should change you just change what you can. What's wrong with 'Go to Work on an Egg'. It's been banned. It sustained the children of the 1960s very well with no adverse effects. Yet even the 'Special One' (Jose Mourinho) was keen to use the egg imagery to describe his team. Now we're getting some serious hard boiled or scrambled theories.

The Church also got caught up in this approach with the 'Make Poverty History Campaign'. Why have a campaign slogan which must ultimately be unachievable. In the old days they would wear a hair shirt or sleep on a rock and at least look like they were suffering for the sins of the world. The Global poverty movement is distorting the picture on climate change and now new business is moving in to create carbon emissions trading, but more of that later.

With Greenism as the new saviour of the world and the politicians thinking that the average citizen is obsessed with it, everyone is jumping on the Chelsea Tractor bandwagon. Yet the reality is in the next 40 years, the two main issues are likely to be, the end of oil and a doubling of the world population. Obviously no 'marketing' term for them yet. And that's another thing, what happened to 'no drama Obama'? Having promoted the positives of deep sea oil exploration he started rushing around like a madman, stamping on necks and kicking arses. But then the tragic Philadelphia shootings took place, and his well rehearsed speech meant he again became the spiritual leader of the world. "Events my dear boy, events".[3]

Well now we've become obsessed with 'strap lines' that hide the reality of the problems. Why are they using jargon to sanitise criminal activity? 'Happy Slapping' (physical assault, usually on children by other children or teenagers). Joy Riding (stealing and possible criminal damage) Anti-social behaviour (usually vandalism, a very old term). Friendly Fire (incompetent, usually conscripted, American troops killing, highly trained British ones). These issues are much too complex to be dealt with by a slogan or strap lines in a society that believes that monetary support 'saves' and the welfare state 'cradles'. Poverty is getting worse and much of current western trade is fuelled from slave labour. It's great, go to a pop concert pay a couple of hours' wages to attend and feel cleansed in the process as you buy into benevolence megalomania and redemption from St Bob.

So whilst knife crime runs out of control, they are busy researching the 'bleeding obvious'. Too much food makes you put on weight. Too much sugar makes kids hyper. Take the contraceptive pill for too long and risks of cancer increase. Take it for a short time and the risks of cancer are decreased. Sussex University concluded, 8 hours sleep can be bad for the heart, 6 hours sleep is bad for everything and 7 hours is just right. The Government seem more concerned to protect our kids from salt than crime. As parents in London buy body armour to go under school uniforms and schools lease metal detectors, the Government tells us that statistics show crime is down. Crime may have receded for many adults, largely because they don't venture out onto the street, particularly, older people who are in a society that terrifies them. Nevertheless all the stats show that our teenagers, especially in the cities, have never been more under threat.

---

[3] Harold Macmillan.

So when Ed Balls was Education Minister, trials took place for 'Happiness classes' in schools to 'help cultivate the right attitude'. Other experts warn that this could 'depress pupils'. Well it's depressed me already. Now there's even a degree in 'Waste Management', to join the list of the other rubbish degrees.

The Green movement is being cultivated by every party and has become the religion of atheists giving them something to believe in when they have nothing else. So as I walk carefully along to minimise my carbon footprint I ponder about the businessman who contacted a Government Department to enquire about tax relief on carbon neutral projects and no one could tell him what the definition of carbon neutral was. Or the Prince with around 70 houses who wants to make a movie about Greenism. I'm sure one is not amused.

The English culture was always capable of being tolerant of deviations from its norms, was good-humoured and gave people a framework to live their lives. A sense of irony, satire and common sense have always been the salvation of the English. Yet when Harry Potter was rumoured to have been killed off by JKR, child line was put on red alert. But when Flipper was caught in that fish net off Cape Cod I just puckered up and carried on regardless in true English fashion. Soap operas have replaced real life for many people who seem to have moved into a parallel universe. When EastEnders decided to show a mad woman throwing herself in full wedding attire from a window onto 'Big Phil's' car, we're asked, at the end of the show "if we have any issues or concerns to ring a certain phone number".

A traditional English response should be to send the number of the nearest panel beater in Essex. It is a sense of proportion which has gone.

But it is a culture well worth keeping as well as still being the natural culture of the majority of inhabitants, including many immigrants who actually came to enjoy it. It might be too late, and not even desirable, to have it fully back but its best features are tried and tested. It will need individuals to mercilessly take the rise out of the pomposity of the new elite and to encourage zealotry to be defeated in any community where English common sense says that they have gone too far!

NATION HOODIES

There is a forgotten
Nay almost forbidden word,
...a word which means more to me than any
other...
That word is
"ENGLAND"[4]

So when did the national identity of the English come under threat? Paxman in his book 'The English' quoted a survey which was carried out in 1951 by 'The People Newspaper'. Geoffrey Gorer had the job of analysing the results and concluded that:

"The English are a truly unified people, more unified I would hazard, than at any previous period in their history. I found I was constantly making the same notes, what dull lives most of these people appear to lead and secondly what good people.!"

Yet whilst Alex Salmond is forging forward with the SNP agenda in Scotland calling Scotland 'a 'Nation' to go forward in the world', the English dare not mention nationhood for fear of being called racists. So why is this?

It is clear that our main institutions have been at the forefront of a fundamental drive away from the celebration of English national identity. The middle class elites have viewed Britain, and in particularly England, being the majority culture, as, by definition, racist and nationalistic. This attitude has made the country vulnerable to minority groups who have promoted their own culture and values whilst the majority indigenous population stood by, too scared to respond and overawed by the scale of the oppressors. The overwhelming tide of the liberal thought police

---

[4] Sir Winston Churchill.

made the majority culture seem to be illegitimate. Secular liberals, often from a Marxist background and political ideology, have now undermined many of our traditions and history. Even the civic role of prayers in Government and Councils prior to business is now under threat from those who want to eliminate this age old tradition.

So when did this eradication of English national identity start? Some feel that it was an outcome of the 1960s. This could be, difficult to prove as the old saying goes, if you can remember it you apparently weren't there. I believe that the 1960s was only the end of the process which started very much earlier. It was a distinct aim of the left-wing intelligentsia to destroy national identity so that 'universalism' could be established. Universalism is the concept that we are all the same and that issues can only be global not local or specific. This is a concept that proves very useful for politicians, as it means when they cock up they can't be blamed, 'it was global' nothing to do with me. This universalism is now expounded by those with Marxists backgrounds like Peter Hain, Red Ken and the Milliboys. When Marxism failed economically, these individuals turned their attention to universal culturalism in order to undermine the national identity and de-stabilise the establishment they had for so long despised. This movement was spotted by a famous, one time, Marxist, but an incisive realist, much earlier in 1941. George Orwell wrote in one of his social essays, 'The Lion and the Unicorn':

"The general weakening of imperialism, and to some extent of the whole British morale, that took place during the nineteen-thirties, was partly the work of the left-wing intelligentsia, itself a kind of growth that had sprouted from the stagnation of the Empire. It should be noted that there is now no intelligentsia that is not in some sense 'left'... Since about 1930 everyone describable as an 'intellectual' has lived in a state of chronic discontent with the existing order. Necessarily so, because society as it was constituted had no room for him. In an Empire that was simply stagnant...

"The intellectuals could find a function for themselves only in the literary reviews and the left-wing political parties. The mentality of the English left-wing intelligentsia can be studied in half a dozen weekly and monthly papers. The immediately striking thing about all these papers is their generally negative, querulous attitude, their complete lack at all times of any constructive suggestion. There is little in them except the irresponsible carping of people who have never been and never expect to be in a position of power. Another marked characteristic is the emotional shallowness of people who live in a world of ideas and have little contact with physical reality. Many intellectuals of the Left were flabbily pacifist up to 1935, shrieked for war against Germany in the years 1935-9, and then promptly cooled off when the war started. It is broadly though not precisely true that the people who were most 'anti-Fascist' during the Spanish Civil War are most defeatist now. And underlying this is the really important fact about so many of the English intelligentsia – their severance from the common culture of the country. In intention, at any rate, the English intelligentsia are Europeanised. They take their cookery from Paris and their opinions from Moscow. In the general patriotism of the country they form a sort of island of dissident thought. England is perhaps the only great country whose intellectuals are ashamed of their own nationality. In left-wing circles it is always felt that there is something slightly disgraceful in being an Englishman."[5]

The loss of the working class culture that held communities together, the work ethic, national self-belief, and the confidence in the fairness and morality of their institutions, has now gone. The English working class have been cut to the bone. They were thought to be too small to be important by Blair who wanted to cultivate the new liberal middle class. They were treated with contempt by Brown who was too arrogant to listen to anyone who did not have his views. There is now an underclass with no pride and the rest are middle class, floating with no roots. Our economic growth in the last 15 years has come from immigration which was

---

[5] George Orwell, 'The Lion and the Unicorn'.

used to keep down inflation by providing a steady source of cheap, non-unionised labour. Our growth was all in financial services with the decline in manufacturing and primary industries. The Trade Unions are more interested in PC issues, like equal pay, flexible working, crèche facilities and paternity rights, than protecting traditional jobs. Yet the old Labour Party owed more to Methodism than Marx. New Labour, are the Lawyers, the middle-class liberalists, they have no conviction other than to win the next election. The Tories and Liberals have the same drive, not conviction but just success at all costs. So we have the civil partnership of Nick and Dave at ease with each other, coming from very similar backgrounds, whilst the parties 'champ' uneasily at the bit.

And Tony is furious that Peter Mandelson stole his fire by getting his book out first, and it is reported that New Labour can no longer return to Blackpool, after it is said that Peter Mandelson went into a fish and chip shop when seeing a green concoction to the side of the chips said: "I'll have some of your guacamole as well please."

The social problems that have arisen out of a loss of national identity are now so severe that some individuals are daring to speak out. Even the national football team has been affected. Trevor Brooking raised this as an issue which needed to be resolved, long before the disaster of the 2010 world cup. With the increasing number of foreign footballers in the premier league, the standards of the English team are bound to diminish as English players struggle to compete with foreign stars who are purchased at massive cost. It's disturbing that the importance of the big premier sides seem to far outweigh the importance of the national English team. The issue of quotas of foreign players was put forward by the FA as an option. However, one official summed this up when he said: 'It's not about numbers, it's about attitudes and the issue is does it matter? Do we want, or indeed need, a national side or are the premier teams the main priority?" The situation is worsening with the academies now bringing in foreign youth players. It could ultimately mean that the majority of the English national team will be players from the Conference league.

The dilemma is that majorities, in the minorities rule culture, are seen as natural oppressors. The majority culture is seen as illegitimate because it is minorities that need protecting from majorities. Yet democracy is based on majorities and functioned effectively here for many years on the basis of tolerance for minorities.

Up until the last 30 years the English had no need to promote themselves or their nation it was all taken in a spirit of self-confidence. Back in 1941 the view was that, "when you come back to England from any foreign country, you have immediately the sensation of breathing a different air. Even in the first few minutes dozens of small things conspire to give you this feeling. The beer is bitterer, the coins are heavier, the grass is greener, the advertisements are more blatant. The crowds in the big towns, with their mild knobby faces, their bad teeth and gentle manners, are different from a European crowd".[6]

It is the English character that Orwell felt was worth preserving, whatever it is, and however we explain it.

"The gentleness of the English civilisation is perhaps its most marked characteristic. You notice it the instant you set foot on English soil. It is a land where the bus conductors are good tempered and the policemen carry no revolvers. In no country inhabited by white men is it easier to shove people off the pavement."

This is the England of the magazine 'This England'. It has a two million circulation and is based on the precept "for all those who love our green and pleasant land".

It is flowery, patriotic and gentle and it reminds me of the England of my childhood. This is in stark contrast to our current broken society where communities live in fear of 15 year olds with guns and knives. As the Government praises the fall in the crime statistics, the reality is that there is such low confidence in the police force that people do not even report crime and when it

---

[6] George Orwell, 'The Lion and the Unicorn'.

37

comes to serious crime those who are victims often live in fear of reprisals if they do. Children and teenagers are the ones who are most at risk in a society that limits their freedom of movement but gives them too much freedom of choice. That promotes all their rights but fails to re-inforce their responsibilities. That gives them no boundaries and expects them to operate with no values.

But what of the British? Is it Britain that has been destroyed or just England? Well the Government seem to want to promote Britishness to attempt to hold together a fragmented society. This is all a bit ironic as the SNP pushes for Scottish independence and plans its St Andrews Bank Holiday. Brown tried to convince the English that they needed a British day, whatever that is. The Welsh have an assembly, the Scottish have their own parliament and the English have nothing other than being part of the British parliament. Tam Dalyell first raised the issue of whether Scottish MPs constitutionally should vote on matters at Westminster, which only affected England. It became termed 'the West Lothian question'. This matter has still not come to a head but surely will do soon. For the English the reality is that they are now left with no anthem and no day. Hence the English more and more, wave their flags of St George in a desperate bid to belong to something which unites them.

This is very problematic for the English. This little Island, which at one point controlled a third of the world's land mass, felt they had done rather well and there was a certain pride. It was easier when the going got hot for the Welsh and Scottish to hold their hands up and say, "nothing to do with us we were victims too". The need to eliminate the English and to make them British is a political fear that the union is breaking up and the powers that be are desperate to hold onto some sort of unity, in a people which include large numbers of other cultures all vying for power.

English culture is distinct but it is a majority culture and hence a threat. It is true that 95% of the values of the English and the British in the past have been shared. The antagonism between the English, the Welsh and the Scots has ebbed and flowed throughout history. It would be common to hear a Scotsman say

38

that in bygone days Scotsmen decided to venture over the wall to go down and get some English Women but decided to bring back some cows instead. Or the Englishmen that said that a Scotsman in England was like a haemorrhoid, ok if he went back up but a pain in the arse if he stayed down. But again Orwell characterised the integral unity of this island.

"Somehow these differences fade away the moment that any two Britons are confronted by a European. It is very rare to meet a foreigner, other than an American, who can distinguish between English and Scots or even English and Irish. The sense of national unity is a substitute for a 'world-view'. Just because patriotism is all but universal and not even the rich are uninfluenced by it, there can be moments when the whole nation suddenly swings together and does the same thing, like a herd of cattle facing a wolf. There was such a moment, unmistakably, at the time of the disaster in France. After eight months of vaguely wondering what the war was about, the people suddenly knew what they had got to do: first, to get the army away from Dunkirk, and secondly to prevent invasion. It was like the awakening of a giant. Quick! Danger! The Philistines be upon thee, Samson! And then the swift unanimous action – and, then, alas, the prompt relapse into sleep."[7]

The Liberalist movement's impact has had a more severe effect on the English, than on other parts of the Union. It is the English that have lost the most. The Scottish were always more old Labour and haven't had the immigration. "You'll have had your tea then?" is still a good joke about their tightness." The Americans have had the Midwest, the rednecks as a bulwark against metropolitan correctness and liberalism and have been used to being a non- homogeneous but aspirant culture for a long time. As a Southern American congressman is reputed to have said: "If English was good enough for Jesus Christ then it's good enough for me."

---

[7] George Orwell, 'The Lion and the Unicorn'.

39

All this is very confusing for the English who always thought British was being English really. The waving of the Flag of St George at England matches is a very recent phenomenon. There was no need to wave the English flag, England was Britain. There was a definite arrogance here. But Britain was only ever a political concept to hold very different nations together. It is only in recent years that the English are starting to understand this.

Would Orwell be surprised to see our current society? I think not. He would have understood perfectly the current 'We' culture from those liberals who feel they are on a mission to save everyone from themselves and re-educate those who deviate from the current ruling elite. After all he did write about them in 1984.

Now with few intellectuals to challenge the prevailing orthodoxy and Big Brother, either unwilling or unable to tap into the mood of the nation, the English feel the need to promote themselves. They feel the national spirit ebbing away in front of their eyes and their forefathers turning in their graves.

The capital city of England, London is now known as a 'World Capital'. Does this mean it is the capital of the world and if so does England need a new capital? With Russian mafia now in control in London the original Londoners have taken flight to Essex. The situation is now that 40% of the London inhabitants are from ethnic minorities and it is one of the most dangerous places to live – where you are 40% more likely to get robbed, drug problems are higher than in any other part of the country and secondary school teaching has become a form of riot control.

I think the problem is that we English in the south used to be represented by what is now an endangered species the 'cockneys'. These individuals used to lurk around hostelries in the eastern part of London ready to pounce on and seize any unguarded piano which they then proceeded to abuse to accompany nationalistic community English singing. The songs that drifted melodically through the smoke filled spit and sawdust inns, included, 'There'll Always Be An England' (Ok So They Got That One Wrong), 'It's A Long Way To Tipperary' (Not Sure How English That Is) and the much loved 'Hokey Cokey'. This tune would be accompanied by grown adults cavorting around in a circle thrusting their body

40

parts about, in a lude manner and would usually involve large, but jovial, ladies exposing their knickers. I believe these creatures are now virtually extinct. How sad.

These people represented the national identity, all be it only in the south. The nationhood of the north had its very own identity and it all came together in cohesive harmony. What we had was a development of National belief, character, attitudes and behaviour which did not exist in isolation but as part of a heritage. It was an organic growth. It is still prevalent in the shires of England but has been lost to the cities.

"For the unbroken life of the English nation over a thousand years and more is a phenomenon unique in history, the product of a specific set of circumstances like those which in biology are supposed to start by chance a new line of evolution. Institutions which elsewhere are recent and artificial creations appear in England almost as works of nature, spontaneous and unquestioned.

"From this continuous life of a united people in its island home spring, as from the soil of England, all that is peculiar in the gifts and the achievements of the English nation."[8]

Yet a panel member on Radio 4, on Any Questions when confronted with the question of national identity stated: "The English are starting to want to be called English. They need to be re-trained to call themselves British."

Common sense has always been the saving grace of the English. From the philosophy of English empiricists to the irony and humour of satire. Satire was always a device for saving humans from themselves. It stopped politicians and other prestigious figures from taking themselves too seriously. Sadly this seems to have been killed off by political correctness. Satirist of the past like Jonathan Swift mocked all in society, he even mocked mankind itself, quite rightly. In Gulliver's Travels

---

[8] E. Powell –St. Georges Day Speech, 23rd April 1961.

politicians were seen cavorting on tightropes to please the powers that be, and wars were waged over which end of the boiled egg should be cracked before eating. Ultimately man was exposed as being a degenerate creature and it was horses that ultimately ruled the world. Nothing wrong with that. He said he wanted to "vex the world rather than divert it".

In his essay 'A Modest Proposal' he put forward the proposal of an eminent professor trying to resolve the food shortages in Ireland.

"I have been assured by a very knowing American of my acquaintance in London, that a young healthy child well nursed is at a year old most delicious, nourishing and wholesome food, where stewed, roasted, baked or boiled, and I make no doubt that it will equally serve in a fricassee or a ragout."[9]

Look out childline! The very point of satire was to be politically incorrect and to shake up the received opinions to look at issues from all perspective and above all to get their feet back on the ground. It's worth pondering how many of our greatest writers would have been silenced by political correctness.

Working class humour is another concept which has been sanitised. Humour is normally a narrative about human fallibility and is usually based on widely understood concepts and stereotypes. The reason for this is that any national culture uses a catalogue of understood or recognisable stereotypes to unify the comic conscience. Working or lower class comedy can be traced back to the bawdy humour of Jacobean and Elizabethan times. Crude and rude. In Victorian times lower class comedy came together with the upper classes in the music halls. Very naughty jokes about all of human life. Think of the comedians of the sixties, perhaps the last decade of old England's working class cohesion. Morecambe and Wise: "He'll never sell any ice cream going that fast."

---

[9] Jonathan Swift, *A Modest Proposal*.

Tommy Cooper: "Two cannibals eating a clown. One says to the other, 'Does this taste funny to you'?"

Nothing political, just designed to titillate. Ken Dodd. Tattifilarious. Bob Monkhouse: "People laughed when I said that I wanted to be a comedian. Well they're not laughing now."

Brilliant timing and self-deprecating. Then there was the show featuring the northern working class club entertainers The Comedians.

"It's the way I tell 'em." Perhaps the most impeccable timing came from Bernard Manning. Accused of anti-Jewish bias, he was always willing to shock his audience.

"Anyway my uncle was killed at Auschwitz. He fell off the guard tower."

But he was thought to be racist and he did nothing to suggest otherwise. The new wave of middle class comedians, who ranted against Thatcherism, had a clear political stance unlike the comedians in the working men's clubs, particularly not the dreadful Manning. It was termed alternative humour or 'alternative to humour' as Manning said, perhaps unfairly as some like Ben Elton and Stephen Fry were very talented. But both were university educated and knowingly clever, not representative of old labour but New Labour elitism. Still today the BBC buys this consensus. That most regional of presenters Jonathan Ross was seen as a national figure and never off the screen, whereas the most popular comedian with mainstream Britain in every poll, Peter Kay from Bolton, came from the tradition of observational narrative self-deprecating humour, but has done his work largely on Independent Television. This is presumably because he is seen as regional, and not readily available in a London studio.

In the 1970s something changed which separated working class comedy from middle class comedy. Shows like the Monty Python series were in stark contrast to very popular shows like 'The comedians' and other non-PC sitcoms. Whilst ex-Cambridge graduates strutted their stuff with funny walks and squeaky voices, the Comedians rattled off non-PC jokes from a genre of working class northern clubs. The jokes were mainly about mother-in-laws, and other at risk minority groups. Drawing huge audiences in the

1970s this programme was later censored in the 1980s and comedians like Bernard Manning banned from TV. Manning denied he was ever racist but believed that in comedy anyone was fair game, and that there should be no sacred cows. On the other hand Monty Python's Life of Brian was also mocking of Christianity but this was on the tide of liberal atheism which ran alongside political correctness, so was deemed to be 'ok'. Manning also insisted that his show was an act and did not reflect his personal views but was a performance based on purely, making people laugh. The new wave comedian liberals called him a 'fat, ugly bigoted racist'. This was because they felt that all human beings should be respected. Manning had the last laugh with his own obituary. The Daily Mail had given him the challenge to write his own obituary and the results reflected the essence of the humour of the man. He quoted old friend Spike Milligan's request for his headstone "I told you I was ill".

For Manning his wish was that he was able to have written on his tombstone, in very small letter so that any visitor will have to get right up close to it "get off, you're standing on my privates".

In the obituary he mocked those who had tried to keep him off the TV, and reflected his own northern English upbringing saying, "My dad was a greengrocer and it was a tough upbringing, for the north was in the pit of depression and money and food were short. I was one of six children and was forced to share a bed with all my siblings, some of whom regularly wet the bed. In fact, I learnt to swim before I could walk. I remember one night my mother asked me 'where do you want to sleep'? I replied 'at the shallow end'".

The important part of his humour was that he reflected working-class northern culture. And in this culture there were issues about feeling threatened. This was a valid response even from a majority culture. He always said he never discriminated against anyone or anything, "I was quite happy to get a laugh out of any situation. All that mattered to me was whether the gag was funny or not."

He would often send up himself and his audience. During the Falklands conflict he joked "we've got a couple of lads in here tonight. They fought at Goose Green".

There was then huge enthusiasm and clapping until Manning added "They're Argentinean".

He was using the same comic devise as Swift by challenging his audience rather than cultivating them.

"They say they want to dance on my grave, that's ok because I'm being buried at sea."

Hence during the 1980s the national culture of working class comedy was under attack. Manning still did his shows in working class clubs but TV was off limits. Friends and neighbours testified to his generosity and kindness. His Asian neighbours were also supportive. Ironically he eventually became a member of a minority group, the white working class northern comedian.

The new Estuary English came into being with comics like Ben Elton with astute social observations and political humour. The 1970s sitcoms like Love Thy Neighbour and Spike Milligan's Curry and Rice were thrown in the vaults, censored out of existence. Whilst I'm all for protecting anyone's sensibility how far does this go. If we ban people from being called Paddy, Taff and Jock the whole British Army will be in the dock. And what about fatties? Can we make jokes about them? Well I'm told it's ok as obesity is one of the few forms of legitimate discrimination. One rather sad lady I met had been told she could not foster children despite being of impeccable character and a long time child minder. This was apparently because she was carrying a bit of excess stodge and took a bit too long to get out of the armchair when being inquisitioned by social workers. These same social workers had left children to be tortured to death with insane parents, but who wants a fatty as a mum? I'm a bit unsure now about who I can make jokes about. Not that I can usually remember the punch lines at my age but with our limited police force I don't want to take their valuable time if they need to come and arrest me, for being inappropriate, or just not funny, whilst teenagers are getting knifed on the streets. But, of course, it would count towards their target figures for arrests and certainly would be much easier than having to go into no go areas of Manchester or London. It says something about our values in society that we shower everyday but STDs are rampant. That the Government keeps telling us the crime figures are down while all the stats show that it is our kids that are under threat .

The problem is that this political engineering is now endemic in the British institutions. Everyone fears for their jobs and indeed, no one dares to challenge this stance. In most places the majority are against this posturing but go through the motions. However, in the BBC this institutional liberalism is a view most people actually hold, which is scary.

This situation was challenged by the BBC Trust who commissioned a report called 'From Seesaw to Wagon wheel'. This report was commissioned to investigate whether the BBC is 'impartial' in its views. The report concludes that it is not impartial but is driven by liberalist views. It is basically anti-nationhood, especially against the English as the majority culture and is pro-multi-culturalist, anti-business and pro-European. It is also generally distrusted by 60% of the population, despite the fact that it is funded by the great British public.

The Radio 4 Today programme has become an annex of Westminster Village. Where Jack De Manio once spoke to the whole of Britain, the Today programme now espouses political jargonese and received PC. To get any sanity on the radio you have to be able to turn to radio 2 and put on an Irishman of iconic status Terry Wogan. The last exponent of common sense and with an estimated one billion listeners worldwide. Too late for that he's retired now, so where does that leave us? Back in depression.

The telly has been taken over by so called 'reality' shows and cookery programmes. The reality TV shows are merely freak shows and cookery programmes are becoming ever quirkier as they struggled to find a new formula to cover the same content. Cooking. The content of many of the soap operas ensures that our kids feel they are freaks if they are normal. Hence a girl I know commented that 50% of her year at school thought they were bi-sexual. This was apparently re-enforced by 'the Brookside lesbian kiss' which was some sort of historical tipping point. Listening to the producer who had been involved with this he stated that there was no room for Brookside anymore as all the taboos were being dealt with by the other soaps now.

The issue over impartiality in the BBC has been exposed and even journalist as respected as Andrew Marr have spoken out:

"The BBC is a publicly funded urban organisation with an abnormally large proportion of younger people, of people in ethnic minorities and almost certainly of gay people than the population at large. It depends on the state's approval at least for its funding mechanism and all this creates an innate liberal bias inside the BBC and I think if we pretend there isn't an institutional liberal bias of that kind, which is much more clearly expressed as a cultural bias than as a party political bias, because as I said at the beginning, the party political bit is relatively speaking, dead easy. Complicated, fiddly, infuriating at times, but fundamentally easy. The liberal bias that we deal with, I think is much harder to deal with."

Jeff Randal, an Essex boy and Journalist on business and sport from the conservative press, explained walking into the BBC in these terms:

"It's a bit like walking into a Sunday meeting of the flat earth society. That's what I felt like, you walk into the flat earth society and of course everybody thinks the earth is flat, and as they discuss great issues of the day they discuss it from the point of view that the earth is flat. If someone overhears this, 'no, no, no the earth is round', they think this person is an extremist, that's what it's like for someone with my views."[10]

In its past the BBC was very representative of national views. It set itself up to have standards, it felt it was the voice of the decent aspects of the nation, of any class. Now it has been exposed as the voice of the Hampstead liberal. So that's why we regularly feel like throwing the TV or radio out of the window. Jeff Randall again:

"The BBC was an unbridled flag waver for multiculturalism. Today there is a strong and robust debate about its values, its upside, its downside. Many people outside the white Anglo-Saxon

---

[10] BBC Trust Seminar, Impartiality: Fact and Fiction, 22.9.06.

protestant community believe that multiculturalism is a threat to Britain; Trevor Phillips has said it, Jonathon Sachs, the chief rabbi has said it. Michael Nazarali, the Bishop of Rochester has said it. George Alagiah, the own, the BBC's golden boy himself has said it, it is a legitimate debate. When I was there this was not up for grabs. Multiculturalism was a good thing, the BBC supported it. Don't take my word for it because when I complained to the BBC about how we were handling multiculturalism, not multi-ethnicity by the way, but multiculturalism, this is what I got back from a very senior BBC news executive, who by the way is still at the corporation, he wrote to me following my complaint about our coverage of asylum seekers. Jeff, the BBC internally is not neutral about multiculturalism, it believes in it."

Some specific cases have been cited in evidence of this; for example when a journalist was reporting on bullying in Feltham Young Offender Institution and found that this was being done by black prisoners he had to go to the BBC, who commissioned the programme, and asked if he was allowed to say this for fear of the programme being axed if he did! On another occasion a black writer, Hilary Salmon, wrote a play for the Dennis Potter Award about black people called 'Shoot the Messenger'. In the words of Sue Lawley at a recent conference on the issue: "The play depicts black boys failing in school and ending up in prison or in psychiatric care. Black women mothering children by several different absent fathers and so on."

Sharon was made to change the title of the play which was initially 'F.ck black people." The play was televised but only because it had been written by a black woman. Sharon explained: "I received an e-mail today on what I call the black internet grapevine about how Bill Cosby, and Reverend Jackson, basically said the same things I've been saying and got slagged off for it but are unrepentant, you know, all we are saying, we haven't lived up to our potential." On being challenged by black folk in Hackney she asked, "If you knew only black people were going to see it how would you feel then?" They responded: "Then I would be fine."

The problem is with the 'We' culture is that the BBC is trying to re-educate us and is falling into the Orwellian role of the 'Thought police' from Orwell's 1984. Mark Ravenhill from the BBC did admit: "We, you know, I include myself in this, tend to think of the mass of the viewers as not being liberal enough. And that TV drama is a medium in which we can enlighten them towards a more enlightened attitude towards gay people, disabled people, or, whatever. And, we think of that as just a neutral impartial thing to do: that human rights, liberation for people, is the right and proper thing to do. So, I think we forgo a lot of the kind of moral complexity of drama for fear that a viewer might empathize with somebody who is racist or homophobic, or whatever."

Jeff Randall again:

"There was another occasion when the BBC broadcast Question Time from I believe Lincoln. Lincolnshire is one of the most white counties in Britain. If you look at the ethnic make-up it's something like 99% white, when they came out from Lincoln I invite you to look back at the tapes, in the audience were dotted lots of black faces, now what's that about? They had bussed them in to create this element of balance. Well surely the whole point of going around Britain is to get diversity, the true diversity of views. If you go to Cornwall you expect some Cornish people and some Cornish fishermen. If you go to Stoke Newington you expect a lot of black people, if you got to Lincoln you expect a lot of white farmers. They didn't do that because they were worried about multiculturalism and diversity."

Helen Bowden, Director of BBC News admitted that they were very late to broadcast any anti-European views, it was not until UKIP came along as a political arm of that voice of the people. Prior to that they considered this to be a 'loony' view. On being questioned about being pro-immigration she replied, "We were late to question this." On being anti-business. "Not really anti-business, but ignorant." Well that's a relief. Yet President Bush, who admittedly can't walk in a straight line and chew gum at the same time, was regularly treated as a loony tune by the BBC. Admittedly George Bush does have a murky Vietnam background, we do know that he was in the national guard so at least he was up for defending Texas from Oklahoma.

As a BBC executive responded after the report: "In the interests of impartiality WE may have to allow views to be voiced that WE do not like."

Hum very impartial.

The tone tends to be institutionally liberal, anti-nation, anti-family, anti-Christian, pro pc and pro metropolitan. So where has this gone and what has been done by the BBC Trust to rectify this? That remains unanswered.

In the good old days the BBC thought of itself as having a role to play in maintaining social standards which were clearly laid down by a society which was clear about what it wanted to be. Now standards are called 'Taboos' in a society that has no idea of what it wants to be but comes from the premise that everything is ok and no one has the right to say what is right. Where everyone has rights but no one has responsibilities. Whilst politicians have helped break the society they were there to protect. It brings to mind a quote I saw recently, "If its not broken, fix it until it is".

Can England as a nation ever recover? Only if it becomes non-PC to be PC.

Political Coercion

"Your worst enemy, he reflected, was your nervous system. At any moment the tension inside you was liable to translate itself into some visible symptom.

"And if all others accepted the lie which the Party imposed – if all records told the same tale – then the lie passed into history and became truth. 'Who controls the past' ran the Party slogan, 'controls the future: who controls the present controls the past".[11]

Political correctness is a tool which manipulates the evolved language of the masses in an attempt to control how they think. It limits language to only terms that the liberal establishment will allow. By restricting the use of words they attempt to restrict how people feel or think. But society, language and cultures evolve over vast amounts of time. If you want to break it, don't be surprised that it seems broken. If you want to undermine it, don't be surprised that it has no belief in itself anymore. A once dignified and proud culture, now mutilated. Big brother is in control and those in charge are the liberal thought police.

This political correctness is promoted by the liberal intelligencia as the language of 'civility' but is seen by others as the language of 'Newspeak' straight out of George Orwell's novel 1984. Their aim is to create a culture where minorities rule through the support of the liberal thought police. A society where you can dress up for a party as a 'naughty nun' but try to dress up

---

[11] George Orwell, *1984*.

as a Muslim in a burka and you can get arrested. This is because 'the party' decides on what IS allowed, not the people, because democracy is now defunct. Not just because people are denied access to vote at polling stations in the 2010 election campaign or because the party that the public definitely did not want to be in charge ended up, in joint control, but because, no voice can be heard but the 'party voice'.

So this PC language seeks to change western society and is viewed by some as the most intolerable abuse of public liberty. It attacks popular culture through cultural Marxism and it's outcome is the political manipulation of the masses. The English have suffered more than most from this concept. Not minority enough to be interesting and quaint, like the Scottish or Welsh whose nationalism has been seen as home grown multiculturalism. Being English itself, or at least daring to call yourself English, has become non-PC. With figures like John Prescott saying that there is no such place as England, and other New Labour politicians saying that the English need to be retrained to be British, the fight is now on to save the English from being buried for good.

With human rights lobbyists like 'Liberty' believing that they are the voice of righteousness in western society and that they speak on behalf of the 'people', there is little hope for redemption. Liberty called for a ban on the use of the Mosquito. This is the high pitched noise that only youngsters can hear and is used in some areas to stop gangs of youths congregating and terrorising the honest citizens going about their daily business. I suppose Liberty must see this activity as a valuable part of the growing up process, and feel that the 'little darling's' human rights' are being infringed. So what's wrong with the good old-fashioned baton charge? And what about those, "we're the ones who know what's right for you, and you lot need to be re-educated to think like us" twittering, oh so sincere voices of groups like Liberty, that only the over 40s can hear??!!

So the English themselves as a nation are politically incorrect as opposed to the all embracing, diversified, and ambiguous but PC 'British'. The English have always reflected a kind of quiet self-confidence and a penchant to mockery and self-degradation.

Generations have taken the piss out of all sorts of issues. In particular the English institutions. We love to mock the monarchy but the majority would fight for its survival. In the spirit of John Bull, institutions are there to be satirised to keep them on their toes. John Bull in the 18th century became a personification of Great Britain, but was not representative of the extremities, so he really became an English Icon, despite his Union Jack waistcoat. The John Bull character was well intentioned, frustrated but full of common sense. Unlike Uncle Sam he was not political but came to represent the shires. He drank beer, ate beef, and mercilessly took the rise out of politics and institutions. But Politicians need to be satirised to stop them taking themselves too seriously and make them realise they are only mere mortals. The problem with liberalism is that it thinks humans can solve the problems of the world and that they are potentially infallible. This is a dangerous posture to take. Someone once said, "The opposite of faith is not doubt, but absolute certainty."

I don't know who but I wish it had been me. Satirists like Swift in Gulliver's Travels mocked society, politics and humanity itself in an attempt to keep a sense of perspective. The Yahoos in the last book of Gulliver's travels, portrayed man as being half human, half horse. Well with the plan to create a half animal, half human hybrid through the use of early cell lines through the vanity of medical technologists, that may not be so bizarre. Thank God for Cardinal O'Brien from Scotland for at least challenging this and making politicians stop and think. Britain has escaped extremism until now because of this mistrust of politicians. Sadly satire is at an all time low and extremism is inevitably marching forward.

In 2007 we saw the closure of Punch which had epitomised this satire so well. As John Major once said: "If the answer to a question is another politician, you are asking the wrong question." Well that's a very sensible quote John and you sound like a man of sound judgement, well until I heard about Edwina. With the rise in liberal extremism, the language of humour and self-mockery, which the English did so well, was removed from them. They lowered voices and texted mass jokes that were deemed politically incorrect. Humour is now driven underground. So, this section may be devoid of humour as this is not allowed. Yet fear not, issues like stiles for disabled people on mountainous terrain, or the fact that we have to ask for the permission of illegal immigrants before we can use of X-ray equipment to seek them out from lorries coming over the channel, as it infringes their human rights. Or the fact that we have to hold known terrorists in this country rather than extradite them to America, because the American prisons are not as nice as ours, provides us with humorous material that no script writer could make up. A recent dictate for any prospective Good Samaritan, 'If you see someone choking you must not just save them but ask them to splutter out "I'm choking" to confirm that they REALLY are chocking, otherwise you could be done for assault. Yet the reality of it all makes you want to weep, not titter, as political correctness may have all but eliminated the English. The politicians may have got their way. So, like the proverbial, leper playing cards, the English may now have thrown in their hands.

But what is the background to this political correctness that has worked so well to destroy the English? The term PC itself goes back to the 18th century and was often used to describe language which was not 'literally' correct. Well that's ok then we understand that. Hilary Clinton on one of the American election campaigns, that go on forever, explained that she had "Mis-spoken". What Hilary had done was describe her arrival at the airport in Bosnia as having to "run ducking snipers' bullets". Presumably she had to run for her life. What she in effect meant was that she arrived at the airport, stepped off the plane and was greeted with a bunch of flowers. Oh dear, and she could end up with her finger on the button! As Paul Burrell, that loyal royal butler to Princess Diana said at the £10m hearing into her death, "I told some untruths".

No Paul, you told lies.

Politically correct language was later used in Marxist vocabulary as describing the party line. Well New Labour is PC labour, a cleaned out, homogenised spinning wheel of platitudes. They scraped that ineffective Welsh windbag, Neil Kinnock off the beach at Brighton, and replaced him with a likeable plastic smile that could win elections. But we would be wise to take note of Orwell's book 1984. It serves as a valuable warning about the power of words to mould popular thought. He drew a frightening picture of a future totalitarian state in which Big Brother's official language of "Newspeak" created its own truths with terms like "War is peace, freedom is slavery"[12] and anyone who opposed the correct or party line was punished. Not a lot has changed then. The problem is that free speech is now curtailed by a movement which stipulates certain topics, expressions, even certain gestures, as off-limits. So we're not allowed to discuss issues like immigration and religious extremism. As Frank Field said we can only say that the recent statistics showing that 85% of new jobs created since 1997 have gone to foreigners, because these foreigners are largely white. What if they had been another colour? In Britain the majority do not have freedom of speech for fear that they may offend minority groups. But does anyone have the right not to be offended? I'm offended every time I put on local radio and hear some spotty youth talking about how he enjoys using a condom and how it gets you respect man! I've never heard such cock, excuse the pun, an unbelievably contrived load of tosh. It's even more nonsensical if you look at the statistics on teenage pregnancies. Liberals do not believe in telling the youth of today what is right and wrong because they have no moral code, only moral relativism, which they believe society should follow. So condoms have become 'essential wear' like a new type of jumper. Yet experience shows us that society cannot function effectively without a structure. Instead we got the Blair Babes pouring out platitudes in pious terms once reserved for an Anglican clergyman 'right and proper', 'hearts and minds'.

So back to Orwell's 1984 and Winston's friend, sorry comrade, who is getting rather excited at the thought of knocking

---

[12] George Orwell, *1984.*

7 bells out of the English language, so that the 'Thought Police' can control the masses:

"The Eleventh Editions is the definitive edition," said Syme. "We're getting the language into its final shape – the shape its going to have when nobody speaks anything else. You think our chief job is inventing new words. But not a bit of it! We're destroying words – scores of them, hundreds of them, every day. We're cutting the language down to the bones. In the final version of Newspeak there'll be nothing else. It's a beautiful thing, the destruction of words. The great wastage is in the verbs and adjectives, but there are hundreds of nouns that can be got rid of as well. It isn't only the synonyms; there are also the antonyms. After all what justification is there for a word which is simply the opposite of some other word? A word contains its opposite in itself. Take 'good' for instance. If you have a word like 'good', what need is there for a word like 'bad'? 'Ungood will do just as well – better, because it's an exact opposite, which the other is not. Or again, if you want a stronger version of 'good', what sense is there in having a whole string of vague useless words like 'excellent' and 'splendid' and all the rest of them? Plus good covers the meaning; or double plus good, if you want something stronger still. In the final version of Newspeak there'll be nothing else. The whole notion of goodness and badness will be covered by only six words – in reality, only one word."[13]

So in the 2010 election campaign we were bombarded with 'New Labour plus'. Back to you George...

"Don't you see that the whole aim of Newspeak is to narrow the range of thought? In the end we shall make thought crime literally impossible, because there will be no words in which to express it. Every concept that can ever be needed will be expressed by exactly one word, with its meaning rigidly defined and all its subsidiary meanings rubbed out and forgotten. Every year fewer and fewer words and the range of consciousness

---

[13] George Orwell, *1984*.

always a little smaller. There's no reason or excuse for committing thought crime. It's merely a question of self-discipline, reality control. The revolution will be complete when the language is perfect. Newspeak is Ingsock and Ingsoc is Newspeak."

Yes that's it, politicians can eliminate any dissent by stopping the use of words that express what the masses think. I'm speechless. Carry on George.

"By the year 2050 – earlier probably – all real knowledge of Oldspeak will have disappeared. The whole literature of the past will have been destroyed. Chaucer, Shakespeare, Milton Byron. The whole climate of thought will be different. In fact there will be no thought, as we understand it now. Orthodoxy means not thinking – not needing to think. Orthodoxy is unconsciousness."

Yes, yes I recognise this…

But the irony of so much of this manipulation of language and expression is that so many people in the institutions have stopped or never did believe in the hype. Many just paid lip service to something which has all gone horribly wrong. Millions of pounds were spent by local councils in translating information documents for minority ethnic communities. They did it because they thought they were being politically correct. However, suddenly all that was changed when they were told they were now just 're-enforcing segregation'. Well you can't get it right all the time. Serves them right. They are now calling for what has always been very English, a 'common sense approach'. But I thought this had been banned. You had to feel for the Liberal Party who lost all their political ground to New Labour, the sanitised version of the Labour party. They foolishly believe that society can be saved by them, mere mortals, and that even Utopia is possible as if a few decades of what they deem as 'right thinking' could change the nature of people. But now the liberal democrats are back in the driving seat, yet ironically they were the last ones the electorate, wanted in power. Oh well, never mind, so much for democracy.

The Christian culture of this country, whether you went to church or not, was ingrained in the moral values and family structure of its people. The secularists sought to destroy this and replace it with... well I don't think they've worked that out yet. Working class hopes of social mobility were taken away by the destruction of the Grammar Schools and Thatcher destroyed the Unions. New Labour is run by public school boys who are possibly delighted that they will never again have to deal with the old Labour working-class kids and trade union leaders who probably ate peas off their knives and preferred beer to wine. Never mind now Tony Blair can go to confession and say penance for a prime minister that did less for Christianity, and in particularly Roman Catholic values, than possibly any other and now counts his millions by working for the commercial sector. That's the true definition of the term Judas. But liberalism had always been about middle-class people with a social conscience, who thought they knew best what the masses needed. No one should have been surprised at Nick Clegg's coming out as an atheist. Atheism is a characteristic of Liberals who are possibly the most PC of all the parties and who believe world salvation to be in their hands. Anyway, his wife's faith did at least manage to ensure he at least got his kids into a decent school.

So in this PC secular society they would love to ban Christmas but then what about the business world? Retailing relies too much on the nativity story. Still they may try to eliminate the Robin. I heard the story on the now unfortunately late 'Wake up to Wogan', about the PCT who were told they should not send out Christmas cards with Robins on the front as they were very symbolic of 'Englishness'. It takes an Irishman to keep our feet on the ground. One of Wogan's listeners came up with a PC Christmas card as follows:

"Please accept with no obligation implied or implicit, my best wishes for an environmentally conscious and socially responsible, low stress, non-addictive, gender neutral celebration of the winter solstice holiday. Practiced within the most enjoyable traditions of the religious persuasion or secular practice of your choice with respect for the religious or secular persuasion and or traditions of others, or indeed their choice not to practice religious or secular tradition at all.

"On the front of the card was the most inclusive nativity scene. A Wiseman going through a metal detector, and a 'safety in the stable poster, in view', a burka and a recycling bin and a fathers, and indeed, mother's for justice protestor at the scene".[14]

So words have been removed, sanitised or morphed into other meanings and reformed into verbal diarrhoea, or Pure Crap. Apparently the latest idea is to change the term Asylum Seekers to Sanctuary Seekers. This is apparently because people do not like Asylum Seekers. Well that's a good idea.

So England became controlled by the politically correct 'Ministry of Truth', which decides all moral values and is involved in a kind of manipulation of the mind. Concentrate now reader. In the novel 1984 this manipulation is mainly done by the Minitrue (Ministry of Truth), where Winston Smith, the main character, works.

'Doublethink makes people accept contradictions, and it makes them also believe that the party is the only institution that distinguishes between right and wrong. So when a person that is well grounded in Doublethink recognises a contradiction or a lie of the Party, then the person thinks that he is remembering a false fact. The use of the word Doublethink involves Doublethink. With the help of the Minitrue it is not only possible to change written facts, but also facts that are remembered by the people. So complete control of the country and its citizens is provided.

Yes that's all clear now George.

So this manipulation of language then gets complicated when terms selected by a particular group as acceptable, then pass into common use, including use by people whose attitudes are those formerly associated with words which the new terms were designed to supersede. The situation is complicated by the fact that members of identity groups actually, like terms that others seek to change. For example, deaf culture has always considered the label 'Deaf' as an affirming statement of group membership

---

[14] Wake up to Wogan.

and not insulting or disparaging in any way. They got it wrong again. The term now often used for the 'deaf', is 'hearing-impaired'. This term was developed to include people with hearing loss due to aging, accidents, and other causes. But 'deaf' people don't like it, so for goodness sake listen! Did you hear me?!

So new terms can then become even more devalued, and a further set of expressions must be created. This happened to the term Gay. This term has now moved into common use, and means 'odd'. This is often used by teenagers. "You're so gay!" is common parlance. At a school I know, the Head threatened to call in the police if teenagers did not stop using the word Gay. Well good for her. Forget about the knives and guns it's easier to call in the police for language crimes. So what about 'Blonde'. I think imprisonment no less if Blondes are discriminated against by being accused of being dippy.

This abuse or manipulation of our language can give rise to lengthy progressions of word such as "negro", "coloured", "black", "and African-American". Apparently in the IT industry lap tops, which indeed are black, are now called Stealth grey so not to be called 'black' for some reason. But of course PC language is not literally correct. Silly me. Back to 1984 and Winston:

"Don't you see that the whole aim of Newspeak is to narrow the range of thought? Has it ever occurred to you, Winston, that by the year 2050, at the very latest, not a single human being will be alive who could understand such a conversation as we are having now? The whole climate of thought will be different. In fact there will be no thought, as we understand it now."[15]

"It was terribly dangerous to let your thoughts wander when you were in any public place or within range of a telescreen. The smallest thing could give you away. A nervous tic, an

---

[15] George Orwell, *1984*.

unconscious look of anxiety, a habit of muttering to yourself –
anything that carried with it the suggestion of abnormality, of
having something to hide. In any case, to wear an improper
expression on your face... was itself a punishable offense. There
was even a word for it in Newspeak: Face crime..."

Winston obviously worked in the public sector.

So Newspeak continues and is alive and well and thriving in
the UK. This can be seen with terms like 'mixed race' which I'm
now hearing termed 'mixed heritage'. The problem is that this is
so vague as to be meaningless and could just as well refer to the
offspring of a Lancastrian man married to a Yorkshire bred
woman. On the tube recently I notice the 'Disabled' seat which
has been renamed several times, is now referred to as, for those
'who have difficulty standing'. Well if they think I'm going to
give up my seat for the next drunk that wanders onto the tube,
well they're wrong! As a vertically challenged, Englishwoman of
dubious heritage, I've had enough. I feel like getting drunk,
getting on a tube pushing a 'person who has difficulty standing'
out of the special chair, sitting in it myself and going on to make a
citizens' arrest on an 'undocumented worker', or an 'alternative
shopper'. No doubt it is I who would be arrested for infringing
their human rights. But hopefully when I get arrested the prisons
will have no places left for me. But then again, I could be hit by
the early release scheme whereby 14,000, probably hardened
criminals have been let out early to make room for me.

So let's do something really silly like ban a 20 year old song,
'Fairytale of New York' by Kirsty McCall and The Pogues for
being non-PC. It has come to something when radio 1, the station
of progressive youth, bans some old gits like The Pogues
considered 'hip' in their time, but now more 'hip replacement'. If
they had banned them for not being able to sing, not visiting a
dentist or being inebriated on stage, one could have understood
this. The BBC soon realised how ridiculous they looked.

The BBC's response:

Radio 1 has now reversed its decision to edit lyrics in the song Fairytale of New York by The Pogues and the late Kirsty MacColl.

Andy Parfitt, Controller of Radio 1 issued the following statement:

"After careful consideration I have decided that the decision to edit the Pogues song Fairy Tale of New York was wrong. Radio 1 does not play homophobic lyrics or condone bullying of any kind. It is not always easy to get this right, mindful of our responsibility to our young audience. The unedited version will be played from now on.

"I want to stress that everyone at Radio 1 and its music team take the issue of language very seriously and enormous care is taken in ensuring that offensive language is edited from records where necessary. I understand absolutely, in a climate where questions about editorial standards are at the fore, the thinking behind this decision. While we would never condone prejudice of any kind, we know our audiences are smart enough to distinguish between maliciousness and creative freedom.

"In the context of this song, I do not feel that there is any negative intent behind the use of the words, hence the reversal of the decision."[16]

And so now even the 3 little pigs are in trouble. Well I've got a copy and if the thought police want it they are going to have to delve a long way down in my loft for it and get over my dead body at the same time.

One important political debate that is being raised and could help save the day is the need for an English parliament. This is the unfinished business of devolution. The promotion of Scottish and Welsh nationalism as something which was positive, just because it was anti-English, could have backfired. Now liberals fear for

---

[16] Andy Parfitt, Controller of Radio 1.

the break up of the union and all that might entail. Well it's a bit too late for that! But still we hear endless debates about being 'British'. But Britain does not exist, it is not a country, it is a political union.

The Campaign for an English parliament has described the situation as it is.

"Devolution has created a United Kingdom in which Scotland has its own national parliament and Wales and Northern Ireland each their own national assembly as distinct nations. England has nothing. The British government refuses to give any such political and constitutional recognition to England. The Scottish Parliament has made Scotland at least 70% independent of the rest of the UK in the most important areas of government like Health and Education, and Wales and Ireland are demanding that same degree of Home-rule. But England as a nation has no such political and constitutional recognition in the UK at all. What is worse, Scottish, Welsh and Northern Irish MPs can now make decisions on the internal affairs of the people of England, even be ministers for England's internal affairs, while no English MP has any such power in Scotland, Wales and Northern Ireland. The United Kingdom is now a most unbalanced Union, in favour of Scotland, Wales and Northern Ireland and against England. It is a great injustice to the English people.

Just consider a small sample of the huge benefits their own parliaments have been able to deliver to Scotland and Wales. Scottish students do not have to pay university fees like English students do, and that even when they are at English universities. Scottish pensioners in nursing homes get free personal care; they don't have to sell their houses to pay for it like English pensioners do. In Wales everyone gets free prescriptions. £1300 more is spent on health, education and social services per head in Scotland and Wales than in England. Little wonder the 1998 Devolution legislation states that the Scottish and Welsh parliaments will be 'the forum to provide a forum for the concerns of the nation."[17]

---

[17] Campaign for an English Parliament.

So Scottish pop singer Amy McDonald can be praised for being cool and Scottish, patriotic and nationalistic, whilst poor old Morrissey, granted a bit dour, is castigated for saying that England has changed beyond recognition. This is of course a fact that everyone knows, but which may be something that some people do not want to acknowledge. Confusion reigned when Gordon told all public buildings to fly the Union Jack, it's a bit like shutting the stable door after the horse has bolted. So Gordon considered getting our kids to swear an oath of allegiance to the Queen to create some sort of national unity. But hang on Gordon what about the Republicans, that'll cause a stir. Well, then he reconsidered. If it can't be to the Queen what about an allegiance to the state? Things became much clearer then Gordon.

A major part of the English culture was to have faith in law and order and indeed they proudly took their system of justice all around the world. Yet the average English person now feels the police to be public enemy number one. The average middle-class person has more to fear from the police than ever before and little faith in justice. They are looking out for the day they are arrested if they smoke in their cars. They fear that they cannot even protect themselves if criminals break into their house or accost them in the street. They are much easier targets than the average criminal because they are basically law abiding citizens who turn up at court and pay their fines. Oh dear another Survey has been carried out. Apparently the over 50s are now causing mayhem abroad doing things they would not do at home, and not just in Thailand. They are apparently going hang-gliding and carrying out other highly dangerous pursuits. Well that's probably because they've escaped abroad away from Alf Ensafety. And another thing, apparently the over 40s drink too much and could be a menace to society. But at least we are not out on the streets causing mayhem, instead we are more likely to fall over or drop off to sleep in the chair. But never mind baring your doors, fear not, the police have put up an emergency phone number if you hear any homophobic comments. They would probably come a lot quicker than the current 999 service.

Born again bikers, the Silver Surfers of the road, who often struggle to hold up their stationary bikes, can be a menace largely to themselves not so much others on the road, who are usually a menace to them. But they feel they are unjustly being targetted. The reality is that police can sit in their panda cars and pick off nice easy targets. They are mostly older men who mostly, once again, would just like a powerful machine between their legs. The threat is now for 6 points for speeding and yet the figures show that in only 5% of accidents speed is a factor. The over 40s are more compliant because their history has taught them that the police are on their side and now they are bemused at what went wrong. So the police achieve their targets for arrests and fines by targeting those who are most vulnerable: the law abiding citizen. A man drops an apple core in the street and ends up in a police cell. Whilst the criminals laugh at the police and the powers they have to detain them. The Government at least has a sense of humour, by telling us that Crime figures are falling. Well they keep telling me how this 'World Capital' is now such a wonderful place. Well done Ken and Boris, it's probably being measured by how good the restaurants are. The reality is crime is spiralling out of control. The fact that people no longer call the police when they are attacked or robbed unless they need a crime number for an insurance claim, is a sad indictment of the confidence they have that any police might actually turn up.

Crime by children and teenagers, on each other are virtually ignored by the police. Instead they target those carrying knives, who will tell you , they are carrying them for self-defence, as ill informed as it might be. Many teenagers carry the weapons because the police, in many areas, are not in control of our street. What the police should really do is deal with the lower level crime by teenagers on other teenagers and makes them feel safe in their own communities. Well our esteemed ex-Home Secretary Jackie Smith gave us much confidence by telling everyone that she was too scared to go out after dark in her area. Well you should have done something about it woman, you were the Home Secretary! Illegal immigrants are at large because if they kick off whilst being departed they are left here. Card crime is out of control but don't worry the Government are now taking them off the crime statistics so things will look better. An amnesty for all illegal immigrants is a lot easier than actually sending them back.

Clegg policy exposed!!

Well, thanks goodness Nick's amnesty plans were exposed by the tabloids.

The message this gives to the millions who are still trying to get in is clear, including a new batch of Iranian homosexuals, who have just been invited in by the High Court. Messages here are vital. Blair got it wrong with cannabis and the trade is now out of control. You must forgive the police as they are a bit busy chasing criminals who are extremely pleased with the legal aid they get courtesy of the tax payer.

If the police are not spending their time chasing terrorists, or scouring rubbish tips for confidential computer discus, or looking for non-documented workers, who are now apparently largely employed in the security business or possibly even the police, they could be investigating your local MP the LDA or the Mayor's office. They are also now tasked to look for exploding houses. You may have one in your area; according to the stats it is increasingly likely.

Of 43 police forces in England, 41 of them have found cannabis farms or 'grow ups' as they are called. They are cannabis production sites in normal domestic houses. In Scotland, of 8 police forces 5 have found them in their areas. This highly lucrative trade is now, according to the Radio 4 documentary, 'The cannabis trade', two thirds controlled by Vietnam's immigrants and because of the huge profits, organized crime is involved. They take over any domestic property, gut it out, and fill it with plants, redirecting electricity, gas and water away from the mains so it goes directly into the houses and not onto their bill. This makes the house a time-bomb and large numbers are exploding all over the country.

This business was very big in Canada and started some 10 years ago and the Canadians also had the same problems of convicting them. However, they got wise and they used Fire Safety laws to close them down and also to recuperate costs. As a result of this action, the criminals have moved out of Canada, and guess where they have come? As one of the Canadian police officers in charge explained: "As long as the problem goes away, we chase them to the UK where they're doing absolutely nothing about it. So let's do that."

Well at least it was reassuring to see so many police on the streets in 2009, even if they were only attending a rally on increasing their pay.

A man gets kicked to death outside his own home trying to stop teenagers, high on drugs and booze, vandalising cars. The Government comes up with the solution that the drink companies need to be tackled about the sale of alcohol, rather than ask themselves why teenagers were at home all day drinking and taking drugs? They were probably claiming incapacity benefit as so many teenage druggies, sorry, victims do, and using it to further feed their habit, compliments of the taxpayers. But then the taxpayers are very generous. The extent of this can be seen by the generosity they show by paying for the welfare benefits to the multiple wives of polygamous Muslim men. By in effect recognising polygamy, Britain is creating parallel legal jurisdictions.

Justice is further demonstrated by the return of 3 Muslims from Guantánamo Bay back to Brent. The Brent MP Sarah Teather commented:

"It is good to see the Government has now agreed to use its influence to bring pressure on other countries to take their responsibilities seriously towards Guantánamo Bay. We can only close Guantanamo Bay if other countries are willing to accept back their refugees and residents. I hope the Government will continue to negotiate for the release of Binyam Mohammed, who has suffered extensive torture at the hands of the US, and that they will ensure the safety of Shaker Aamer."[18]

Richard Littlejohn commented in his column in the mail, rightly or wrongly:

"For the record, Binyam Mohammed is an Ethiopian soon to be put on trial for terrorism. Shaker Aamer is a Saudi citizen

---

[18] R. Littlejohn – Daily Mail, 21st December 2007.

negotiating repatriation to his homeland, where they will probably chop his head off after a decent interval. They are about as British as I am French on the strength of spending a long weekend in St Tropez. It is beyond me what any of this has got to do with either the Lib Dem MP for a scruffy part of North London or the British Foreign Office … but for a Government, which is letting people die on the NHS because life-saving drugs are too expensive, spent £100,000 chartering a private plane to fly the three Gitmo 'residents' back to Britain, needs a public enquiry".

So political correctness is subjective, and corresponds to the sponsored view of the Government, to protect minority, or special interest group by silencing contradiction. These views then become orthodox, and presented as 'truth' because freedom of thought requires the ability to choose between more than one viewpoint.

So back to our Sage Orwell and his essay on the English language…

"When there is a gap between one's real and one's declared aims, one turns as it were instinctively to long words and exhausted idioms, like a cuttlefish spurting out ink. In our age there is no such thing as "keeping out of politics". All issues are political issues, and politics itself is a mass of lies, evasions, folly, hatred, and schizophrenia".

So we must question why words that have been evolved over centuries are being eliminated and expressions taken from us.

"It follows that any struggle against the abuse of language is a sentimental archaism, like preferring candles to electric light or hansom cabs to aeroplanes. Underneath this lies the half-conscious belief that language is a natural growth and not an instrument which we shape for our own purposes."[19]

So let's use a new term to manipulate the language 'Positive Action'. In Newspeak this means, well, social engineering. In old speak this means 'discrimination'.

---

[19] George Orwell, 'Essay on English Politics and Language'.

Even Science is dominated by politically correct thinking. Subjects like evolution, aids and global warming need a complete reappraisal to sort out the issues. But how long can we wait. Most argue that the majority of non-mainstream scientists or pseudo-scientists claim bias within the scientific community as an explanation for why their theories remain unaccepted. Never mind, the Government are arranging to whip our bits away without even asking us, hopefully after we're dead, but of course they are no good after we're dead. Ah then there's the problem of how we define dead and so on... well I just hope they allow us to at least stop breathing first.

The English unfortunately are the majority group in a minority focused culture and have suffered from the terminology which has in effect sought to bury them. It would be more convenient for Newspeak if the English would agree to be British as this is more inclusive. Inclusively means that the thought police can define you down to what they want you to be. And it is working. How often do you hear people say, "I'm not allowed to say that now...?"

Though this may not be true, the fact that people feel it to be so is a bit scary and means that we are in a sort of police state. This social engineering is particularly focused in party politics, the public sector, and academia and is distorting the emphasis of our vital public institutions.

We need to understand that the Government, big enough to give you everything is also big enough to take it away, including freedom itself. Language is at the root of political consciousness. We can only know what we understand and our understanding is limited by the words and phrases used to frame an issue. The constant repetition of imprecise politically correct language is sure to have a cumulative effect upon a target audience, eventually we begin to accept what we are told.

Indeed the main goal of political correctness, is to diminish the choice of words and thereby reduce the range of thought. This is demonstrated in academia. Ironically the liberal intelligencia now control academia and censor those concepts which are deemed as non-pc. Hence academics who write about issues which, in many cases have been stated many times before in other research, lose their jobs if they state anything which is deemed non-PC. Debaters at the Oxford Union are harassed by liberal Nazis demonstrating against free speech, and intellectual challenge and rigour have gone from the education system. Once the quote "I may not agree with what you say but I will defend to the death your right to say it"[20] would have defined our politics and culture. It was taken away without us even noticing. The only right now is for the human rights of minority groups. If human rights means protecting the rights of minority groups by not offending them, then freedom of speech is no longer a human right for the majority.

The irony is that past liberal concentration on free speech has now become silencing speech unless it is liberal. Freedom is now interpreted as an issue of human rights for criminals or potential criminals or minority groups. The mass no longer have the same rights of freedom. The liberal intelligencia now speak for the British public who they want to retrain to think like them. This is demonstrated by politicians constant reference in pious terms to 'the public will not accept' issues that in reality the great masses have no interest in at all like terrorists being locked up uncharged for 28 days. Or indeed a referendum on the voting system when what the people wanted was a referendum on Europe! The politicians are so out of touch with the public, who largely couldn't care about the welfare of terrorists, and who would probably string them up there and then and save on their taxes. They need to educate the public to have the same concerns as the Bien Pensant. Yet they will not let the public have a referendum, in case they make a choice that is truly democratic. And the English can't have their own parliament because it would mean that in effect New Labour would probably never regain power in England.

---

[20] Voltaire.

71

An indication of how far we have now moved away from this freedom is demonstrated by the English teacher who called the Teddy Mohammed. This fear not only focused on the likes of writers like Salman Rushdie but innocent victims who get caught up in the rhetoric and then have to keep a low profile for fear of reprisals in a country, which was once meant to be the safest and freest in the world. Another author who was planning to publish a book with Mohammed the Mole quickly re-wrote the title to Morgan the Mole. The irony is that he was probably thinking he was being politically correct and embracing multiculturalism; well that serves him right!

The people who really do believe in the rhetoric are often those in the media. Radio 4 is full of twittering females, in particularly programmes like 'Woman's Hour', which I suppose is positive discrimination, and the tone of sincerity and concern for every victim group is predictable and boring. The individuals that promote this tend to be females, who work in the public sector, who often live in Hampstead and it would be a distinct advantage to them if they came from a minority group.

How refreshing it was to listen to Julie Birchall who went on the programme to be asked the normal predictable probing question about how she was inspired to be a writer. I can't quote Julie verbatim but it went along the lines that it was the only profession where she could lie in bed, go to the pub and get pissed at lunchtime and do a few hours work in the afternoons. Not a conventional woman's hour interview. But it brought to mind a lecturer of mine at college who said that the thing which most motivated the Americans was the need to be seen as 'sincere'. But for the English the key motivator was 'not to be boring'. Oh what did happen to that?

The hairy females that promoted feminism as a liberal freedom for the oppressed female in the 1960s are now a bit confused. Women are now seen more as sexual objects than they have ever been. So what went wrong, let's ask an expert.

'Gender feminism', which is essentially based on a form of Marxist theory that substitutes "gender" for Marx's category of 'class', or simply adds the two together, usually with "race" thrown in. This sort of "race, class, and gender" theory is typically a dangerous form of political moralism, with the same totalitarian characteristics as other versions of Marxism have proven to display".

Well I think I probably agree with that. Put simply, some, mostly middle-class females saw themselves as missing out on some of the pleasures of the men folk. They then set about breaking down the conservative establishment, which they saw as tying them to the kitchen sink. Ultimately this became 'girl power' and was responsible, in the 1970s, for hideous shoulder pads and power dressing. In the 1990s this became the laddette culture of the Spice Girls. So 'hey' now women were liberated, or were they? What they really got was the opportunity to be treated like one of the lads. Laddettes were supposed to then enjoy uncommitted sex, and loads of booze. Hey guess what, the boys were really enjoying this. They now had no need to give women any respect, open doors, or indeed to even woo them, which to be fair was what a lot of women loved. The feminists are gob smacked. What happened? The marketing men took feminism, commoditised it, and threw it back at them. Female rapes are on the increase, and prosecutions are difficult to make. That's possibly because the girls are acting like boys. Hence rapes are at their highest and convictions low because the men believe that the girls are equally enthusiastic, or at least should be. And no doubt the liberated women of this era can go off to Goa with their 'partners' and allow their 15 year old daughters to be abused by men, as part of the joy of freedom. The Brits now have a new reputation abroad, and it's for 'child neglect. And now large numbers of children call Childline every day because their innocence has been taken from them and they feel under pressure to have sex. As pole dancing clubs hit the high streets, the feminists are in a quandary, they would want the right to dance with the Pole, well there are enough of them, but are they being exploited? And in France it was the Female liberation movement which played a fundamental role in the campaign to ban the burka.

The individuals who do not go for the language of political correctness are largely white working class males, or even those from the private sector who after all are 'money grabbing entrepreneurs' who need to be re-educated, like us all, to understand the real issues as promoted by the 'we' culture. So get them on a diversity or equal opps training course. The public sector has been totally consumed by Newspeak and meaningless targets, which are often used to just re-enforce Newspeak. Yet the uncontrolled growth of the public sector under New Labour, has had to be pulled back by the Coalition Government. For example, millions of taxpayers money was spent on promoting Welsh language, and now it seems that Welsh is set to become the first language of Wales. The Welsh language, how multicultural is that we have some other ethnics right on our doorstep. In many ways the bizarre drive for meaningless targets has led to most Government departments being unfit for purpose. Whilst talented individuals of 20 years ago would have gone into the public sector they have now gone into investment banking. There is no challenge against decisions or policies because they are all created by the same mindset; and no one has the freedom of speech to question, daft policies or systems. So the public institutions and Government departments are now unfit for purpose, not just the Home Office but the NHS, Local Authorities, Police, Education, the lot. Hospitals are killing people daily with C.Diff and MRSA as a consequence of lack of attention to detail. Secondary school education is a form of riot control, fortunately without tear gas, but with tears. And now we can all rejoice in the news that hospitals are sending patients home to recover. Well that's a relief at least the hygiene standards may be better.

So, shock horror, it was exposed that 12 illegal workers were employed to guard Metropolitan police cars and one had overseen repairs to the one time Prime Minister, Tony Blair's, car. The Daily Mail also published emails between Jackie Smith and top civil servants in which the Home Secretary agreed the problem was "not ready for public announcement". Smith told the Commons that the SIA had written to 10,500 people who hold its licenses informing them the authorization may be withdrawn, but there was a "minimum 42-day period for that process to happen". Well it's a relief that no one was blown up in the meantime.

The one department we did have some confidence in, in as much as we knew they would be capable of hounding us to death for every last penny we owed them, was the Dept of Tax and Revenue. So the police spent thousands of pounds scouring rubbish tips for computer discs, holding details of all those who get family allowance, which the public sector has lost. Prisons let out prisoners to kill innocent folk, police arrest pensioners for cutting their conifers back too hard, or someone drops an apple core and is put in a police cell. All this enables the police to defer going into no go areas of crime and arresting real criminals. I was told by someone who had his car stolen and had later spotted it in a gypsy camp, when he went to the police they said that it was "much too dangerous to go in there"! No, just send two squad cars and 7 policemen to deal with a bunch of pensioners on a bowling green, having a peaceful protest because the council has raised their rent. The police then threatened them with a criminal offence. So alas, we see ambulances in the Midlands, queuing up outside hospitals with patients inside because they are using them as beds. And January 08 didn't start too well with details of 600,000 individuals who have applied for the armed forces being found on a roundabout in Devon. Well at least the police did not have to search too far to redeem the data.

Then there is the incompetence of 90 people dying in Kent hospitals, well I suppose they were mostly oldies so they didn't matter that much. They are the ones who fought wars in the hope that this country would survive and be a land fit for heroes. Kent police launched an investigation into whether the Maidstone and Tunbridge Wells NHS Trust should be prosecuted for the deaths. The Healthcare Commission said a "litany" of errors in infection control had caused the "avoidable tragedy".

The trust said it had not been prepared for "an outbreak of that size and complexity" but had learned lessons. Well that's very reassuring for those who lost their relatives. The commission's report said nurses at the trust were too rushed to wash hands and left patients to lie in their own excrement. Mr

75

Johnson said he was shocked by the findings, but denied accusations that the problems were caused by staff being put under pressures to meet government A and E targets. The trust's chief executive, Rose Gibb, finally did resign. How relieved she was to get her £75,000 pay-off.

So the public sector is sinking fast and is obsessed by targets and PC postures with much time spent on promotions about how Homophobia and Racism should not be tolerated. How about a new one, "incompetence should not be tolerated"!! The Coalition Government is now cutting the public sector to the bone, but let's just hope it cuts the right bits.

Mrs Thatcher seemed to believe everyone who worked in the public sector was no good. Hence she went on to make a significant number of the top bosses in the public sector multi-millionaires to repay them for their services. They became what are known as 'fat cats'. They profited from the taxpayers and took the money and ran. Blair picked up Thatcher's economic policies and just gave them a PR work over. Twenty years ago the top civil servants were highly intelligent individuals, reading classic degrees and PPE at Oxford. For those now in the civil service it is almost impossible for anyone who holds even mildly non-socialist views or who is willing to make them known, to survive. They chase meaningless targets, and paperwork rather than concentrating on the effectiveness of their management. Major political decisions about the public sector, like the expansion of funding in the health service, are unmanaged and undirected, hence the main money that went into the health service ended up increasing the salaries of those who were the most highly paid in the first place. And the Government then asked, very nicely, if GPs would mind doing some out of hours surgeries, as they have had a significant pay increase for doing less work. Someone made a mistake I think.

This means that two generations of professionals have done harm in the public sector, and you have to look back to the 1950s to get any common sense. New Labour itself is a sanitisation of the Labour Party. Gordon Brown's concept of the. 'Ministry of all talents' was a far cry from a mature democracy. Sir Digby Jones became Minister for Trade and Investment without being a member of the Labour Party or even declaring his politics. I'd like to know what 'Brand Britain' really is as we don't seem to make anything but are looking more like a transit camp for the rich non-doms and terrorist groups, and a dumping ground for cheap Chinese goods. Well of course, this did help hold the inflation rate down for the New Labour Government until the whole thing crashed around them. And our politicians are exceptionally kind to the EU even selling our North Sea Gas to them, in the summer when the demand is not so heavy here; they then store this and sell it back to us at a higher cost in the winter when we need it. Well it would take a while to sort out gas storage facilities, especially at the rate we make decisions here, and the Europeans have got to be patted on the back for their enterprise. This country is increasingly looking like it couldn't organise a piss up in a brewery, if we had any left.

So what went wrong? The 1960s teacher training colleges and the new universities, so ably characterised in the History Man by Malcolm Bradbury, became places where anyone naturally Tory was not considered capable of doing a Sociology course. Clearly the Gilbert and Sullivan view that everyone is either born 'a little liberal or a little conservative', which is apparently now backed by genetic research, is still not accepted in academia. The Grammar school boys went on to destroy the chances of other working-class kids. Secondary education has been dumbed down so much to ensure that 50% of kids go to university and do meaningless qualifications and end of stocking supermarket shelves, whilst we import tradesman from abroad.

But you should never underestimate the power of education in this process. Any tyrant be they fascist or liberal know that they have to control the education process. When Blair pronounced 'Education, Education, Education', the master of spin knew the power of Educational doctrinarian on the masses in the same way as Mao or Stalin, whilst, of course, giving his own kids a solid traditional Catholic education.

He certainly was not going to give his kids an education with no moral position, which he just inflicted on every other child. It is now said that childhood in this country is over by the age of 11, how sad an indictment is that of this society. Blair's Catholicism was only for his personal life, his public life seemed devoid of moral stance.

I've heard that some Government ministers are concerned about the numbers of parents getting their children into church schools. This they view as a problem because it increases segregation. Well why don't they just come out and say that they do not want their kids mixing with the kids of plebs!

'Golden' Brown, when in Government got Ed 'Balls-up' to fiddle with the system to enforce his own Doctrines, no doubt more Presbyterian, and to put 'happiness' on the school curriculum. As for Ed Balls, his father is a professor at Nottingham University and he was sent to Nottingham High, an outstanding Independent school, from where he went to Oxford and Harvard. Ed is determined like many of his generation, and political purist persuasion, that children of future generations will not be allowed to benefit from the advantages he enjoyed. Hence what he saw as 'pushy parents' were to be stopped and punished. Ed was keen to downgrade education and get back to what he called 'core issues', which included child poverty and child welfare. Hang on a minute Ed, schools were struggling to deliver education. But now schools were expected to play the role of the family, which New Labour policies helped to eliminate Schools were being told they needed to provide childcare from 8 a.m. to 6 p.m. Ed was understandably concerned when he heard the Head of the Association of Teachers accusing parents of devolving their responsibility to schools.

They are now saying that too much English history is being taught in England. I must have missed something whilst watching Alex Salmon look for Scottish independence, hopefully if that comes the English will realise that their own history is actually important. Apparently history teaching does not now have to be based on characters like Churchill but on nebulous 'causes and consequences' of conflicts. Is this move away from historical knowledge something to do with the lack of teachers with a first degree? The way things are developing the whole curriculum could be delivered in media studies mode, which would solve the teaching specialist shortages. Ironically the same has happened with the Science curriculum at GCSE where laboratory work has been cut down and children are asked to look at science issues in the newspapers. Ok media studies. So much so, that Imperial College London has said they will not accept this as a sound standard. Mind you Imperial College are also bemused about the current inflow of supposedly 'A' star pupils who can't spell fairly straightforward worlds like 'occur'. But all this we're told will make education more relevant to our youngsters. We could start doing maths using the amount of cannabis or English using phone texts. LOL

It's OK it's all coming back to me. As a student teacher at training college in the 1980s, we were told we should not correct spelling mistakes, as this would 'offend' the children. Not that I took any notice of that, the more I offended them the more they seemed to like it, something to do with giving them time and being honest I suspect. Hence the outcome was around 5 million illiterate, sorry children with non-functional literacy skills.

As each part of our once renowned system of exams are dumbed down and seen as failing, we discuss setting up another one. The old O levels which prepared students for A levels with such tasks as 'essays' were eliminated because not everyone could do them. But I thought that was why we had CSEs to assess different types of abilities? So then GCSEs were born, which everyone could take but unfortunately never prepared students for A levels. So the chasm between the two exams opened up. We must congratulate those children for doing well in meaningless exams, and so we should it's not their fault the politicians have mucked it up. Speaking to one of these students I was told if you get a 'D' on Coursework you just re-do it until you get a higher grade. A friend of mine was bemused when her daughter was predicted a grade C in RE as she was particularly interested in this subject area. The child replied, "It's OK mum, I spoke to the teacher and he said I'm going to get an 'A' but if he puts me down as a 'C' when I get my 'A' he will get a bonus." Hence then we had to make A levels easier to come in line with GSCE standards.

A major factor here was that the exam Boards were privatised by Mrs T and they then became businesses which meant they needed to vie for trade. How do you do that? You make everyone want to do your exam syllabi because they are so hard to pass. And schools will want to do your qualifications even though they are measured purely by the number of good grades they achieve. To put some reality into this without the hype, to compare in the 1980s 5% of Students at A level achieved grade 'A' whilst in 2007 25% achieved. And in 2010 A-Level pass rates reached 97.6%, and an unprecedented 27% of entries achieved an 'A' grade. So this must be because everyone is getting cleverer and of course the school system is working so well, instead of actually being in melt down. I think not. Hence we now look at A star grades to tell the top universities who is really clever, and we're still not quite sure, so just to be safe they make them do their own tests.

In the 1970s 6% of the population went to university, now 43% go, and get into huge amounts of debt for the privilege. But why did Blair want 50% of our kids to go to university? Was it him who assumed that if you didn't go to university you were a failure? When I was a kid, tradesmen were respected with some famous people from that field not least Jesus and Shakespeare's dad. And what was wrong with kids who were not academic or good with their hands, working in shops? It was honest labour. But our kids have been told they are obviously too good to do these jobs, which immigrants can be brought in to do, more New Labour voters, of course, and that they need to go to UNI. Why? Was he looking at it from his public school, middle-class socialist stance? If we can get 50% of our kids to university, socialism has arrived? Hence whilst major portions of our own youth take on ASBOs because they didn't go to university and have no other role in society, we pull in foreign labour to plug the skilled labour trade gaps, and also to do the low paid jobs. And when the Coalition came into power there were still arguments about needing immigrants to do our jobs even though students are coming out of university with no hope of getting jobs. Those who did media studies can end up having to stack shelves in supermarkets, but then it is probably a better way forward because if they actually got a job which paid more than £15k they would have to pay back their loan and this way they don't. Bring on the budgeting and financial capability courses so the Government can explain to them why they should not get themselves into debt.

Well now the money's gone. Our kids thought they were too good to do menial jobs so foreigners were brought in and now, in the cities especially, there are no lower paid jobs for them to do even to enable them to gain any work experience or work skills. They can no longer be sent off to do meaningless studies at college because the funding has gone and there are now far fewer places. Reality arrived when the New Labour Government left a note saying the money had all been spent.

So let's just warehouse 16-18 year olds, keep them off the streets by compelling them to stay in education, which has failed them from the age of 5. So at 16 you have the right to get married, and are positively encouraged by the welfare system to have babies, but New Labour proposed a Bill to make you stay at school or college until you're 18. Well that's a good way of increasing the teenage pregnancy rates! The reality is that issues that are driven by moral decisions like, sex, drugs and rock and roll cannot be taught without any moral position.

Hence if you teach kids about drugs and sex without any moral message you are wasting your time. What you are in fact doing is normalising behaviour that would have been seen by past generations as morally and socially wrong. But as no moral posturing is allowed now no boundaries can be set. It used to be called social stigma. But social stigmatism has been banned so anything goes. The liberal posturing does not allow for any moral view because 'hey man, we're all free to make our own decisions and no one has the right to say that anyone else is wrong, they just have a different perspective'. The reality is give them information and they will know how to do it more. Bring in celebrities and they will glamorise it. Education is not the answer to all issues, far from it.

Well we all know what a success sex education has been. More money is spent on drugs and sex education and both are getting much worse. Britain is now at the top of the league table for teenage pregnancies. With over 50,000 babies being born each year to teenage mums the figures are the highest in Western Europe – twice as high as in Germany, three times as high as in France and six times as high as in the Netherlands. Norman Wells, of the Family Education Trust, told the Sunday Telegraph that the Government had allowed the "systematic removal of every restraint that used to act as a disincentive to under-age sex".

Norman said: "The problems associated with teenage pregnancy will never be solved so long as the Government persists with its reliance on yet more contraception and sex education."[21]

So let's have another Government Minister explain where it all went wrong. Viv Crouch, a former advisor to the Government on the issue, said 'better sex education in schools was needed'. Oh dear!

So, the UK is at least top of a league table, if only for teenage pregnancies. Still if we can't teach kids that this is in effect, not a good idea, perhaps we can culture them up. So there is little enough time to teach them to read and write but let's put 5 hours of culture into the curriculum. Possibly the Minister for Ballet can work out how to do this. Party politics is at an end and political rhetoric has taken over. This is now termed 'the progressive consensus'. Vote by panel but don't let the BBC run this or you could be in trouble.

In the good old days members of parliament represented social and pressure groups which had clear political interests. The 'toffs' from the shires and the working-class trade union leaders. The view of 'plastic toffs' and 'plastic plebs' performing on the Westminster stage, created entertaining dramas. The Beast of Bolsover and Basher Healey were formidable figures but did at least say what they meant. Now, all 3 parties are led by men with

---

[21] Norman Wells – Too Much Too Soon: Family Education Trust 2009.

very similar backgrounds. Public school twits. Gone are the days when it would be possible to get a working-class prime minister. They went when those who could afford to pay for private education made the political decision to stop working-class kids getting a good education. The liberal elite fixed that one by getting rid of the Grammar School system, the only way that working-class kids could get into positions of power. We may never now see a working-class prime minister like Jim Callaghan or Harold Wilson. Increasingly MPs comes from within politics, speech writers, and marketing men. The A list has meant that politicians in power tend to come from certain inner circle groups. The Blair Babes epitomise those put into power because of the equality agenda not on merit. Censorship is endemic. The party line is held by career politicians and social mobility has never been worse.

Marxists like Red Ken and Peter Hain became establishment figures promoting a new form of Universalism, but now they are in the back row waiting for their comebacks. This 'universalism' concept, seems to assume that there are no local or national issues to any problem and that everyone is the same and even Utopia is possible. Marxism was meant to release the people but it just suppressed them and suppression is the want of most politicians who do not support the democratic process. So Brown said 'no more spin' but poor old Gordon looked permanently dizzy. When he first got into power he managed to get himself into so much PR difficulty he was soon reaching for the spin men. PR is used like PC, it closes down debate in problematic areas. So while Red Ken starved to death the pigeons in Trafalgar Square and eliminated any last trace of indigenous Londoners, Peter the Hain forgets the odd £100,000 that's been given to him, and still stays an 'honourable member' in parliament. His colleagues called it an 'honest mistake'. When Red Ken needed to find a new Race Adviser for his London Development Agency, he should have recruited Seb Coe who seems to personify 'Team Britain'. One thing is for certain, Lee Jasper, his ex-Race Adviser will now find it hard to get a post with the Olympics, as his salary rose from £40k per year to £100k per year under Ken. And we all know that the Olympics budget is likely to go 'tits up' with the initial costs put at £4.5 million they are now estimating the costs at £9.3 million. If you were in business with these skills you would certainly be out of business by now. Still there could be a surplus of out of work bankers who could get the job sorting the chaos out. If only the Olympics officials had concentrated a bit more and pushed the correct button, Paris would have got the prize.

So political correctness is subjective and is the view of those in the powerful elite who aim to silence any opposition. This is a major problem as it means that the masses, or the majority, in democratic terms, are alienated in their own society. Even the wealth creating part of society is alienated from the political classes but will of course toe the PC line with anything that will create them more wealth. Hence they are currently great supporters of immigration, which gives them a cheap supply of non-unionised labour, not only to create production in their businesses, but to clean their houses, do their gardens and look after their kids. Sorry, not PC, not sure why, something to do with goats. I have to say 'children'.

The PC concepts are promoted in the 'right on' media as part of the 'We' debate and by academics and social services managers. These are more often than not, middle class, and middle-aged. This is in contrast to the tabloids which are seen as 'Tribalistic' and representing the masses who 'know not what they think' and are deemed to be 'irresponsible'. The Dockers who supported Enoch Powell believed that they spoke for the working class and were not interested in party politics purse. The working class became an embarrassment to the Labour Party and the cultural Marxists took over and New Labour was born. New Labour was a project to get Labour back into power after so many years in the wilderness. Blair was style not substance with his 'metrosexual' Newcastle accent and his dodgy stories about absconding from Public School and watching Jackie Milburn play for Newcastle. More romance than substance, but that is what Labour wanted. Their aim was to change society for themselves not the lower classes. The Marxist economic debate had died but they could destroy the English culture instead and with it the

Conservative establishment. Hence democracy is on the decline and the masses are alienated. The metropolis which tends to be populated by these PC groups and the minorities they promote is alienated from the shires. Hence divided society.

Party Politics has now given way to single issue campaigning, one of the most distorting practices of our current time. The problem is that the domination of one issue promoted by an individual whose sole aim is to sell the theory, means it distorts truth and silences debate. It looks at an issue, or problem, from only one angle. For example, if you take an issue like abortion, the Catholics are clear it is wrong and want to protect the unborn child, the feminists are clear it's OK if the woman wants it as she is the priority, whilst others are in the middle. Not terribly clear cut.

Des Wilson of Shelter had the drive to push the housing issue up the political agenda but only from one angle, that of the homeless. They then marketed the view. No one can say that he's not been successful, on the contrary. But anti-road campaigners argued from the opposite, demand led solution. If you build more roads you're just going to fill them up and build more and fill 'em up and so on. Strange this angle hasn't been considered, discussed or even thrown out as an answer, with the housing debate. Instead the Green belt is likely to be destroyed, but then it is probably England we are hitting so who cares, the English have no voice. Hurray for Sir William Probey of the National Trust, who has come out and said that the National Trust will fight this policy if no one else has any power to, and at least create a debate about the issue. Don't worry Sir William, the failed economic miracle and the issues of the sub prime market will probably save use from all that.

Hence one angle of an issue distorts the other. Both Friends of the Earth and other Green campaigners have been anti-nuclear power for many years. And yet many scientists feel that the dangers of global warming far outweigh the risks for the nuclear industry. So how do they escape from their own single issue morality and be pragmatic? In 2008 crisis management took over and nuclear power stations have at last been commissioned. It's just a shame that we've lost all our own skills and will have to employ the French to run them. Political correctness had stopped the nuclear power debate and now we've hit crisis point and our much needed skills have been lost.

Human rights legislation is making loads of money for lawyers and undermining the rights of the mass of people who now have no rights at all. The Philosopher Bentham, analysed this issue back in the 18th century. He attacked what he called 'natural rights' particularly in his *Anarchical Fallacies* (a polemical attack on the declarations of rights issued in France during the French Revolution), According to Bentham then, the term 'natural right' "is a 'perversion of language'. It is 'ambiguous', 'sentimental' and 'figurative' and it has anarchical consequences. He noted that at best, such a 'right' may tell us what we ought to do; it cannot serve as a legal restriction on what we can or cannot do. The term 'natural right' is ambiguous since "what is every man's right is no man's right". No legal system could function with such a broad conception of rights. Bentham said that the idea of a natural right is "anarchical". Such a right, he claims, entails a freedom from all restraint and, in particular, from all legal restraint. "Since a natural right would be anterior to law, it could not be limited by law, and (since human beings are motivated by self-interest) if everyone had such freedom, the result would be pure anarchy."[22]

He was right. He concluded that the term 'natural rights' is simple nonsense.

"Natural and imprescriptibly rights, rhetorical nonsense – nonsense upon stilts."

An illegal immigrant breaks the law by coming to this country and commits a crime against our society or individuals. The issue is that if we send him back to his own country to protect the residents of this country from his crimes or for paying for his prison sentence, if he is likely to get hurt by his own Government he can stay here and continue to cause risk to our population as

---

[22]Bentham, *Anarchical Fallacies*, 1816.

his right to crime is obviously higher than our right to safety. Hence Abu Hamza cannot be extradited to the USA to answer crimes there because the prisons are not nice enough.

"But none of this would have happened had Britain simply deported him back in the 1990s when he first became involved in radical Islam. Hamza was an immigrant to this country who acquired citizenship through marrying a Briton, but he has since brought only pain to his adopted country. I can see no moral, as opposed to legal, reason why we cannot revoke the citizenship of people who have committed crimes or, in cases such as Abu Hamza, are a menace to the public. Ever since 2001 the Americans have started deporting foreign-born citizens if they commit crimes, a measure once only reserved for Nazi war criminals and other outstanding crimes. Were Britain to impose such a policy it would be considered a gross breach of human rights by the tiny section of opinion allowed on Radio 4."[23]

But not to worry we are busying 'bigging up' the case against the slave trade, whilst openly supporting the goods from countries that have 'slave labour' as it is to our economic advantage. We have to keep in with them you know. So let's focus on aspects of history that are being picked out by possibly well intentioned, or not, individuals or groups and raised as issues that are suddenly a threat to the world. The bicentenary of the slave trade was a prime example; slavery has existed and been practiced in various forms throughout history. But slavery can take many forms from men chained to large constructions to children who carry out bonded labour in the current boom economies of China and India, which of course we must embrace.

China is turning huge numbers of areas into special economic zones, laboratories for the communist regime experiment with capitalism. One area, Guangdong Province, now has a booming economy and accounts for half the GDP of China. An economy

---

[23] Ed West World News, July 8th, 2010.

powered by millions of workers who have migrated from the country to cities. More than 100 million rural Chinese have moved to cities, the biggest movement of people in human history. They do jobs with long hours and low pay because it is better than no work at all. Many regret their lots but there is no alternative. These goods are flooding into western markets and are eagerly encouraged by Governments who are thankful that their own economic inadequacies may be sheltered by cheap imports. So the West rushes to embrace this miracle, oh no not another one, of social engineering, whilst issues like the Chinese links in Africa and Darfur were just embarrassments for Gordon. So when the Olympic torch debacle came to London, Gordon and Ken chose to keep a low profile and avoid the issues. But never mind, this other economic miracle is so polluted it is a wonder that the marathon runners even survived the course.

Gap may have been embarrassed by the exposure that their clothes were being produced by children but one only has to look at the amount of goods coming in from China and India to know that this is widespread. The hypocrisy of the western free market is its rush to embrace these new slave driven economies. The mass population benefit from cheap goods and produce and the Government benefits by holding their own inflation down through cheap imports. So it is even more vital that you switch off that light and bath together, survival of the planet is in your hands folks. And of course, a New Labour view now is that 'sport is sport so let's just get on with the games'. Well that's a very new posture for liberalism, I must have missed something since the last time they caused anarchy on the cricket pitches.

But all this liberal posturing about the slave trade does not help the case of disenchanted black youths who are being told that they are indeed victims of this terrible ordeal, despite the fact that they never knew this, and that white people are the devil incarnate, and that they should actually be given reparations for what there ancestors must have suffered. I heard a black Tory A list candidate state that much damage was being inflicted to the black youth community by white liberals avoiding the real issues with the youths. He said what they needed was 'tough love'. Any left footed papist, should consider a case against the Queen for the problems Henry VIII caused, but I'm not sure I'd be able to pin her down on this one.

The church also got caught up in this approach with the Make Poverty History Campaign. In the old days they would wear a hair shirt or sleep on a rock and at least look like they were suffering for a cause. The Church of England once held the reigns of English culture but the liberal leaders, or wets, have given up the plot. Nicky Gumbel, the creator of the Alpha courses, said "even God has left the church of England". The Church of England was the pillar of society but it has repositioned itself so many times in an attempt to be politically correct that it's in danger of disappearing up its own bottom. So much so that whilst the Christian movement is expanding rapidly the growth is not in the established churches but in school halls and community centres. The new evangelical Christians feel they do not need an institution to get in touch with God, particularly one that is founded on sand not stone. The problem is that the church needs to have a structure, and an effective hierarchy if, as an institution, it is to have an impact on social change. It needs coherence and moral codes at least as a guideline or anarchy will prevail. This new anti-institution Christianity is counter productive in a nation where the church had always supported the culture for the masses. The city church vicars are now often just glorified social workers with no 'hell fire' messages, even some of the traditional institutions like the YMCA, have left the Christian message behind, and seem almost embarrassed by it. But people need a 'still point in a turning world'.

But the fashion for saying 'sorry' even when the people who are saying it have not actually done anything, which of course means that any genuine penance is missing, continues. Even the locals of Papua New Guinea in August 2007 did say sorry for eating 4 Christian missionaries 150 years beforehand and having a good old do in the process. This is what you get when you try and over simplify complex historical issues.

The Global poverty movement is distorting the picture on climate change and now new business is moving in to create carbon emissions trading, but more of that later. The silly season then tips over into humour when we see vicars parading through the streets yoked together in self-flagellation, or self-gratification, on the anniversary of the abolishment of the old Colonial slave trade. Good job someone else has taken over this trade so we can now feel better about ourselves. Sorry seems to be the easiest word.

Still it is also easy for our middle-class youth to attend aid concerts on the issues of poverty. Our own economy itself is boosted by a cheap immigrant labour force, whilst the youth of our own indigenous 'underclass' population languishes in the lap of the welfare state, no longer part of the economic structure and falling into so called 'anti-social' behaviour. The irony is that whilst some sections of immigrants are being encouraged to rediscover their roots, the English culture is being dismantled and our own youths are becoming rootless people with no identification. The reality is that they are a problem too difficult to deal with in a society that believes that no one actually has responsibilities. They are now the underclass. Businesses now capitalises on the cheap labour that has not been there since the rise of the trade unions. Marx said that any access to cheap labour will ultimately result in a more polarised society with increased rich and increased poor. He was right for once. Immigration was being encouraged by the Government and the business world to keep down wage inflation and provide cheap resources for the so called economic miracle.

The New Labour Government silenced the debate on immigration for fear of having to actually deal with it and it is still to be seen as to whether the Coalition Government can do any better. Thousands of jobs that were created in this economy have largely gone to foreign workers. And now that the bubble has burst the Government has a dilemma. It was only in quite recent times that this has been exposed and even discussed. However, as Frank Field said "how would this discussion have taken place if the immigrants had not been white"? Would we even have been allowed to discuss the issue? The case of the shooting of Charles de Menendez was in stark contrast to the case in 1983 when police shot the innocent film director Stephen Waldorf, and in 1999 when the innocent man Harry Stanley was also shot dead. These tragedies happened in a period of far less strain for the police than the traumatic period of counter terrorism when Menendez was also accidentally shot. Yet the fallout for the police was very different. They were both white.

So Greenism has now become the religion of atheists. Now that Marxism is dead, its followers have had to find a new belief system. And just as the Marxists had a hidden agenda of controlling other people, it is arguable that most of the professional Greens also do. After all, at least in the West, they are largely the very same people. Protecting the earth, as important as it unquestionably is, serves as an excellent pretext for almost any controls. This opens the door, as with Marxism, to 'the end justifies the means'. Absolutely nothing is more important than saving the earth. Global warming, a Government Minister recently told us is a bigger threat to the world than terrorism. Now we're told that obesity is a bitter threat to the planet than global warming. So it follows that fatties are about to destroy the world. Whether it is from gasses or from some kind of earth movement who knows. So why are they showing us all those bloody cookery programmes? I know Nigella has her 'knockers', but we had Fanny and Johnny and that was enough to put you off food for life and kept us so much slimmer.

The problem is, the Liberal posturing, does not want to confront the real issues, that are all about lifestyle changes, which would be much too difficult to deal with. So just make a gesture instead. As Andy Kershaw explained. "I am coming, reluctantly, to the conclusion that Live 8 is as much to do with Geldof showing off his ability to push around presidents and prime ministers as with pointing out the potential of Africa. Indeed, Geldof appears not to be interested in Africa's strengths, only in an Africa on its knees."

St Bob was criticised for using Africa as "a catwalk" which was more about reviving the careers of aging rock stars than about helping the poor. As Damon Albarn suggested it would be a good idea if the performers' record labels should have to pay "a tariff" as the accompanying publicity would increase future record sales and hence their profits. Live 8, it is important to note, was not a charity event. More criticism was leveled at some of the performers based on what they took home for participating in the Philadelphia concert. Because whilst they received no monetary compensation some were given gift bags containing lavish gifts and designer clothing. Some bands including the Who and the Artic Monkeys dubbed Live Earth as "Private Jets for Climate Change". It is estimated that the performers flew the equivalent of nearly nine times around the plant, and this does not include transporting all the technicians and support workers! It was also estimated that 100,000 trees needed to be planted to offset the total carbon emissions produced during the entire event, as well as the fact that a key sponsor was Chevrolet who were promoting a new hybrid four wheel drive car!

Spurred on by fears over security of oil supply from the Middle East, the United States has seen the biggest recent switch to bio-fuels and grain is being converted to gasoline on a vast scale. So then we got, the tortilla riots in Mexico.

Over the last fifteen years cheap American grain had ruined the Mexican maize business, millions of farmers had left the land, leaving the country hooked on imports. Critics of carbon trading, such as Carbon Trade Watch argue that it places disproportionate emphasis on individual lifestyles and carbon footprints, distracting attention from the wider, systemic changes and collective political action that needs to be taken to tackle climate change.

In the UK, wind power is the fastest growing renewable energy sector. The Government is investing massive amounts of money in its future. But some experts seem to think that the power of the wind to deliver electricity is being overestimated by companies keen to cash in on big subsidies. What a surprise!

On paper, wind power is a great proposition. We are the windiest nation in Europe not surprising with all the fatties – but despite the Government having subsidised the wind industry to the tune of half a billion pounds, so far it's failed to deliver half of one per cent of our electricity needs.

So the gestures are masking the real debate as the gestures are more palatable than the solutions. So Greenism is the latest PC party game. You can have lots of lovely fun calculating your carbon footprint; it's the latest middle class pursuit. You drive a Jeep, and you shouldn't. Yes but my jeep is a 1.3 engine whilst your car is a 2 litre engine. Well OK but you have a conventional boiler and I have a combi. Yes but your house is lit up like a Christmas tree, at Christmas. But I know you leave your TV on standby, and so on. So why not measure your own carbon footprint. You could stop smoking indoors and polluting everyone else's space, but don't go down the pub as if you smoke outside in colder times the patio heaters will need to be full on to keep you warm. You can recycle your carrier bags but perhaps you should not be buying so much food, especially those Scottish prawns that are transported to China for processing before being transported and sold back here. So like the Liberal MP on Radio 4 question time said: "I do think we all need to take on some responsibility. I do have a large BMW but I do lots of other things to compensate and I do take the train when it's not too inconvenient for me."

Well that's a relief, that will save the planet. And good old Jackie Smith, on the same programme, when she was a Minister, we can always rely on her to be the tour de force for saving the planet.

"My New Year's resolution for 2008 is to remember to take a carrier bag to the supermarket."

Wow, just the one Jackie?

The other great force infecting the world is said to be 'globalisation'. Sometimes it means Coco Cola replacing Tizer on the supermarket shelves, but normally it's about the economy being worldwide with no individual nation accountable for its own follies. So as our economy went into nosedive, Gordon held his hands up and said "this is nothing to do with me this is global". So globalisation had distorted all the rational debates we used to have. In the past the balance of payments figures and the value of the pound would have made headlines on a daily basis and could make or break Governments. Imports and export figures are now virtually ignored by politicians and yet

93

supposedly if a nation is buying more than it's selling then it has a problem. Well economic nationalism is making a comeback. With the crash of the UK's miracle economy, the Americans and the French have decided that they are going to look after their own economies rather than follow the supposedly 'highly successful 'Anglo Saxon' model of 'free enterprise'. Are they allowed to say 'Anglo Saxon'?

There was always something very scary about the whole thing really. The assets of the nation were being 'asset stripped by foreigners' with money'. Non-doms were big business for the removals and rehousing companies. They come here and as they don't have to pay tax on earning elsewhere, they buy up our big houses. Hence the arrival of a new rich elite.

And as for current immigration, the immigration lobby claims that there is little the government can do, it is all down to some mysterious force called Globalisation.

"Hold back the immigrant flood."[24]

"The crucial wake-up call was publication of the Government's latest population forecasts. They were truly shocking. They showed that if immigration continues at the level the Government now assumes, the population of the UK will grow by more than 10m in the next 25 years – that is equivalent to 10 cities the size of Birmingham; 70% of the increase will be due to immigration.

The public were taken aback by these numbers. They are now beginning to realise that we face the most critical decision for a generation. Not since the referendum on the Common Market in the 1970s have we confronted a decision that will so greatly affect the lives of our children and grandchildren. Do we set about a massive building programme, constructing a virtual Birmingham every 2.5 years and do we accept the fundamental changes to our society that will flow from immigration on this scale. Or do we take action now to cut immigration sharply?

---

[24] Sir Andrew Green, Migration Watch, 4th November 2007.

It was not long before we had Labour and the Conservatives competing to sound tough on immigration – an extraordinary transformation from the days when people hardly dared mention the topic for fear of being accused of racism.

The third event – if such it be – was the farcical episode when the Government's count of the new jobs taken by foreigners changed three times in a day, ending up roughly double where it began. The outcome was another blow to confidence in the Government's ability to manage immigration.

The genie is now well and truly out of the bottle. Public opinion is extremely strong – 80% disbelieve the Government honesty and 75% want to see an annual limit, two thirds fear that our culture is under threat. Only one in three believes that immigration brings economic benefit to Britain. The immigration lobby claims there is little that the Government can do. It is all down to some mysterious force called 'globalisation'. They are wrong. In fact, immigration to the UK took off in 1997. The prime cause was a series of policy errors by the present Government. First, it abolished such border controls as it inherited. Then it trebled the number of work permits to 150,000 a year, plus dependants. Finally, it hopelessly miscalculated the inflow of east Europeans.

Failure to act now will mean that our society will be changed beyond recognition – and especially our cities. London is one-third immigrant and half of all babies born there have a foreign parent. Other large cities will follow. According to one academic study, the ethnic community in Britain will grow from 9% to 29% by mid-century.

There is every reason for concern. The Commission for Racial Equality's final report spoke frankly about growing segregation and of our society 'fracturing', with bonds of solidarity across different groups weakening, and tensions between people increasing. These are serious warnings. The CRE was in denial about the role of mass immigration in all this but the rest of us can see it clearly.

We can now at last speak about the elephant in the room. But when will our political leaders respond to the deep anxieties that so many of us feel? And will they get down to some serious action before it is, indeed, too late?"

So Sainsbury's decided to allow Muslim workers who are working on checkouts, to have the option not to sell alcohol to customers. Presumably Catholics may now opt not to sell condoms? Why not concentrate on the real problems over the next 40 years, the loss of oil, the increasing world population and the collapse of western economies. The world's population has actually doubled to 6.5 billion over the past century. It is predicted to increase to 9 billion by the year 2050. In the 20th century, life expectancy increased from 45 years to 75 years; global population increased by one billion people every 12 years. We need to plan for 9.5 billion people who will be aspiring to the same standards as the West and using the same amount of energy. The Optimum Population Trust believes that the only solution is to gradually decrease the global population by 25% a year. The experts are warning the UK Government but little notice is being taken because of the unpleasant reality.

"The supreme function of statesmanship is to provide against preventable evils. In seeking to do so, it encounters obstacles which are deeply rooted in human nature. One is that by the very order of things such evils are not demonstrable until they have occurred.

Above all, people are disposed to mistake predicting troubles for causing troubles and even for desiring troubles; if only, they love to think, if only people wouldn't talk about it, it probably wouldn't happen. Perhaps this habit goes back to the primitive belief that the word and the thing, the names and the object, are identical. At all events the discussion of future grave but, with effort now, avoidable evils is the most unpopular and at the same time the most necessary occupation for the politician. Those who knowingly shirk it deserve, and not infrequently receive, the curses of those who come after."[25]

---

[25] E. Powell – Rivers of Blood Speech, 20th April 1968.

The power of political correctness to stifle democracy and free speech, and also silence any debate over crucial social issues over the last 30 years has led to a people who are only allowed to express themselves in the way the political elite would like. "Your worst enemy," he reflected, "was your nervous system. At any moment the tension inside you was liable to translate itself into some visible symptom."

All this social engineering has led inevitably to the breakdown of democracy because only the liberal thought police decide what is politically correct. This amounts to no more than political coercion and with terms like 'positive action', any common sense approach should ask, who decides what is 'positive', WHAT IS the moral or ethical position? This should always be declared. In the past we always knew, but now we don't. Who decides what speech is allowed and what is deemed as politically correct, or 'compliant'. The anti-nation, anti-christian, anti-family, secularists have stolen the show and dismantled the English institutions which we may have mocked, but we relied on to give us our stability. If the liberalists are so keen to dismantle England, why just not rename it. London was renamed by the Americans as Londonistan and this ultimately was proved to be very appropriate. It was just a shame people had to die before anyone would acknowledge this.

So this once proud nation is now renowned abroad for 'child neglect'. A place where a child dies at the hands of their parents or carers every 10 days, where the number of 8 year olds in A and E for alcohol problems has risen to epic proportions. Where, poor Aaron Douglas, died at the hands of his parents and when concerned neighbours rang social services to alert them to the issues, it was said that their comments were 'judgmental' so no one took any notice. What did they say? That they thought they were probably 'bad parents' because they were killing him! Obviously not pc ENOUGH. So another child dies. And now new statistics show that in the UK childhood is over by the age of 11. How sad. And the figures in 2009 on teenage pregnancies have again risen, another great success for sex education. They have decided to look at why this is happening, again, but one thing they made clear, it must not be deemed to be 'wrong' because that would be judgemental. They, 'teenagers', need supporting, and presumably more social payments, to encourage them to have another one!

Thatcher believed the market solved everything. She certainly made some millionaires out of privatisation for public sector bosses. But it was kindergarten economics and Blair just continued with her policies. Thatcher created unemployment and in so doing solved inflation and destroyed trade union power. Blair increased immigration in order to cut wage inflation and provide cheap labour for business and in so doing increased growth. Neither policies have taken any account of longer term economic problems or seen the wider picture of social problems. The costs of immigration have been hidden by counting GDP growth not per capita (per head) but as just one figure overall which is a nonsense considering the increased numbers that any extra wealth would have to support. Hence the pressure and demands on education, the health service, housing, the benefit system, prisons and all other services. And that is not even considering the future demands on all these areas plus pensions. So the ambulances at Midlands hospitals are queuing up with patients inside as there are no beds. The police are spending time chasing terrorists, searching rubbish dumps and investigating MPs. Free speech, even for politicians in a democracy has been stopped. So what did Nigel Hastilow say that he was forced to resign as candidate for Halesowen and Rowley Regis. Well, because he gave a view that was considered non PC. He said, "When you ask most people in the black country what the single biggest problem facing the country is, most say immigration... many insist Enoch Powel was right".

Enoch, once MP for Wolverhampton South West, was sacked from the Conservative front bench and marginalised politically for his 1968 Rivers of Blood speech, warning that uncontrolled immigration would change our country irrevocably. He was right. It has changed dramatically. Can anyone deny that?

We live in a minority rules society. Political correctness deems that all minorities must not be offended. I recently saw an advertisement for a job looking after problem kids who were getting into crime. In the advert it said that the job was working with those "at risk of offending". They may be at risk of becoming criminals but we, the majority, are at risk of being offended against! It seems like the whole language has been distorted to say something it does not really mean.

The outcome of all this was that we ended up with 3 liberal parties, all led by career politicians, rather than those of conviction. With no choice between parties democracy has died. The takeover of the education system by the political elite sealed the fate of democracy and silenced debate. Anyone who spoke out against the political elite would be bullied into submission. The bullying would be carried out by the self-righteous and any academic who dared to pose an alternative view would lose their job. Sounds starkly familiar to fascist and communist states.

The Labour Party liberalists had to eliminate the trade unions and the working-class lobbyists to be electable. Blair took over and silenced debate in his own party and MPs delivered on the promise of a job and an income. Plus of course, quite good expenses. Blair was a safe option he was a man of image not substance. But who needed substance, image was far more important. He looked like a Yuppy rather than, legend has it, a mediocre barrister. A clerk was reportedly quoted speaking to a client when both Tony and Cherie worked in the Inns of Court. "No I would not recommend young Mr Blair Sir, you would be better represented by Miss Booth."

The Tories having failed another election were in the same position as Labour several years earlier. So they elected a Blair lookalike clone and all opposition was silence on the promise of getting elected. As Rory Bremner once said, "I only imitated Blair, Cameron did the whole career."

Happiness is not something you can be taught. It is not something you can sort out by putting it on the school curriculum. Happiness is a state of mind, it comes from feeling safe, having an identity, being in a family and having a belief in yourself and your country, It comes from family, security, spirituality, faith and a belief in your culture. All this the majority of the over 40s took for granted. It was what English culture was all about.

"Our ancient culture was a forest that took a thousand years to grow and less than half a century to cut down. Now that the trees are all flattened, the people who massacred them find that they are shivering in a howling wilderness that they are powerless to restore to its formers shape...

"All the funny money, private finance initiatives in the world, all the taxes they can raise, all the concrete and plastic they can buy, cannot rebuild a forest... Is this any surprise in a country whose leading minds have devoted the past half century to dismantling absolute morality, the married family and the idea of punishment? They claim to be concerned about the planet – in the abstract. But in reality they preside over the gross foul-smelling uglification of a country that was within living memory, one of the most beautiful on Earth." So that's why they are planning to sell off English forests and not Scottish or Welsh ones. They would not allow that to happen.

But fear not, political correctness has not completely destroyed this once proud culture. The English can still be seen, not in Metroland, but in the shires. Shopping in Marks and Spencers, in a Country pub, at a whist drive, at the WI, or at a cricket match.

The real split for the English is between the city and the shires. The indigenous Londoners of the blitz, had no confusion about their allegiance. They fought for the monarchy and their country. The liberals took over the cities and built them on sand. They drove out the indigenous population and built a society where the most fearful attack on it would come from within. London has no cohesion, but no doubt they will set up some social cohesion centres, that should sort it. The London boom was fuelled by the city. It was built on Russian and Arab oil money. Its basic utilities are owned by foreigners and as the city collapses so does the economy.

We make very little, we own even less. Our assets have largely been sold off to foreigners in an attempt to balance our

100

imports and exports. London has been fuelled by large capital inflows and the result is our total vulnerability. In the English Premier league, we may have top Premier teams competing in Europe but far fewer Englishmen on the pitch. So the root and branch review of English football promised by the FA after our failure in the European cup, turned out more like lots of gestures but not even much pruning. They just grasped the first passing foreigner and appointed him as the England manager. And after the 2010 World Cup fiasco, they are promising, yes, more root and branch reviews.

Fabulous Fabio's English skills were so poor that they were considering that it would be easier to teach the English footballers Italian. Well that's a real progressive move. The English have battled to make English the language of the world, and our footballers may have to learn Italian to play for England. Still let's not be negative. We could always create a little phrase book for Fabio, with essential phrases like:

The lads done well
Football's a game of two halves
We waz robbed
I've never met Ulrika Johnson
When is the next flight to Milano?

This may all help towards breaking down the English attitude towards Johnny Foreigner, well it's certainly about time. Our ancestors were obviously all racists and fascists.

But to be fair we weren't the only ones to be humiliated in the world cup. There can be no excusing the French performance and, more significantly, their attitude at this World Cup. A squad featuring players from super clubs like Barcelona, Manchester United, Chelsea and Arsenal played like a bunch of amateurs and acted like a collection of spoiled children.

When Nicholas Sarkozy came here and showed off his new wife to us he returned to France talking of a new 'entente cordial'. Well let's be honest the French have always been there when they needed us. They were the only nation during the war to get sunburned armpits. The Americans are reported to have said

101

during the Gulf War, "going to war with the French was like going to war with an accordion."

And we English do have other things on our mind apart from our own extinction. We've got illnesses we never knew we had. There are 'uisms', 'obias' and 'axioms', coming at us from all angles. Now even 'anger' is apparently an illness, as is 'sex addiction'. I'm thinking about retreating to my sick bed, as I know I can leave the Government in charge, they know how to sort things out. They often come up with some cunning plans. Hide cigarettes under the shop counters so children don't see them. Yes, that should fool them. Lock the school gates, to stop the little darlings escaping and buying junk goods, which is a big threat, especially if they start attacking each other with it rather than using knives or people's heads as footballs, which seems to be the latest sport. That should do it.

They may even be able to save the planet by closing our post offices, libraries and local schools. That's a very Greenist notion. This is very logical and fits in well with the demise of the health service which is being looted by health tourists who come here to get free treatment, whilst we fly to Poland to get a dentist or a hip replacement. Good thinking.

Society is broken and the politicians live in a state of denial. They know not what to do. Hazel Blears when she was a Minister had a good idea, she wanted all the Labour Ministers to have sessions stocking supermarket shelves, as she did herself, as a way of connecting with the people. Well I hope she reminds Jackie Smith to take her carrier bag with her. Thanks goodness they are now looking for new jobs.

What really defined the English was 'wit' and 'tolerance'. Unfortunately, political correctness called for the English to be tolerant but took away the wit. The irony is that the tolerance was about the wit. Wit is not allowed, because all humour is about man's fallibility, his reach that exceeds his grasp. The problem is that the elite believe that Utopia is possible. And that actually it is by being re-educated like them that we can achieve it!

Yet the one thing that has protected us from totalitarianism be it liberal or fascist, is humour. As Orwell once said 'Every joke is a tiny revolution'.

So let's end this political coercion section with a few words from the Master of political wit, who I'm sure the Blair babes would have considered as extremely 'rude'. The problem with feminists is that they believe they are 'women' before they are human beings.

As Lady Astor said to Mr Churchill after a heated commons debate: "How rude Winston, if I was your husband I'd shoot you." Mr Churchill retorted: "Madam, if I was your husband I'd shoot myself." Possibly Lady Astor would have had enough dignity to have realised she had left herself wide open to that. But a Blair babe would no doubt have been rushing to a highly paid lawyer for legal advice.

CULTURE CLUB

"Error creeps in again and again through our tendency to think of culture as group culture exclusively, the culture of the 'cultured classes and elites'. We then proceed to think of the humbler part of society as having culture only in so far as it participates in this superior and more conscious culture.

"To treat the 'uneducated' mass of the population as we might treat some innocent tribe of savages to whom we are impelled to deliver the true faith, is to encourage them to neglect or despise that culture which they should posses and from which the more conscious part of culture draws vitality."[26]

The thing is, when I was a kid I thought culture was something that had nothing to do with me. It was for people who went to the ballet, ate lunch at dinner time and had dinner at tea time. Then when I got an education I discovered that culture is really everything that makes a nation what it is. So my mum's bingo nights at the local palaise de dance, and our annual holidays to Hayling Island on the bus, in a caravan with no hot water, counted equally as part of the English culture. So, socks and sandals, knitted swimsuits, fat ladies paddling in large bloomers, stripy deck chairs, rainy days, sing songs, and knees ups; bawdy postcards and humour that dates back to Elizabethan times. They

---

[26] T.S Eliot, *Notes Towards the Definition of Culture*.

were all part of what made England what it was. It was our cultural identity. The sum activities of the nation. We never had a Minister for Culture, community centres, or even social cohesion committees. We were proud of being English and always suspicious of Johnny Foreigner.

But now, whilst English culture has been destroyed, other cultures are being encouraged to revisit their roots. The liberalist political agenda encouraged the demolition of English culture which it saw as symbolising the crimes of the West. Hence, English culture has been destroyed by ethnocentric separatists who see the history of the West as corrupt and get redemptive input from non western cultures, plus a few good restaurants thrown in for the bargain. Well except of course those aspects which are deemed distasteful, to the 'We know best' brigade. Foreign food, delicious, 'so difficult to find a decent restaurant in England pre-1980'. Fashion, very nice and much cheaper now what with the Chinese and globalisation. Jewellery startling. Carnival, magnifique. But arranged marriages, not really darling, Suttee, that's a bit horrifying and honour killing, well honour is always good isn't it?

So the celebration and pride in our culture which the over 40s took for granted has been lost. Our once proud cultural identity is being dismantled by those who have taken over our institutions and we sit by and watch, as our places of social congregation, where we used to freely debate these issues, disappear. As post offices, local pubs, working men's clubs and local schools are destroyed by Government policy, we just return to our front rooms and watch programmes that disturbingly seem to symbolise our current mass culture. Programmes like Big Brother and the Apprentice. It's no wonder we question what went wrong. To get on Big Brother you need to be a sexual exhibitionist, being dysfunctional is an advantage and a disability is always useful. And as Big Brother gets louder and brasher than ever, and that's just Davina, we sadly reflect back on our TV programmes that used to unite, rather than divide, the nation, like Morecambe and Wise.

We now have men 'working their tits off' and women, surprisingly enough, 'with balls'. To lie on your CV is OK as long as you get the job but hopefully you won't be a surgeon or an airline pilot. But all this is to miss what we really mean by our culture and its gift. It is to devalue what was once precious. Our culture is what holds us together. It's our beliefs, our faith, our attitudes, our community, heritage and our ancestry. It's what helps us to decide whether to jump into a lake to save a child or cross the road to help someone in distress.

It is a sad indictment of our cultural confusion that we are now told that the British are less likely to be 'have-a-go heroes' and to intervene in any dispute or problem in a community, than anywhere else in Europe. It's as if we don't share humanity with people from other races or classes or even the next town or village.

"British people are the least likely in Europe to be 'have-a-go heroes' and get involved if they witness a crime," research from a think tank claims. "Crime has become so 'nationalised and politicised' that the Home Secretary and the Prime Minister are held responsible for every assault," says the report. "Maintaining lawfulness should be seen as part of the duty of every citizen," it says. The report quotes a survey which studied public perception of anti-social behaviour in six European countries – France, Germany, Italy, the Netherlands, Spain and the UK. It found six out of 10 of the people questioned in the UK would be unlikely to challenge a group of 14-year-old boys vandalising a bus shelter, more than any other country surveyed. In Germany, six out of 10 said they would challenge the group. The public policy group Reform says that Britons have become 'passive bystanders' in the fight against crime".

The English, in particular, seem to have become passive bystanders in so many issues mainly because the loss of their culture has undermined their confidence to know who and what they are, what to do and how to behave. Well perhaps if the Government's bizarre, and of course very expensive, legal system didn't allow people to be arrested who challenged victim groups (criminals) and have them for assault. And if health and safety did not intervene when the normal Christian concept of the good Samaritan raised its head, perhaps we would be clearer about our roles as citizens! When we were subjects we didn't seem to have this problem. Perhaps we've all switched off from society and retreated behind our locked doors. The saddest aspect of all this is the loss of working-class culture. This was built on a 'poor but proud' belief system, which did not base happiness on money, but on community, family and faith. Marxists may have tried to undermine this by talking about 'the oppression of the workers' and in the process destroyed what was precious and ironically what held them together.

So let's look back to sounder times. "When you come back to England from any foreign country, you have immediately the sensation of breathing a different air. Even in the first few minutes dozens of small things conspire to give you this feeling. The beer is bitterer, the coins are heavier, the grass is greener, the advertisements are more blatant. The crowds in the big towns, with their mild knobbly faces, their bad teeth and gentle manners, are different from a European crowd. Then the vastness of England swallows you up, and you lose for a while your feeling that the whole nation has a single identifiable character. Are there really such things as nations? Are we not forty-six million individuals, all different? And the diversity of it, the chaos! The clatter of clogs in the Lancashire mill towns, the to-and-fro of the lorries on the Great North Road, the queues outside the Labour Exchanges, the rattle of pin-tables in the Soho pubs, the old maids hiking to Holy Communion through the mists of the autumn morning – all these are not only fragments, but CHARACTERISTIC fragments, of the English scene."[27]

Our heritage was built on Judea Christian faith, Roman administration and Greek democracy. It is what our forefathers died for and our history has shaped over 1500 years. To destroy that is to undermine the sacrifices of generations that went before

---

[27] George Orwell, 'The Lion and the Unicorn'.

and to betray our forefathers. Now it is the mass identity which is seriously under threat, it has been destroyed by those who despised it but don't know how to replace it.

Margaret Hodge was the New Labour Minister for Culture, Creative Industries and Tourism. So why couldn't she get a proper job? In 2009 Margaret's attack on the Proms caused such embarrassment to the Government that they were forced to deny her words. She did later admit that it's not so much the music she has a problem with but the audience, and I suspect Jerusalem. She was quoted as saying that everything must be as diverse as possible. Whatever that means. Perhaps there should be someone at the box office carrying out ethnicity stats on entry, or possible sexual preferences? There was a very different take on this from an Italian official who attended the proms and raved about them saying that they should be replicated in all countries.

New Labour also had a similar issue with those dissident fell walkers in the Lake District. Lakeland fell walkers suddenly entered the category of cultural extremists and lost their lottery grant to provide guides for walkers, as fell walking was considered 'much too English'. Ok, look nobody is going to support them for carrying national geographic bags on their backs, or smelling like wet socks but suicide bombers they aren't. Ethnic minority groups may well not want to walk up steep hills in the rain, but then an English person may not want to do things that they like to do. So let's try and re-educate the mass plebs and, well, make them more like the liberal elite. Give them some 'real culture' not that English peasant stuff. The cultural elite had a good crack at this in West Bromwich by commissioning 'the public' a state of the art gallery that went £12 million over budget and opened 2 years late. A bemused pensioner seen to be walking past when it was opened was asked what she thought and she just said "West Bromwich is not the place it used to be." Sad really.

The Arts Council has come to represent everything that is batty about our society. They are now allocating grants by the diversity of the sexual orientation of the Board. Just how much different sex can you get? They stated that "Diversity is not just about ethnicity, race and Religion."

"Theatreland will have to give up its bedroom secrets in the quest for funding, under new Arts Council requirements. Organisations applying for grants are being asked to state how many board members are bisexual, homosexual, heterosexual, lesbian or whose inclinations are 'not known'."

Audrey Roy, the director of grants, said that the council needed to understand who its audience was and to whom its funding was going.

"We see diversity as broader than race, ethnicity, faith and disability," she said. Question 22 of the Grants for the Arts forms, relating to sexual orientation, was not compulsory, she added, although the form states that it must be answered.

The question caused anger and bemusement among leading figures of the arts world yesterday. The Oscar-nominated actor Sir Ian McKellen, who is openly gay, said: "It sounds extraordinary. It shouldn't be on a form. It's quite inappropriate."

Vanessa Redgrave, the actress and human rights campaigner, said: "Everyone should put down 'trisexual', whoever you are. Britain has become the world's leading population of trisexuals." I agree Vanessa.

As Woody Allen once said: "Bisexuality immediately doubles your chances for a date on Saturday night," so trisexuality must be a bonus. And I'm sure there must be loads of people who would be only too willing to 'try sexual activity of one sort or another'.

So let's hear from Colin Tweedie from Art for Business who seems to think that art is about to save the nation from its cultural extinction and in so doing seems to represent the deluded. So here's a snippet of Colin speaking on Radio 4.

"Every child should have a right to listen to Beethoven, to hear a Mozart opera, to see the magic of a Titian, etcetera, etcetera. And that's not just a poncey, middle-class man like me talking."

Oh Yes it is Col...

"But it's also about getting feral kids off the street, give them hope. A child who is understanding the energy of their own body in a dance class, I would argue is going to be more comfortable in their skin and successful in life than kicking around a football." Oh dear.

So new ideas are all the rage singing and dancing in schools is making a comeback, and of course competitive sport. Well shock horror. Perhaps they should not have sold off the school playing fields after all. Of course singing and dancing should be part of the curriculum in school and it's a crime that they ever stopped. When I was at primary school we certainly danced in class, 'stand up, sit down, turn around, keep moving'. But we sang and danced for a reason. There was no heating. We enjoyed patriotic songs and did traditional English folk dancing and played playground games that have been passed down from generation to generation. This was our culture and we were proud.

Art should not be used for social engineering but to enlighten inspire and challenge. The role of art is to make one think, not as a form of social engineering. Art is about the voice in the wilderness not a political movement. Once art becomes the political agenda it is no longer art.

The Brown Government suddenly became so concerned about our lack of identity, which they had destroyed, that they then decided to debate the break up of English culture but only in terms of high culture. So the liberals have now snuck off with the term culture and ironically turned it back into elitism and rant on about everyone having access to Mozart and Beethoven regardless of whether we want access, we will have access, they know what is best!

So the mission of the political elite now is to save our feral youth from the streets by turning them into Billy Elliot's rather than Edward Sissorhands. So when the Government mentions 'culture' it dare not mention indigenous English culture but only the high culture with which the 'We' brigade can identify. The high culture is the only aspect of culture that the liberals are prepared to raise. If they delved into the issues around current English culture and what has happened to it, the questions would be too difficult to solve and the blame too much to take. The irony is that it is often those from other cultures who came here to embrace ours that most laments its passing. They had viewed it

110

from afar and stood in awe of it. The Anglican church, has at least two things in its favour, two bishops who are fierce supporters of English culture, thank God. The Archbishop of Rochester and the Archbishop of York, both Johnny foreigners, have a clear understanding of what we really mean by culture and what we have lost.

"I fear that we are in danger of losing the formative Christian inheritance and foundation of this great nation, a foundation upon which our laws, society and culture have been built, but which is in danger of being undermined – a foundation of meeting the other person halfway... Reinventing the wheel is not the problem; it is reinventing the flat tyre that is the killer."

The danger is if we don't celebrate the indigenous culture it may become too dysfunctional to save. So I'm staying with T.S Eliot's view of culture as 'the sum activities of what a country is'. What makes them, laugh, cry, what they believe in, how they act and what they do. It unifies a nation and creates a collective consciousness that holds it together. We will discover at our peril that a unified culture is more necessary in times of trouble than ever before. The problem is that when you break a culture that has evolved over at least 1500 years and you have nothing to replace it with, then what you get is a cultural vacuum for the masses and the liberals may want to fill it with Beethoven but what they are getting is Big Brother.

"But here it is worth noting a minor English trait which is extremely well marked though not often commented on, and that is a love of flowers. This is one of the first things that one notices when one reaches England from abroad, especially if one is coming from southern Europe. Does it not contradict the English indifference to the arts? Not really, because it is found in people who have no aesthetic feelings whatever. What it does link up with, however, is another English characteristic which is so much a part of us that we barely notice it, and that is the addiction to hobbies and spare-time occupations, the *fate* of English life. We are a nation of flower-lovers, but also a nation of stamp-collectors, pigeon-fanciers, amateur carpenters, coupon-snippers, darts-players, crossword-puzzle fans. All the culture that is most

111

truly native centres round things which even when they are communal are not official – the pub, the football match, the back garden, the fireside and the 'nice cup of tea'. The liberty of the individual is still believed in, almost as in the nineteenth century."[28]

It may be this concept of the privateness that Orwell describes and of the 'individual' life which makes us retreat to our front rooms and hope it will all go away.

We were awe inspired by the spectacle of the Beijing Olympics but it seems likely that GB 2012 will be a very different affair as things become more gloomy. So when the American stock market moved into 'negative momentum' and as the British economy is in meltdown, £9.2 billion. has been set as the maximum budget for the Olympics. And now the marketing men are thinking of as many ways as possible to positively express 'broke'. Let's try 'cosy', 'intimate', 'different', and of course, 'funnier'. Bozzer calls it 'intimate' and "humourous". Whilst Seb states: "The 2012 event's mission statements will be about Creativity and the British Capital's cultural scene... sure it is about sport (smarmy voice). "But we will take the chance to showcase the creative capital that London is... and let's have a bit of fun with this."

Well you're making me chuckle anyway Seb. When I saw Becks kick a football from a grassy knoll that had morphed into a bus, onto some unsuspecting Chinaman, it set the scene. As Bozzer then turned up looking like he'd forgotten about it and had to be dragged away from the bar it all started to make sense. My only query is where were the hoodies that normally terrorise people on London buses and shouldn't there have been two buses both on their way to the depot? The so called 'Green' Olympics has managed to destroy all the allotments located in the East End of London by the goodwill of Victorian philanthropists. The only thing Green about the Olympics is possibly the pigment they are

---

[28] George Orwell, 'England Your England'.

putting in the cement. So why not liven things up with Ken Dodd and his tickling stick, in the Olympic colours. That should make em run a bit faster. He is, after all, from the 2009 capital of culture.

Well in my memory Liverpool was a place full of 'scousegits' who were notoriously friendly, humorous and lively. "Who's the woman in the white shell suit at a Liverpudlian wedding? The bride." They placed great importance culturally on family and faith. When they became a centre for culture they may have lost some of the culture which held them together. The killing of Rhys Jones stunned the city but the fact that it happened should have been no surprise to locals given the gang culture that has developed in many parts of the city. It was said that Rhys Jones died because of Sean Mercer's hatred for members of the Strand Gang. Sean Mercer's hatred was so powerful, he was willing to fire shots in full view of the many customers who had gone there for a quiet drink or to watch the England versus Germany football match which was taking place that night.

As Liverpool was reported to be having a year long party as part of their Capital of Culture celebrations, the council were reported to be £29 million in debt and those most vulnerable, the old people, were having their care homes pulled down. The old and infirm in Liverpool found it hard to get excited about the big party. Still they could get ready for the 2012 Olympics, and start training with the free swimming the Government is promoting for the over 60s. Even though I suppose they may not still be around. At least this would allow them to escape from the old people's homes, which according to experts have 'serious problems', due to the fact that the inspectors are told not to flag up any provision which is poor because of the Government targets which the CSCI need to meet. Well then with a bit of luck they will be pulled down. Never mind a right wing think-tank has come up with a solution to problems of unemployment in the area; they can all move to London. Hopefully they still have a sense of humour.

Well back to the Olympics. With no security costs even considered within the budget, we are still looking for an economical way to open the celebration. The Red Arrows were considered for a fly past, but they were considered too British. So I'm not sure what they want, possibly some Kosak dancers, I'm sure Mr Putin would oblige, although I hear he's keener on Abba, but that would be appropriate as the Russians run London anyway. But it's OK, apparently Danny Boyle has been tasked to organise the opening ceremony, so whilst Beijing does pageant, we will probably be doing some scenes of self-imposed misery.

But let's not be too gloomy Danny. If intimate, funny and cheap are the bywords, let's go for something more discrete, a little less noisy and full of the real cultural traditions of the English capital. Radio 2 audiences have suggested Chas and Dave singing 'Rabbit' or 'my old Dutch'? We could always surround them with a range of pearly Kings and Queens all eating jellied eels. Bozzer Johnson could perhaps do a rendition of Gercha. They could perform on the top of an open top route master bus with dambusters playing in the background. We could use Barbara Windsor to serve up the jellied eels in true Old Vic fashion. Just to put the icing on the cake, we could see if Dick Van Dyke is still available to add some local vocal authenticity to the whole scene. If not we may have to resort back to Dicky Ticker and the red arrows. Then Cliff Richard could be on standby in case it rains. Now that should just about be within budget. Or on the other hand, we could always get the pretty little girl who opened the Chinese games to appear and then dub Chas and Dave onto her, that would be very multicultural. Or perhaps we could just get the whole thing boxed up and sent over from China, like everything else. Gor luvva duck what a scene, cor blimey.

The rot seemed to set in when the financial stability of the western world relied on the fortunes of Fanny May and Freddie Mac, who sound like two reprobates from the Jerry Springer show. Perhaps these highly respected leaders of the financial world should have made a start by changing their names? The UK banks have now found a way forward, they just provide their customers' information to be sold on eBay. So Gordon mumbled on about a very new concept 'waste not want not' and tucked into his 20 course meal at the G8 at a cost of over £220 million whilst he told us not to throw food away. Well perhaps he should have eliminated the 'sell by date' police to sort this little problem out. Alternatively you could just remove the 'sell by date' labels before the kids catch you. What was wrong with the old sniffing method? It never did my mum any harm. Well I had a few soft tomatoes and a few rotten eggs I would have loved to have given Gordon. Gordon always claimed to be a dour Scott, who favoured Prudence, but did his wife know about it?

Our once proud history and culture have now been denigrated and we need to ask how did we get to where we are now. How did it all evolve and whose fault is it?

I'm not sure if one can begin at the beginning and no one quite knows where the Beginning is, and if you get all philosophical about it is there any such thing as beginning? And no one knows the real truth other than those that were there, but you can bet your life that if you did get those that were there together you still wouldn't get one Version of the event. Similarly, if you laid a group of economists from end to end you would still never reach a conclusion. All we can ever know or understand about history is interpretations of documented evidence and events. And anyone who passes this evidence forward is coming from a distinct set of values, cultures and attitudes and even sides. Politics is the key to many historical debates taken from a position of right, left, centre and barmy. When history has been written it can be rewritten to please an individual in power, or sanitised so as not too offend. It is extremely unlikely that Richard III would have ended up with a hunched back or indeed disabled, as we would now say, if Shakespeare had not been trying to please the Elizabethan Queen and been keen to keep his head attached to his neck. And even our attitudes towards a hunched back from our current society would have been totally different than if it had been written as history now rather than as a view from the Elizabethan stalls.

History can be manipulated. The Scottish played a significant role and capitalised greatly out of the British empire, but when the shit hit the fan they held their hands up and said, "We were

115

victims too, and look how we suffered for the highland clearances..." Then there are the groups who only believe history becomes real or of importance when their own social theories were born, like Marxists and feminists. They portray history from their own political ideology. Past renegades and ex-Marxists like Ken Livingstone and Peter Haine become establishment figures whilst Ian Paisley and Martin McGuiness share a cuddle and Peter Mandelson had more comebacks than Frank Sinatra.

Then there is the added complication that history writers will find it difficult to sell the books they write, or indeed get anyone interested at all, unless they take a different slant on history to previous writers. So we have an added dimension, history is often written just because it is controversial so books on the Battle of Britain and the Holocaust overturn traditional history and make 'loads of money'. One theory has it that it has been scientifically proven that Adam and Eve were black! The original man was black! The Egyptians were black! Moses was black! The original Jews were black! Abraham was black! Jesus is and was black! In the book of revelation it tells you that God himself is black! But your white supremacist thinking will keep you from acknowledging or accepting the truth!

So, Hitler was misunderstood, Christ married a prostitute, Leonardo di Vinci didn't like young boys, and Dan Brown understands history.

Whichever way history is surely just one bloody thing after another. And those who have destroyed our narrative history have definitely lost the plot. To get at the true history of the English you've got to fight your way through a lora, lora battles. Throughout history war is a consequence of man's innate need for territory and his tribal instinct. Should we not put hoods on prisoners but just kill them in battle? Should we protect the right of one individual over the rights of thousands that could be in danger of dying? There are no absolute solutions to these questions and, in the past we never would have been arrogant enough to think there were. We would have only used a term called 'common sense'. Now we think we have answers, but they make no sense at all. But then the Coalition Government asked for a 'common sense' approach to health and safety, but do we still have the ability to do this?

But when we look back self-righteously and retrospectively at wars, were they bad wars, were they bad people, who knows. How do we define this? What standards are we looking at? Were they effective, did they succeed, were they nice, did they care, are they sorry? The real truth is always illusive but the heritage of it all makes us what we become. History is a record of events but it is tradition that holds society together that which is passed forward by generations. Those social links with the past, present, a future that marks one culture out from another and gives social cohesion and collective harmony without any sign of a social cohesion committee, or a Minister for Harmony.

History gives each nation, and has always given the English, a sense of themselves. So understandably those of a certain age are bemused to see, what their forefathers celebrated as victories now demeaned as irrelevant in a world where victims' rule and minorities are sacrosanct. We now seem to be in a structure where majorities are seen as natural oppressors, and minority groups, natural victims. The Falklands war was a prime example. It was a traditional war; they invaded a land which we believed was ours. It was part of our country and our lads saw them off. I remember the euphoric scenes at Portsmouth docks as our lads sailed out with the task force. Buttocks were brandished and breasts were bared. A fine English tradition. We were proud, the Argentineans had dared to invade our territories and the justification was fairly clear, or was it? What about the Argentineans who died, well in any war there are casualties on both sides. Ironically it is believed there were more Argentineans who died of suicide after the conflict ended than actually died during hostilities. The celebrations were somewhat muted. We should not celebrate wars. Who can now even remember or care what happened to those who went off to fight for their country or what it was about 'lest we forget'. In any war there are always people who fight and lose their lives, or limbs, on behalf of the Government. If people lose faith in the armed forces in a democracy, they lose faith in themselves and their own identity. The armed forces ultimately represent the people. If our culture is fragmented this is not possible. After the Iraq war, which was so unpopular with the masses, and with multiculturalism being promoted, attitudes towards our troops became confused. There were 1000 ex-soldiers sleeping rough in London on any night and there were examples of our own hotels banning our lads from staying with them. The Brown Government rightly became concerned that something in the culture was breaking down. He put out a dictate that the Union Jack should fly from public buildings and Wootton Basset became the centre for welcoming home the troops. But his actions were inadequate. When the people of Luton turned out to celebrate the homecoming of local soldiers the scene turned ugly when a group of Muslims protested against the celebrations and it started the formation of the English Defence League. Whose nation was it now?

The reality is that no one can have an absolute perspective of history but anyone can sit with a self-righteous glow. Who do the islands actually belong to, and no one can really answer that either, they just have views. Throughout history senseless wars have been fought by often ill-informed people. Nationhood may be the cause of wars but it is also the drive or existence. Men are territorial animals and territory and God are the main motivators. History is cyclical and nothing much changes, only borders and sometimes causes, but Man never learns. Soldiers are increasingly being used to police political situations, to be peace keepers or social workers in broken societies that we are arrogant enough to believe we can fix. To insist on democracy in countries that have no use for it, as it is not part of their culture whilst our democracy is defunct and our culture truly broken, is the final irony.

So should we ask what wars are 'just'? Who should we fight? Who should decide who we fight or whose side who is on? Is it about the country you live in, or the one you have an allegiance to? This is a complex new question that has not arisen before to any great significance. If you are encouraged to revisit your culture, go back to your roots and demonstrate how diverse or different you are, when you are in another land, then why should anyone be surprised when you want to fight for your own

118

homeland and culture? Why would you rather belong to some other culture, which its own intelligentsia has deserted and which has become so watered down that its own youth are alienated and have dug their own hole on the scrap heap?

Part of the English culture has been, strangely enough, about celebrating our failures, because failure teaches us things that success never can. Yet now we are in a culture where no one is allowed to fail only to achieve different ways of not succeeding. So let's just lower the bar for our kids so they can all be meaninglessly successful.

In the past, blunders have scarred our history and resulted in pointless deaths. Perhaps we could look back to the Victorians for inspiration. They celebrated their failures based on the Victorian belief that failure toughens the resolve and feeds the spirit understanding that our weaknesses and failures makes us stronger and enables us to understand our flaws. The problem with Liberalism is that it believes in Utopia. A fundamental blunder. Failure inspired the Victorians to write powerful poetry, like the 'Charge of the Light Brigade' to honour the fallen.

The Brigade had set off down the valley but were apparently going in the wrong direction. One of the commanders, Nolan was seen to rush across the front, possibly in an attempt to stop them, but was killed by an artillery shell, so they carried on through the valley of death. The futility of the action and its reckless bravery prompted the French Marshal Pierre Bosquet to state: "C'est magnifique, maid ce n'est pas la guerre." (it's magnificent, but it isn't war.") Rarely quoted, but he continued: "C'est de la folie" – "It's madness." The Russian commanders are said to have initially believed that the British soldiers must have been drunk. The reputation of the British cavalry was significantly enhanced as a result of the charge, though the same cannot be said for their commanders. Heroes led by donkeys once again.

The evacuation of Dunkirk became know as 'The Dunkirk Spirit' and also became a significant part of our culture and is quoted as having got us through some of our more difficult moments. J.B. Priestly felt that it symbolised part of the character of the English. He said in his postscript broadcast of 5th June of that year:

"Nothing, I feel, could be more English than this battle of Dunkirk, both in its beginning and its end, its folly and its grandeur... What began as a miserable blunder, a catalogue of misfortunes and miscalculations, ended as an epic of gallantry. We have a queer habit, and you can see it running through our history, of conjuring up such transformations. Out of a black gulf of humiliation and despair, rises a sun of blazing glory."[29]

Churchill had a more pragmatic view. Before the operation was completed, the prognosis had been gloomy, with Winston Churchill warning the House of Commons to expect "hard and heavy tidings". Subsequently, Churchill referred to the outcome as a "miracle" and exhortations to 'The Dunkirk Spirit' are still heard in Britain today. The British press presented the evacuation as a "Disaster Turned to Triumph" so successfully that Churchill had to remind the country, in a speech to the House of Commons on 4th June, that: "We must be very careful not to assign to this deliverance the attributes of a victory. Wars are not won by evacuations."

But the rescue of the British troops at Dunkirk provided a psychological boost to British morale which ended any possibility that the British would seek peace terms from Germany, since they retained the ability to defend themselves against a possible German invasion and of course showed a united culture. One wonders in our multicultural society how many would now go, or if the Titanic had sunk in 2008 how many women and children would have been pushed out of the lifeboats.

To look at the history of the English all you can do is look at what has been passed down as evidence and not be too precious or purist. This world is a more dangerous place than it ever was but what we had was a national belief, character, attitude and behaviour which did not exist in isolation but as part of a heritage.

---

[29] J.B. Priestley.

It was our culture. One of the main causes of our loss of culture has been mass immigration since the 1970s.

In order to justify the mass immigration over the last 40 years, which can be blamed for diluting the indigenous culture, much has been said about the English being a mongrel people, but we need to explore this issue further. The Romans had named 'Britannia' as a single Roman Region but by 410 Rome had fallen so the outposts of empire had no support. Hence this island was made up of Angles, Saxons, Jutes, Frisians, and Franks from around 400-600 AD. In the writings of Bede he tells us that the race of the English, or Saxons, came from three very strong tribes of Germany. Christianity was reintroduced by St Augustine who converted Aethelbert to be the Christian king. Bede's poetry tells us that England became a centre of Christianity and missionaries went out to convert mainland Europe. The Celts were pushed to the extremities by the Rhineland marauders, and the language, law and Government we now know were developed. The move from tribes to nationhood arose out of the need for effective leadership.

The establishment of kingship by inheritance enabled the ultimate stability of the role of kingship. The success of the Norman Conquest was pure luck. If the Norwegians had not attacked in the North, Harold's army would have been waiting for William in Kent. But unfortunately they had to traipse back from Northumberland to Kent and then fight for their land. The Normans took over an England which had a stable Monarchy and a reformed church. This land then became ruled by men whose main concerns were external to this country. The English were taken over by a non-English ruling class.

Writing of the Norman invasion and Continental takeover, Paul Johnson writes: "When William dismissed his mercenaries in 1070, nearly all returned to France. The probability is that the Continental settlement did not involve more than 10,000 people – and perhaps as few as 5,000 out of a population of well over a million. England simply acquired a new ruling class."

Until quite recently the Jews represented the only substantial non-Christian presence in Britain. The first definite settlement, was after 1066 and there are even suggestions that they may have helped finance the invasions. But their main activity was money lending. In 1290 the community of around 5,000 to 15,000 were expelled by Edward I. It has been said that English agriculture suffered from the absence of Jewish finance. In 1650 Manasseh Ben Israel published 'The Hope of Israel'. which was aimed at Christian fundamentalists arguing that before the messiah returned, Jews needed to be spread throughout the world including England. Cromwell favoured this, so Jews began to resettle in the late 17th century. William of Orange also encouraged wealthy Dutch Jews to finance his operations in the Glorious Revolution of 1688.

Other immigrants were small in numbers. Lombard's, were small numbers of merchants from Italy. There were Gypsies from 1500 from Egypt, but again in small numbers. Huguenots, were protestants from France from 1560-1720, and around 80,000 are believed to have come in but only around 40,000 remained. There were only small numbers of Africans who came via the slave trade, much to Elizabeth I annoyance in the 16th century. However, towards the end of the 18th century at the height of the slave trade there was a larger black population of 10-20,000 located mainly in London and around dock areas. The numbers of West Indians coming to Britain was small and did not gain any momentum until around 1954. Hence 1066 was the last hostile invasion of this Island in the history of the English people until quite recently".

The English had an identity which eventually was held together by a central authority of kingship and a unified ideology of the Christian church. The pride and self-confidence of the English grew especially during the days of empire and the Victorian era and can be blamed for the jingoism of the First World War. But who are we to judge. I suppose pride goes before a fall. This is the cyclic nature of history and no one could support the folly of the First World War, but possibly they could understand its inevitability.

The English mass culture has not really been driven by art but relied much more on the 'word'. Be it the 'Bible', the 'Book of Common Prayer' the plays of Shakespeare or the Victorian poets.

Common words and beliefs were embraced and treasure by all sections of society. The word was carried by all classes uniting communities. Kipling was read in the barrack rooms by all ranks. Whatever folly they may have been sent upon by politicians, it did not undermine their own self-belief, sense of honour and responsibility to their nation.

The church and the parish were the basis of communication right back to medieval times and the birth of English folk songs came from pagan rituals. The church, prior to the reformation, provided the roots of carnival and entertainment as expressed through the writing of Chaucer. Even Henry III was entertained by champion farters 'with a jump a whistle and a fart'. The main problem with champion farters is that they often need to clear their throats when their nerves get the better of them.

Minstrels songs were developed by the peasants and passed from generation to generation down to Frankie Howard and Benny Hill. English folk songs always belonged to the people. The songs of all folk in one culture which inspired united and provided solace. Deep in the heart of us all there is a love of songs and singing, much to my children's unrelenting embarrassment. In the 1920s when times were hard, the community singing movement was a distinctive feature of English popular musical life. The movement was seen by both its organisers and contemporary commentators as providing an antidote to the widespread social tensions following from the post-First World War economic dislocation and industrial unrest that led to the 1926 General Strike.

Community singing, had its roots deep in the Victorian age. It represented both literally and symbolically, a socially united nation in which people were working in harmony, irrespective of their social position. This movement was demonstrated by the enthusiastic chorus-singing beloved of Victorian music-hall audiences and the impromptu singing sessions enjoyed by British troops during the First World War.

The First World War songs mere music-hall songs, with 'It's a Long Way to Tipperary', 'Pack up your Troubles' and 'Take Me Back to Blighty', particular favourites, although Ivor Novello's

'Keep the Home Fires Burning' was one of the most moving and strongly favoured. Christmas carols were widely sung and 'Abide with Me', was soon to become central to the culture of community singing particularly for football supporters. Indeed, something close to a separate community hymn singing movement emerged in this period, organised mainly within religious communities but held both in churches and in secular settings like the cup final.

In 1957 the play write John Osborne commented: "The music Hall is dying and within it, a significant part of England. Some of the heart of England has gone: something that once belonged to everyone, for this was truly a folk art."[30]

Some saw the final blow when Moss Empires the largest British Music Hall chain closed the majority of its theatres in 1960 followed by the death of Max Miller in 1963. Yet the English love of this type of entertainment continued in a different context and The BBC Good Old Days ran for 30 years and TV variety shows and programmes like the Muppets were popular particularly amongst the working classes. The culture was that of unity and camaraderie for the working classes and the music hall traditions were carried on in holiday camps, coach trips and working men's clubs. Children in schools, all did community singing. Sea shanties, great stuff, patriotic songs, well good, hymns, timeless. Knobbly knee competitions, hokey cockey we knew how to enjoy ourselves.

Music and words were always seen as a way of uniting the English. Well now Seb has rediscovered our history of community singing and wants to try and get some harmony into the nation for the Olympics, but I wonder what they will sing?

From the turmoil of the First World War through to social unrest and back to stability, it was necessary for popular culture to be understood and respected by all parts of society and especially by the politicians. The clear view of the English in the 1940s

---

[30] John Osbourn, New Statesman, 1957.

developed from the historical self-confidence in the populace and the unity of understanding amongst all classes that had developed through the Victorian era and which was epitomised in films like 'In which we Serve,' and 'This noble breed'. There was an attitude of 'stiff upper lip' and 'don't make a fuss'. 'I've lost my leg old chap', 'by gad sir so you have'. Some classic films of the time reflect the English attitude to life which was about order, self-control dignity, honour and pride. The moral in 'Brief Encounter' was all about the fact that we are not put on earth to enjoy ourselves. It was all about doing the 'right thing'. But everyone had an understanding in those days of what the 'right thing' was. It was a common understanding in our culture.

George Orwell writing in 1944. "An imaginary foreign observer would certainly be struck by our gentleness by the orderly behaviour of English crowds, the lack of pushing and quarrelling and except for certain well-defined areas in half a dozen big towns, there is very little crime or violence." Those were the days.

The war years developed a more intense aspect of popular culture, the need for each other. The essential aspect of belonging to a community. The Queen Mother seemed to symbolise much of this spirit. She is quoted as saying 'the children won't go without me, 'I won't leave the King, and the King will never leave'. This made her much loved by Londoners. To many it is remembered as her finest hour. During the dark days of the Second World War, the Queen Mother served as an inspiration to a country battered and bloodied by the Blitz. Together with Winston Churchill, she had come to personify the fighting spirit which saw Britain through those troubled times to emerge victorious in 1945. While the King endlessly inspected lines of military forces in his own naval uniform, and worked at his stammer, his wife was pictured carefully treading her way through the rubble of Buckingham Palace and other bomb-hit sites in the capital. She famously said: "Now we can look the East End in the face."

The London of the Blitz has long gone, the community has fled and it is now a very different place. So many boroughs house a chaotic and fragmented transient society with no community to support each other and no protection for the weak from the incompetence of social services, which are equally fragmented and chaotic.

Harringay: where no one will hear you cry.

Neil Tweedie visited the seemingly respectable streets in which Baby P endured a private hell and found no trace of a community.

"The woman taking her children home from school in the early darkness of the afternoon did not realise the significance of the dilapidated semi-detached council house. "In there, was it? I knew it was around here, but I didn't know that. You don't know, do you – what goes on."

What went on in that council house in Tottenham, north London was the slow torture and eventual death of a young boy by the man he had just learned to call "dad" – the newly acquired boyfriend of a mother who preferred to spend her time on internet chat and poker sites, chain-smoking while her children resided in squalor.

A very Victorian word, squalor – redolent of the gin bottle and the slum. But it was just as relevant to Baby P's existence. In his 17 months of life he lived as the children of the Victorian slums did, in a house stinking of urine and faeces and riddled with rat holes; neglected, unloved and subject to arbitrary abuse.

The crumbling semi was a private little hell in which his 32-year-old tormentor, imported by a 29-year-old mother who had herself suffered neglect in childhood, was free to indulge his simple-minded sadism. Later on, a second man, Jason Owen, the only one of the three who can be named because of legal restrictions, moved in to the four-bedroom house. He was 36 and had a 15-year-old girlfriend.

In this demented world Baby P stood no chance. From November 2006, when his stepfather moved in, until August 2007, when he was found dead in his blood-stained cot, the boy suffered appalling violence. His back and ribs were broken, and the nails torn from his fingers.

The case of Baby P is one of those routine shockers served up by modern British life, but not just because of the way he died.

The London Borough of Harringay, in which he lived and died, is not Victorian England, and Baby P did not suffer in secret. Everyone in authority – social workers, doctors and police – knew something was wrong. Baby P was visited 60 times. At the same time, everyone who lived nearby, the people who formed what was once known as a neighbourhood, knew nothing.

Baby P's mother was first arrested in December 2006, after doctors reported suspicious bruising. The boy was put into care – and then returned to his home. Chocolate smeared across his wounds was enough to deceive the social worker and health visitor monitoring him. The registered child-minder appointed to look after him four days a week claims her warnings were ignored. In the wake of the scandal surrounding Victoria Climbié, the Ivorian girl tortured to death in 2000, Harringay social services, the body responsible for her safety, underwent a major overhaul. Accountability, or rather bureaucracy, became all in the wake of a public inquiry conducted by Lord Laming. Scores of recommendations issued from his pen and new procedures were put in place. But no amount of form-filling could make up for a lack of on-the-ground experience and wisdom.

Eileen Munro, who specialises in the study of child protection at the London School of Economics, puts it simply: "Harringay had a beautiful paper trail of how they failed to protect this baby."

Baby P's mother, anxious that her flow of welfare benefits should not be interrupted, kept her son's torturer's presence in the house a secret".

In another period, neighbours would have provided another line of defence. Sarah Wise, author of *The Blackest Streets*, a study of Victorian slum life, explains:

"Some commentators in the final years of the 19th century pointed out that since the poor had to huddle together in extremely overcrowded districts, it was in fact harder to keep neglect and child assaults hidden away from inquisitive neighbours than in districts where privacy and seclusion were more highly valued. Being a nosy neighbour could be a very good thing, and the NSPCC in the late 1880s relied heavily upon neighbours to be vigilant about child neglect and assaults upon children within the home. Well over half the initial complaints to the London branch of the society were made by neighbours."[31]

Things seem to have gone backwards. A transience population and with it an ignorance of what goes on next door, particularly in our cities.

The houses that flank the semi in which Baby P died are occupied by East European families, the one opposite by a Turkish family newly arrived in Britain. Harringay ticks the boxes of relative social deprivation (fifth most deprived authority in London, 18th most deprived nationally) but when one walks its streets the problem is more one of alienation, of head-turning, of not knowing the people who live next to you.

Michael Gephard is 73 and has lived in the neighbourhood where Baby P died for more than 20 years. His council house, and those around it, are not dilapidated – plenty of money appears to have been spent on their upkeep.

"It's not a neighbourhood and we are not neighbours," he said, walking his dog in the dark along the wet pavement. "People here come from all over – Turkey, Africa, everywhere. You might see someone move into a house with a big bag and then move out again a few months later. I know one or two people, good friends, but that's it. That little boy had his fingernails pulled out and nobody knew."

It is a familiar story, and not only in London. There was the case of Khyra Ishaq, the seven-year-old who allegedly starved to death at her home in Birmingham. The next-door neighbours knew nothing of her awful existence until paramedics arrived in the early hours, and many more, far too many, sadly to mention.

The 1950s was remembered as a peaceful decade full of hopes of domestic bliss. Women became empowered as 'customers' by the advertising men. In 1950 Macmillan said they never had it so good, some think they never had it, but that's

---

[31] Sarah Wise, *The Blackest Streets.*

nonsense. They definitely had it, some say the war years were the most promiscuous of all times as people felt on the edge of extinction. The difference was that social structure was felt to be essential for social cohesion. So they had it but knew they shouldn't have. Whilst they may have strayed they ultimately knew the importance of keeping the family together, and individual responsibility was expressed as my mother would have said "you've made your bed you lie on it".

The real changes were in the 1960s. Values were turned on their head and knickers were exposed, as skirts became belts. The era of the see-through dress had arrived. Everything was tried, 'art for art sake' promoted by middle-class students in the Art Colleges. This was truly a middle-class Revolution. It was always useful in the past to get the middle classes off out of the country into the army or the Empire. But now they had become troublesome, setting out to destroy the culture their forefather had made them respect. The bulldozing of Victorian architecture symbolised the destruction of the moral values which had held society together. Victorian architecture was destroyed and replaced by concrete 1960s buildings some of which lasted no longer than 15 years. Temporary architecture, temporary society. Works of art like the Tricorn in Portsmouth were pulled down in the 1980s, just temporary scars on the landscape.

There were some heroes that stuck their necks out to satirise what was happening. Sir John Betjeman, who was Poet Laureate from 1972, satirised this social revolution through his poetry. Burgess Hill, Aldershot, Bath, Bristol, Oxford, Newbury, Leamington, the Lake District to name but a few English places that were included in his odes. His poetic commemoration of so many quintessentially English towns and buildings – including Westminster Abbey and the Hackney Empire – may go some way to explaining his continuing reputation as England's best-loved poet. Of course, the burghers of Slough may beg to differ: it was their town that, in a 1937 poem, Betjeman called for 'friendly bombs' to fall on Slough, on the contentious basis that "it isn't fit for humans now". I wonder what he'd say if he saw it now?

The 1960s era was bursting with working-class youths who had benefited from a Grammar School education which had given them social mobility. These same youths joined the ranks of the middle classes and pushed for what they saw as outdated moral standards to be overturned. The conservative establishment was under threat. The old guard was holding back but liberalist tyranny was on the way. Nationhood was one of the key concepts that was under question.

The liberalist search for Utopia was one that was firmly ground in their own pleasure rather than penitence. Heaven could be found on earth and there was no room for rules. It was a largely middle-class revolution, but probably finished off the working classes, which had been built on the protestant work ethic and Christian morality.

The 1960s represented the 'get down and get dirty' era. Sexual freedom was all about having sex instead of going to war. Hum strange. The Grosvenor riots in 1969 were a total clash of cultures. Dixon of Dock Green versus the Sex Pistols. The police, who were attacked by protesting revolting students, were from a different era. The cry of the HO HO HO, laughing policeman, was replaced by the 'HO HO HO chi min' cries of the students. Not that many knew much about him. For the police there was no strategy, no planning, and no understanding of why the people would fight them. Up until this time the police, were largely seen as the protectors of the people, other than a few notorious cases. The 'Bobby' was an affectionate term, even when they were 'feeling your collar' 'ello 'ello, 'ello'. Very different to the 'Pigs' we use now. In those days the policeman's belt was to hold up his trousers, not for guns and CS sprays.

Feminism, was the cry of middle-class liberalist females and this movement was epitomised by novels such as the *Female Eunuch*, which was of course, full of explicit sex, which meant it was a bestseller. So good fun was to be had through sex, without any consequences because the pill would sort it all out. In the 21st century many female libbers bemoan what went wrong. What the Pill took away was the strongest empowerment of women, the reason and right to say 'No'. So over to Woody Allen: "I want to tell you a terrific story about oral contraception. I asked this girl to sleep with me and she said 'No'."

This whole movement led to more promiscuous women and more feckless men. Women are now seen as sex objects rather than to be put on a pedestal and wooed. They are now part of the laddette culture where they can drink like men and fall flat on their face like men. But with laddered stockings and smudged eye make-up they look a lot more unsightly than our male warriors, who have carried out this type of behaviour since ancient times. Feminism has made us all equal at last.

But there are consequences. The head of a police officers' association has warned that rising crime among the female population is putting a huge burden on the force's resources.

Speaking to BBC News, Police Federation of England and Wales chair Paul McKeever said figures for England and Wales for 2006-2007 showed that 240 women were arrested every day for violent crime.

"Statistics from the Youth Justice Board also show that offences amongst the female population are on the rise. According to the body, the number of breaches of the law committed by girls between the ages of ten and 17 had increased by 25 per cent in three years to 59,000. The offences included minor assaults, robberies and criminal damage.

There is also evidence to show that young women are now joining violent gangs and inevitably putting a strain on police resources".

So this was a very high cultural revolution. Up until 1968 the Lord Chamberlain since the restoration had the right to censor the theatres. 'Hair' was put on the London stage and it challenged all the old sexual taboos and in the process took away all our perimeters of behaviour. As Peter Cooke once said: "I don't want to see rape, sodomy and drug addiction in the theatre when I can see that at home."

The ball was now firmly in the court of liberalists. But the days were not yet born when Sikhs would storm a theatre and writers would have to go into hiding, whilst Government Ministers seemed to accept this as normal behaviour.

131

Sexual energy was meant to transform the world. Soldiers involved in fighting were said to be taking out their sexual frustrations through war. So if they had sex instead that should sort it out. Now what had gone on behind closed doors in the confines of a relationship and fitted into a social context and structure now went on in public. Sex became a statement of peace and love rather than a shag. The girls hoped they were being liberated and the guys, well they just enjoyed it as usual. The theatre was at the forefront of the middle-class revolution. 'There's a girl in my soup' epitomised a working-class swinging chick of the 1960s having an affair with an older man. It was the generation and class war personified.

The fact is that sex is, and always has been, a power game. From Cleopatra to Helen of Troy until now, nothing has changed. Men have always chased women who sprinted, jogged or had a poorly leg but the whole mating game was played out under the umbrella and perimeters of social behaviour which were understood by all and policed by social stigma. But the whole sexual revolution fiasco has put in jeopardy the social order and the family unit which has become a tragic-drama played out on the cultural stage.

Those who thought sex and fun were the way forward set about undermining the social values that had held society together. The only way to create a social revolution was to undermine the Victorian values that held it all in place. This was a political movement based on Marxism. They looked at the past and saw what they classed as the crimes of the West. They then set about using this as a basis for a future Utopian society. But economic Marxism failed and cultural Marxism took over and the State replaced the family.

"And if all others accepted the lie which the Party imposed – if all records told the same lie – then the lie passed into history and became truth. "Who controls the past" ran the Party slogan, "controls the future, who controls the present controls the past."[32]

---

[32] George Orwell, *1984*.

Some saw the worst coming but felt powerless to change its course. The social rebellion was from the Public Schools and the Art Colleges largely upper and middle-class youths. But it was the split in the generations which was to cause possibly the most damage. The lack of respect for experience and age accelerated the development of the youth culture which was very anti-establishment. Some saw the danger coming, The Kinks sang the Village Green preservation society and Alan Bennett mumbled about the crowds being let into the secret garden. Dad's army, which was a send up of the Home Guard, struck a chord in the hearts of the people who still loved those they saw as 'honourable souls'. Alf Garnett from 'Til Death Do Us Part' was written by a Marxist who wanted to expose what he saw as the bigotries of the Tory working-class. What he got was a population who loved Alf. He reflected much of what they believed and definitely what their fathers and grandfathers accepted. Could they really undermine our heritage with their own political views and change society? As articulated by Jimmy Nail in an episode of Auf Wiedersehen Pet when the gang were working in Germany. 'These are the bastards that bombed me Grannie."

We are all Thatcher's children. She dismantled our state owned industries, sold off our assets and laid the stage for our current economy of boom and ultimately bust, which Mr Brown promised us had gone forever. Short termism was born. The building societies that had provided the equity for home ownership on a mutual basis for generations were de-regulated and we all became enmeshed in the myth of the dream of free enterprise. Working-class people purchased council houses and became part of the free enterprise economy and of course voted for Mrs T. Everything can be purchased including happiness and the 'market' became the new God. The 1970s saw the ultimate destruction of our manufacturing industry, largely by the greed of powerful labour groups and the self-interest of politicians and businesses. What the Victorians had built up and made us proud over 100 years was destroyed. They understood that to be powerful you had to actual MAKE things. British industry had been destroyed by Mrs T. Uncle Jim Callaghan, the last real

Labour PM had tried to resolve the issues by taking on the unions but failed in the winter of discontent. Mrs T made a famous speech which often came back to haunt her but was misunderstood by many. She said there was no such thing as society, what she meant was that we all needed individual responsibility, but what she got from her policies and her legacy was the culture of individual rights and the destruction of social interdependence and indeed the institutions that supported them.

She believed the 'market' would solve everything but she was also on her own ego trip. I think she didn't really care so long as she could destroy the powerful unions and knee-cap Arthur Scargill.

Mrs Thatcher was in no way a traditional Tory. Her first cabinet were unable to deal with her. The Wets came from a different generation. They were middle and upper-class gentlemen who were not used to women using their female wiles to get their way in cabinet, throwing tantrums and handbagging any opposition. She dismantled our state owned enterprise, sold off our assets and laid the foundation for Blairism and ultimately the destruction of the economy. So the new God has now become the devil and I'm now the proud owner of a bank but I've never had more trouble getting a loan. And now whilst the Blairites have become the pantomime villains, the legal industry multiply their profits almost unnoticed.

Our places of social congregation and support like the trade unions and working men's clubs, were destroyed. Solid institutions that entertained, trained and protected our kids, like the Boy Scouts and Girls Venture Brigade and many others were seen as old-fashioned. The cheap lamb that had sustained working-class families for Sunday roast, was replaced by the CAP and the whole UK became based on a transient economy built on short term capital, and consumerism. The UK became an economic staging post. Mrs T saw herself almost as a republican and at times forgot herself with "We have a granddaughter." On one occasion rumour has it that she wrote to the Queen to ask what the Queen would be wearing so they would not clash at an event they were both attending. She got a curt response from the

Queen along the lines that "the Queen does not notice what other people are wearing." No love lost there then. Good on yeh Mam. But the final nail in the coffin of English culture was about to be promoted.

The term Multiculturalism is inevitably entwined with immigration. Where you stand on immigration and multiculturalism depends on where you sit. To some, multiculturalism is a lovely bijous restaurant in Hammersmith, to others it's a housing estate in Oldham. It ultimately means a number of separate communities in one land with different beliefs and loyalties and it's a recipe for Beirut. Multiculturalism is a favourite of the chattering classes and is promoted by those interested in ethnic separatism.

Multiculturalism can be dangerous in that it destroys national unity and stops social integration. It is an ideology itself and as such challenges democracy. Ethnic awareness can be good but when it becomes the cult of ethnicity it can endanger the cohesion of society. The problem is that, multiculturalists are usually liberals or ethnocentric separateness who sees English culture as symbolising western crimes. But the English culture was one which people came from all over the world to embrace. In order for multiculturalism to win English culture must be destroyed first. By that I mean its history, beliefs, religion attitudes and lifestyle. Or even more, its humour, irony, pathos, what makes it laugh, what makes it cry, what holds it together.

Surprise, surprise other nations have realised the folly of multiculturalism a bit more quickly than us. An anti-immigration one nation party was formed in Australia in the late 1990s because they feared that multiculturalism had been promoted by self-interest groups into a philosophy that put allegiances to original culture ahead of national loyalty. This, it was said, led to a range of ethnic cultures, not one community, what became termed a "cluster of tribes". This emphasised what was different and emphasised the rights of the new minority rather than the old majority. In January 2007 the Howard Government took the 'multicultural' out of the Department of Immigration and

Multicultural Affairs, changing its name to the Department of Immigration and Citizenship.

The Netherlands experience is one from which we should have learned. If ever we feel that we must be the battiest society in the world we can always look at the Dutch to make us feel saner about ourselves. Yes, 'double Dutch' of course our ancestors understood. So now they've banned smoking in all public places, they have a team of inspectors out sniffing at the local cafes and bars to sniff out tobacco. Cannabis is OK but tobacco is a 'no no'. I've even heard there's a place in Holland called Fondle Park where you can have sex in public, but there is also a sign saying 'dogs must be kept on a lead'. This brings a whole new dimension to the concept of taking the kids to the park. But wait a minute, oh dear I knew it would come in this country, please excuse the pun.

'In his new guidance, Mr Cunningham told officers to ignore dogging – where strangers meet in public for sex – as well as cruising and cottaging, when gay men meet in parks and loos.

He warned that arresting offenders would alienate the gay community. Mr Cunningham – the lead at the Association of Chief Police Officers on gay, lesbian, bisexual and sex-swap issues – said it was not the role of officers to act as "moral arbiter".

And he warned police officers to avoid a "knee-jerk reaction" when responding to complaints.

Arrests should only be made as a last resort, he says. Instead, he said officers should study specialist sex websites – to see what is taking place in local parks, toilets and car parks.

Mr Cunningham, Lancashire's deputy top cop, told officers to ease off on open-air sex addicts in a new 21-page rulebook. He advised: "Our role is to ensure that any complaints are dealt with fairly and professionally and that where individuals are engaged in lawful activity they may do so safely."

Well at least it will allow the police to study specialist sex web sites and could help recruitment, and I suppose we are also letting dogs off the lead!? So parks have become no go areas for dogs, but 'doggin' is apparently encouraged as it's minorities that enjoy it and there are far too many dog owners; so there!

In the 1950s, the Netherlands was a much saner place, but in the 1960s mass immigration started for them earlier than us and they seemed to lose their marbles. In the 1970s multiculturalism was the mantra of the political classes, based on the usual folly of the, so-called, 'need for unskilled labour'. In 2006 one fifth of the population was of non-Dutch origin about half of which were not western. In Amsterdam 55% of young people are of non-western origin. Major immigration began in the 1960s, and increased in the 1970s. From the 1970s, multiculturalism was a consensus ideology among the 'political class'. Paul Cliteur saw multiculturalism as an unacceptable ideology of relativism which he believed would lead to the acceptance of barbaric practices, including those brought to the western world by immigrants. He listed infanticide, torture and slavery, the oppression of women, homophobia and the death penalty. Feminists had an issue too, political theorist Susan Okin argued that a concern for the preservation of cultural diversity should not overshadow the discriminatory nature of gender roles in many traditional minority cultures, that, at the very least, 'culture' should not be used as an excuse for rolling back the women's rights movement. Ironically the same has happened in France with the women's rights movement supporting the banning of the burka.

Oh, so culture is not about embracing the whole social activities and beliefs of a group of people, it's only about what the 'we' brigade find acceptable. This is a dilemma for the English. One of the most liberal countries in the world suddenly found that to bury your own ideology means that the ones you embrace are often not compatible but you no longer have a forum for making that judgement. You make decisions about other cultures based on your own culture. To have no perspective on right or wrong good or evil is the liberal dilemma.

So back to the Dutch. As all was going tits up (in fondle Park of course) some Dutch politicians began to promote the view that a society does have a finite 'absorptive capacity' of those from other cultures, and that, the capacity had been exceeded in the

137

Netherlands. Dutch society also experienced a range of social issues such as school drop-out, unemployment, and high crime rates. This led to more voices daring to speak out. Pim Fortuyn was one of these. He believed that a society which does not respect itself (its Dutch national identity) also has no value for immigrants.

Afshin Ellian also stated, "A liberal democracy cannot be multicultural, because multiculturalism is an ideology and a democracy has no official ideology." He went on to explain that "There were 800,000 Muslims in the country, with 450 mosques, and that the Netherlands had legalised the feudal system of the Islamic Empire".

Hence Democracy and the rule of law could only be restored by abolishing multiculturalism. Pim Fortuyn led a populist revolt against the political elite. He fought against what he called the "Islamisation of the Netherlands". Fortuyn actually came close to being Prime Minister of the Netherlands. When he was assassinated in May 2002, his supporters saw him as a national martyr in the struggle against multiculturalism. Following Fortuyn's death, open rejection of multiculturalism and immigration ceased to be taboo. Politicians announced that Holland was 'full'. Had Fortuyn not been shot dead before the election many believe he would have gone on to lead the country. Fortuyn led a populist support with his makeshift party and was so successful at the polls that the Government adopted a more stringent immigration policy, with a proposal to repatriate 26,000 failed asylum seekers.

One of the most prominent figure in the post-Fortuyn debate was Ayaan Hirsi Ali. Her first criticisms of multiculturalism paralleled those of the early liberal-feminists in the United States – the emphasis on group identity and group rights threatened individual liberty for those within the minorities, and especially for women. As time went on, her criticism was increasingly directed at Islam itself, and its incompatibility with democracy and western culture. By 2004 she was the most prominent critic of Islam in Europe. When she scripted a short play for the Dutch Van Gogh more blood was shed.

"Dressed in an oversized coat and the traditional Arab cloak known as a djellaba, he stood close to the bicycle lane. At around 8.45 a.m., Van Gogh rode by and was knocked from his saddle by a volley of shots fired from a 9mm handgun. He struggled to the other side of the road, where he collapsed in front of a shop selling washing machines. Terrified onlookers ducked behind cars or fled down side streets as the young man crossed the thoroughfare to where Van Gogh lay, and opened fire again. Eight bullets were later found in his body. Bleeding heavily, the 47-year-old father of a 14-year-old boy had pleaded with the gunman: 'Don't do it! Don't do it! Mercy! Mercy!' A woman with a young child also screamed out to the assailant, begging him to stop. He listened to neither appeal, but instead produced a long sharpened knife and proceeded to slit Van Gogh's throat so deeply that his head was almost severed. One witness described the young man as behaving with the methodical detachment of 'a butcher'. His final act was to affix a five-page letter to the corpse by plunging another knife into Van Gogh's chest. It was addressed to Ayaan Hirsi Ali, a Dutch MP from Somalia who had collaborated with Van Gogh on 'Submission', a film that suggested that the Koran sanctioned domestic violence...

"The small country with a global reputation for tolerance had witnessed peacetime Europe's most extreme act of intolerance. The whole episode lasted little more than a minute, but its aftermath continues to reverberate in Holland, and may do so for some time to come. It was as if the very savagery of the attack was aimed not just at an individual but everything he represented. As such, the murderer and his victim have been cast as symbols of conflicts now reshaping modern Europe: those between freedom of expression and the protection of ethnic minorities, national laws and religious authority, multiculturalism and integration, rationalism and faith, permissiveness and absolutism.

"As one of the most densely populated nations on earth, the Dutch had evolved an attitude known as 'gedogen'. The word translates as a kind of pragmatic tolerance – legislating to put up with something – which is probably a necessary outlook when you live, as it were, in your neighbour's face. It's this concept that has led to Holland's renowned hash-selling coffee bars and legalised red-light districts, as well as initiatives like police protection for gay cruising zones. In many ways, gedogen has created an environment that ill suits a traditional culture like Islam. It does not take a social scientist to see that a veiled woman might have problems living next to a live sex show."[33]

The problem of liberalism is that it makes no sense. It liberalises society to the point where anything goes, and becomes itself the fascism that it seeks to eradicate. The elimination of any culture or boundaries allows a void that is usually filled by some sort of extremism. After all fascism is only the idea that you must be absolutely right, and who epitomises that more than the liberal PC brigade.

Britain has continuous high immigration rates, among the highest in the EU. Most of the immigrants of the last decades came from the Indian subcontinent or the Caribbean or from former British colonies. In 2004 the number of people who became British citizens rose to a record 140,795 – a rise of 12% on the previous year. This number had risen dramatically since 2000. The overwhelming majority of new citizens come from Africa (32%) and Asia (40%), the largest three groups being people from Pakistan, India and Somalia.

Prominent critics of multiculturalism include Yasmin Alibhai-Brown, Ugandan-born author of After Multiculturalism, and one-time black activist Trevor Phillips, the chairman of the Commission for Racial Equality. In 2006, Phillips was criticised by the then London mayor Ken Livingstone, who accused him of fuelling hostility towards ethnic minorities by criticising the principle of multiculturalism. But then look what became of Livingstone and Sir Ian Blair. Livingstone then accused Phillips of being so right-wing that he would 'soon be joining the BNP'. Wow perhaps he would be a little more charitable to a man of the cloth?

---

[33] The Observer, 5th December 2004.

In November 2005 John Sentamu, the first member of an ethnic minority to be appointed as Archbishop of York stated, "Well, St Bede writes, that the Christian Gospel gave nationhood to England. So the things that have come out of a fairly strong Christian tradition, have shaped these traditions, our schools, our hospitals, the rule of law, and the worry that I've got is that these very strong Christian traditions on which this society was built, slowly people are actually undermining them. But I think, what I think about the English, having lost an empire; they haven't yet re-discovered a big enough vision to sustain this great nation. And I think the bigger vision has got to be those wonderful virtues of decency, of truth, honesty of fair play, and clearly believing in God, because if you don't believe in God I think they're going to find the place is still empty. And I think if people did reconnect with Jesus, reconnected with each other, loved their country, loved their neighbour, chances are this would be a great nation." On the question of multiculturalism Sentenue replied:

"As long as the main dominant culture is safe in its traditions, it is possible for other cultures to thrive. But as long as it is insecure, doesn't know what it believes, doesn't know what its goals are, there will be such confusion, and there will be even some people who say, English culture doesn't matter anymore after all we are multicultural, but what are you going to integrate into? Multiculturalism has seemed to imply, wrongly for me: let other cultures be allowed to express themselves but do not let the majority culture at all tell us its glories, its struggles, its joys, its pains."

Criticisms have also been voiced by bishop Nazir Ali of Rochester.

He has received a number of threats against him and his family since he stated that Islamic extremism has turned some communities into no-go areas for non-Muslims. In a message posted on his website, the Bishop said he was aware his views would cause a debate on the issue but he added:

"I have been surprised at its scale: yet if violent Muslims can be tolerated in the UK and nuns can be murdered in response to the Pope's Regensburg speech, threats to the bishop are just par for the course."

The Bishop retorted in a similar fashion to the Pope who was also said to have made anti-Islamic comments.

'I deeply regret any hurt. Britain currently seems to be in a state of permanent uproar about its national identity. Home-grown Brits don't seem to know what it is any more, while immigrants flock to these shores in vast numbers to claim it for themselves."

So Gordon started to fret about recreating a sense of national solidarity which he finally realised had been lost. He then proposed erecting hurdles for immigrants to jump over before they could join the Great British project. He looked enviously at the way every American pledges allegiance to the Stars and Stripes and considered similar loyalty oaths to our own national symbols of Britishness. But as usual missed the point:

"Their flag doesn't make Americans patriotic. They rally to it so emotionally because they have enormous pride and belief in their country. That's because they believe that America's defining characteristics of freedom and equality, based on Judeo-Christian ethics, are simply superior to anything else.

"So they love their country for what it represents and, accordingly, are prepared to fight and to die for it. That is the essence of a shared sense of national purpose. Just to state this about America is to realise the depth of the problem in this once-great United Kingdom. This country has simply lost belief in itself.

"I do not wish to cause offence to anyone, let alone my Muslim friends. But unless we diagnose the malaise from which we all suffer we shall not be able to discover the remedy."[34]

In August 2006, the Community and Local Government Secretary Ruth Kelly made a speech, which some saw as signalling the end of multiculturalism as official policy.

---

[34] Melanie Philips.

She called for a "new, honest debate" about rooting out extremism and argued it was "not racist" to discuss immigration and asylum.

She said Britain had moved away from a "near-uniform consensus on the value of multiculturalism" and was facing challenges that threatened its record on uniting ethnic groups. Well whatever happened to Ruth? She cleared off and it seems the institutions have not caught up yet and are still promoting multiculturalism, even though Dave has questioned its role.

So over to Richard Littlejohn:

"Mail reader Barry Gower from the Isle of Dogs, suggested I catch up with an item the programme broadcast about the suitability of women for police firearms duty. The officer in charge explained that there were no barriers to women being deployed in specialist weapons units – bar one.

"Young black males and Muslim males don't react well to being told what to do by a woman," she said. "So we adapt and overcome and use a male officer."

So that's all right, then. What happens if a female member of SO19 confronts an Islamic suicide bomber about to blow himself up on the Tube?

Does she shout: "Armed police! Put your hands on your head and get down on your knees NOW!?"

Or does she say: "I'm so sorry to trouble you sir but would you mind awfully not detonating your device until I have had the opportunity to summon a male officer who will be able to arrest you in a manner appropriate to your cultural sensitivities?"

…Bishop Nazir-Ali is bang on the money when he talks about 'no-go' areas for Christians in fundamentalist Muslim ghettoes in Britain. But he could have gone further still.

This country is littered with 'no-go' areas, not just physically, but culturally, spiritually, intellectually and academically, too. Our very liberties are being torched in the name of 'diversity'.

The pernicious doctrine of multiculturalism has turned us into a society where people are frightened to speak their minds and justice has been flipped on its head.

To express an opinion contrary to the ruthlessly enforced, politically motivated conformity of the Fascist Left is to risk a vicious campaign of character assassination which, if you work in the public sector, will almost certainly cost you your job...

We have reached the ludicrous position where a Pakistani clergyman is facing demands for his resignation and is being accused of stirring up racial and religious hatred simply for speaking the truth.

All Bishop Nazir-Ali did was state the bleedin' obvious. Yet even William Hague has attacked him, saying the idea that Christians are made to feel uncomfortable by Muslim extremists is not a Britain he recognises.

In which case, I suggest Hague heads a few stops east of Westminster, along the Mile End and Whitechapel Roads, where Muslim mono-culturalism holds sway. Or visits Leicester, Bradford, Burnley, Oldham or parts of Birmingham."

When Channel 4's Dispatches programme exposed the sermons of hate and violence against 'kaffirs' and 'infidels', the West Midlands police not only refused to act, they launched an investigation into the programme-makers.

"LONDON'S busiest mosque has been accused of promoting Islamic fundamentalists who vilify Jews, call for Sharia law in Britain, blame Christians for deliberately spreading Aids in Africa and preach intolerance towards all non-Muslims.

The allegations against London Central Mosque in Regent's Park follows a 12-month investigation by the Channel 4 Dispatches programme. It found the mosque's official bookshop sells DVDs containing the speeches of two radical preachers, Sheikh Feiz and Sheikh Khalid Yasin.

They also claims western powers are behind the Aids epidemic in Africa, and "Missionaries from the World Health Organisation and Christian groups went into Africa and inoculated people for diphtheria, malaria, yellow fever and they put in the medicine the Aids virus, which is a conspiracy."

Both men are linked to the Wahhabi brand of Islam, which is dominant in Saudi Arabia and well-funded. Wahhabis are some of the most radical and fundamentalist Muslims, believing in Sharia law and interpreting the Koran literally. Moderate Muslims are deeply concerned about its spread to the UK.

But the paranoia has spread to the East end.

"Furious Muslims (when are they ever not 'furious?) have issued threats against EastEnders bosses over a storyline that showed an Asian character breaking his Ramadan fast. Postman Masood Ahmed was spotted snacking on a chapati during the holy month. BBC chiefs said the incident was supposed to show the 'fallibility' of Masood – played by Nitin Ganatra, 40. But hundreds of angry Muslims have accused the soap of mocking their religion. And some have even threatened the show's bosses on internet sites."[35]

Well apparently Muslim license fee payers have threatened to blow up EastEnders. Rumour has it that it's something to do with Big Phil bearing a resemblance to a young Winston Churchill.

Well at least foreign sex traffickers are putting their best foot forward in the interests of multi-culturalism. Apparently Lithuanians bring in the girls, Albanians set up the brothels. The Chinese supply drugs. And I suppose the British tax payers pay for the imprisonment of the offenders and future support for the girls. Very benevolent. An excellent example of multicultural co-operation.

So let's go retro and try and redeem some bits of our once great culture to stop us slipping into anarchy and chaos. Community singing, bringing it on back, let's put singing back on to the national curriculum for primary school kids. But what will they sing? What will unite communities that are divided with no national identity to hold them together? Community singing was part of our mass cultural activity. So let's pay parents to be good parents. Enid Blyton may be off the menu but nanny is alive and well and living at number 10. The social cohesion that characterised most of the 20th century was based on a shared culture. The solid institutions like the scout movement, the WI,

---

[35] Katie Begley, The Sun.

working men's clubs, local pubs, local post offices, and local schools. In the chaos that Governments have created lurching from one initiative to the next, they don't know how they redeem what has been lost. Now, even what we thought of as our solid, self-confident institutions have been sucked into the malaise of self-doubt and Government initiatives. Plans for scouts to be issued with condoms and taken on trips to sexual health clinics have been condemned by family campaigners.

Under new guidelines issued by their Scouts Association, they say that leaders should feel able to hand out condoms and that visits to sexual health clinics may help older scouts feel more confident seeking family planning and health advice.

But I thought that the values the scouts were founded on were about responsibility and self-control. Whatever happened to cold showers?

The current social malaise may be beyond repair as society is in tatters but when we only had 3 or 4 channels to watch television viewing was a shared experience. From the Queen down to the poorest, we would all watch Morecambe and Wise. Even earlier the Home Service unified the nation and listening to radio programmes was a national social activity. As the smell of roast dinner wafted through the house on a Sunday, Family Favourites, was followed by Round the Horn and the Clithero kid. Coach trips were again collective experiences with lots of sing songs. Regional identity was always there, but with no discussion about devolution. It was a joint culture with Paddy, Taff and Jock who all seemed to accept this as a term of endearment.

Sack races, egg and spoon races, we knew how to enjoy ourselves. The cities were held together by collective unions. The trade associations that had made men proud of their work had been around since the Norman conquest.

The 1980s was the start of the short term credit fix, with service sector jobs being the cornerstone of the economy. The financial chaos had started and the Blair bubble took over where Thatcher left off. I might be able to forgive Blair for the war in Iraq or Afghanistan, even for the London bombings and the decline of the economy of the western world, but the Blair babes, never!

Now we live in a culture where everyone has rights but no one seems to have responsibilities.

'Just wait until your father gets home' was a cry of many housewives in the earliest part of the 20th century right up until the 1960s. The woman's movement led us to believe that father's don't matter and could be dispensed with. They were pure sperm donors. So when super heroes camped on Harriet Harman's roof, middle-class fathers showed they were kicking back against a change of culture which has encouraged them to take their turn in bringing up baby with the 'parenting means you too' cry, but then to be dispensed with when mothers move on with their own right to 'change partners'. It is as if they were in some sort of catastrophic type of social dance. As society changed, women kept the traditional view of the father as remote when it suited them, a perspective that was very Victorian. Yet they had to change men and make them more like women in terms of 'new men' and then expect them not to have any rights. Very strange. So as the middle-class men fight for their rights as parents the underclass of men are happy to carry on the liberal attitude that there are no responsibilities, only rights. So all rights have been taken away from legitimate fathers, whilst others spread their seed with no responsibilities and the State has become the new 'father figure'.

"In the earthly hell inhabited by 'Baby P' – life financed by £450 a week of other people's money, filthy rooms and clothes, infestations of lice, the house stinking of human waste and overrun by smelly, aggressive dogs.

"The mother, constantly watching TV or staring at rubbish on the internet, was so unmoved by her child's death (the little martyred corpse was actually blue) that she asked the ambulance men to hang on while she fetched her cigarettes.

"And, of course, there's an ever-shifting queue of serial boyfriends lurking just out of view, hoping for a slice of the benefits.

"But we cannot own up to this problem. Officially, we aren't even allowed to disapprove of this way of life or be 'judgmental' about the people who lead such lives. Why? Mainly because the Left cannot admit that these things are bad. Because to accept that would be to accept that it has made a terrible mistake."[36] Shannon Matthews mother had 7 children by 5 different fathers but it was said that she needed support because she was unable to be a good mother. Ah so was it 'she' who was the 'victim' not little Shannon?

So now anyone constitutes a family there are no specific roles or genders. Marriage is out of date and let's just give them some money to make them better parents. That'll sort it. Yet they miss the point. The family was the most important unit in our culture and marriage the most important constitution. Forget religion in this context even forget fidelity. It was the belief in the institution that mattered and its structure. A structure that provided two individuals with commitment before entering into the process of having children. The creation of a life should not just be about a bonk. Those 1960s theorists that saw the pill as the answer to liberated sex, missed the point. Individuals enter into a relationship be it for 24 hours or much longer for a range of reasons. Loneliness, desperation, the need for love, alcohol, drugs and desire. The most vulnerable are the young. For the young, the lack of a social structure has led to an abyss of sexual abuse, alcohol and drugs. For children, caught in the middle of this the cry has become, not, 'wait until your father gets home', but your father won't be coming home and I'm not even sure who he is! All this at the blessing of the taxpayer. The beliefs which held the institution together via the populace have been undermined. As the Archbishop of Canterbury addressed the Lambeth conference in 2008 he claimed that 'Diversity' was the big success of the Church of England. But it was the Church of England which held the community together on these social issues and that's why we

---

[36] Peter Hitchens, Daily Mail, 15th November 2008.

have a cultural vacuum. The Church of England have deserted their people and become the most dysfunctional family of all.

The role of the father had to go when gender bending became the norm and a succession of 'partners' replaced Dad. So now the statistics shock us of children under the age of 5 self-harming. The cult of children's rights has undermined the effectiveness and indeed confidence of many adults. Children's rights and a 'child centred' culture, has led to children being in more danger than ever before. As children become the centre of their own universe, we should lament the passing of the family culture and the safety net it provided for children. But now we have the cult of the expert as adults abdicate their responsibility to 'Super nanny'. So as Trinny and Suzanna grapple with women's boobs, when 'Britain got naked' burst onto our TV screens I started to wonder why I ever invested in a 40" TV set. If I want gross in my front room I don't need a licence. Children are killing each other in the streets, the lost causes in our cultural breakdown. So now, no cuddles, no photographs of your kids by the pool on holiday in the UK and Nitty Nora has been banned. Esther Rantzen's plaintiff cry of 'what went wrong' can be heard echoing through the jungle.

The problem is that political correctness has made children more vulnerable. In Wakefield, in 2007, the case of two homosexual foster carers who abused a string of young boys demonstrated that they had been viewed as 'trophy' carers by the local authority who thought they were being 'right on' PC. As a result they abused a number of boys put in their care and when suspicions were raised by one of the mothers, she was ignored, they seemed to be untouchable. Two paedophiles who repeatedly abused children in their care were given a free reign with the blessing of the authority who should have been protecting the children because social workers feared being accused of homophobia if they investigated complaints".

So social workers are more keen to be PC and to champion the cause of 'victim or minority' groups, Of course there are rather a lot of children and they do not deserve the protection a minority group might deserve in our confused culture.

Never mind Tony Blair was onto it, he knew what children needed. He started the campaign to eliminate childhood poverty. Now how rational is that? He declared that as a result of tax and benefit changes, 700,000 children would be lifted out of poverty.

Mr Blair was proud to promote his new initiative, "the historic aim will be for ours to be the first generation to end child poverty".

But Mr B how do you define poverty? Is money now the root of all happiness? How much should each child have? Is it food, or a PlayStation? Is it mental, physical or material.? Or was it another soundbite? Whatever happened to the 'we may be poor but we are happy' culture. Childhood happiness is what is at stake not bloody poverty!

"According to the inquiry by the National Institute for Clinical Excellence, the proportion of young people who self-harm in the UK is now among the highest in Europe. But the report failed to investigate incidents among children aged 10 and under, believing that was the minimum age at which a child could be involved in self-harm. The report's authors and other experts have now admitted this was a mistake...

"'We are treating one boy, aged just five years old, who has been biting himself so badly that we are all very concerned about him,' said Peter Wilson, clinical adviser to the Place2Be, a charity which supports young children, and the former director of the Young Minds mental health charity. 'It is not yet common for children of that age to self-harm, but we are seeing it increasingly often...

"'I have worked with children all my life, but I find this increase a shock and a mystery,' Wilson, a consultant child psychotherapist, added. 'The only thing I can link it to is the increased rates of mental health problems we are now seeing in children as a result of the ever greater levels of stress, unhappiness and insecurity they report suffering'."

So now family trips have taken on a new dimension, there is apparently a new movement where suicide bombers take their children with them.

So sound bites, political gestures and meaningless words have come to epitomise our political culture. Individual responsibility and thrift is old hat, the market needs your money and the language of marketing pervades all aspects of our culture to our social, and indeed financial, cost.

Thatcher had to market herself to the people so she lowered her voice, and raised her hair. She needed to increase her own market share so she sold off our council houses and our state industries to the highest bidder just to increase her vote. She was the Queen of short termism. Blair was a positive student of Thatcherism, he took on her economic madness and took it to its final conclusion in 2008; chaos and failure. New Labour was a marketing project and with its success the market seemed to become a new type of God.

This same language of marketing pervades all aspects of society and allows us to accept meaningless soundbites and political gestures as reality: Clive James sums this up on the ordeal of taking a simple journey:

"My problem, as I ran with a heavy bag in each hand from the barrier end of the platform, was to find the first second class carriage in a train all of whose carriages were marked 'First'. I cursed 'First' in the worst language at my command, but my outburst at First was nothing beside the imprecations I rained on 'One'.

Yes, what used to be simply called Anglia Railways is now even more briefly but far less simply called 'One'. This leaves the way clear for the railway station announcer to inform potential passengers that one 'One' train will leave from platform two and the other 'One' train will leave from platform three.

"If the first' One' train leaves at twenty to one it's the twenty to one 'One' train and if the other one leaves at ten to one it's ten to one on that it's the one 'One' train one actually wanted but one couldn't understand the announcement.

Except, of course, that it's never now called a 'train', it's called a 'service', just as the passenger is now a 'customer'. Linguistic philosophers have already written theses about how the vocabulary of marketing has invaded the realm of transport, which logically should have no need of marketing, because people know exactly what they want and demand nothing except for the means of transport to be safe, clean and on time. But the language of marketing spreads inexorably because it gives those who use it a chance to be creative, which everybody has been taught is a desirable thing to be.

In fact, the last thing that a passenger who has already been outraged by being called a 'customer' wants to hear when he is sitting, or probably standing, in a train running late, or probably not running at all, is a voice on the public address system calling the train a 'service', when providing a service is exactly what it is currently in the process of not doing. Nor does the voice on the public address system show any sign, once it gets started, of wanting to shut up. The voice apologises for the delay caused to your journey, a way of softening the fact that the delay had been caused, not to your journey, but to you.

The voice continues to audition for a career in broadcasting by pointing out that the first 'One' service to arrive at the next station will be the last 'One' service to continue any further until the engineering works have been completed. Where did it all start? Well, it probably started when the name British Railways contracted to British Rail.

Sometimes the total cost happens twice. History has forgotten the brief period when the name Royal Mail, which everyone understood, was changed to Consignia, which nobody understood. The cost of changing the name on every facility and product of the Royal Mail to Consignia was astronomical, and the cost of changing the name back again was astronomical twice.

Such changes of name were once made by freshly appointed executives who wanted to announce their arrival, and who, unable to change what they should, changed what they could. But by now, surely, it's done out of a kind of desperation, as if words can work magic. It happens throughout the culture, and the misguided use of the word 'culture' is a disturbing further development of what is essentially voodoo. Regularly now we hear about young men shooting each other, and sometimes shooting their own girlfriends, as a response to what they call 'disrespect'. The misuse of the word 'disrespect' is just a pitiful sign of the vicious stupidity by which young men demand to be respected when there is nothing to respect them for. But when the up-market newspapers run worried articles about what they call 'the gun culture', that's something else. Calling it 'the gun culture' not only solves nothing, it actually compounds the offence, by tacitly conceding that the responsible authorities can't be expected to confiscate the lethal weapons from the individual boneheads waving them, but should wait until a complex sociological phenomenon has been explained in the appropriately elevated words. And you can't blame the responsible authorities for waiting. Actually to do something about a young crack-head fidgeting with a gun takes more than high-flown language. It takes bravery. But that's another subject."

So now we have another marketing package, the civil partnership of Nick and Dave. But words crack and strain and indeed multiply and retract. Government ministries now don't say what they are like Education, Health, and Defence. They have dynamic and pro-active names like 'Innovation' and 'Creativity' the, so called, creative sector now employs two million workers but what does it mean? I think lots of jobs for consultants. Harriet Harman is also now the Minister for Women. I wonder who is the Minister for Men?

The cultural shift has been hard on the over 40s. They are bewildered, not just through the loss of their spectacles and dodgy dancing, they cannot relate to current generations. There has never been such a cultural divide amongst the mass population in generations. The most extreme clash of culture is in the generational split. Older people cannot understand the current culture.

In fact anyone over 40 is finding it difficult understanding much of what is going on other than the liberal elitists who initiated it and now grapple around for something to rectify its chaos. And grappling around is not an understatement. The politicians are grasping at straws. If you want good parenting you have to give the parents 'money'. Give deprived kids 'computers'. Give teenagers terrorising others with crime 'a chance'. After all they are the outcome of a failed liberalist social policy over the last 30 years. It can't be their fault can it?

So in this shallow and superficial culture, the new role models for our youth are now celebrities. When I watch Celebrity chef I live in hope that one day I may possibly know who they are. Instead we rely on euphemisms, like 'a celebrated actor' 'a much loved soap star' but who are they?

Celebrity culture in the past was always about celebrating success and achievement. Now we pull down and humiliate celebrities as a validation of our own mess. The celebration of degradation. Celebrities don't inspire or elevate us, we wait to watch them fail to make us feel better. That's true democracy. The bar is lowered so we can aspire to failure. There are now no role models for our kids. So where do they draw their values from? John Sentamu shows his concerns.

"In a recent survey for National Kids' Day, 'Being a celebrity' has topped a list of what children under 10 believe to be the 'very best thing in the world'. The poll of just under 1,500 youngsters ranked 'God' as their tenth favourite thing in the world, with celebrity, 'good looks' and being rich at one, two and three respectively.

And it is not only kids. Many of our young men and women are prostituting themselves at the altar of idolatry in a bid to become famous or a celebrity in the belief that through this they will find meaning and happiness. The sales of gossip and celebrity magazines have never been higher, our news is as celebrity driven as the programmes it reports upon, whilst the head of documentaries at the BBC was recently reported to have said that 'it was not ideas he needed for new factual programmes, but celebrities to present them'."

For at least 1500 years the Christian culture has held this Island together. A large proportion of the population still call themselves Christians. When people say this is a secular society who decided that? The reality is that liberal secularists are now in control of the major institutions and are making that statement on behalf of the people. But they are making this assertion not on a

154

democratic basis but from a position of moral superiority which amounts to a form of fascist dictatorship.

Yet since the protestant reformation the priest did not mediate over an Englishman's communication with God. It was a personal communion and was part of the whole anti-clerical movement. The current evangelical and growing wing of the church, do not believe in institutions and are more likely to meet in warehouses and cinemas. Yet the church developed the culture which it now seems content to throw away. The church was the drive even pre-reformation, on the social aspects of the community with the parish as the unit of social gathering. The Parish was the root of carnival and popular entertainment as graphically demonstrated by Chaucer through the Miller in the Canterbury tales, and this grand tradition is carried on in the bawdy humour that pervades much of our entertainment from Frankie Howard down to Benny Hill and the Royal Family.

The Christian culture still underpins our society and institutions. The Commons' proceedings always starts with prayers to seek the wisdom to make the right decisions. Soldiers still pray before they go to battle. The Queen's church attendance on Sunday is without questioning, and guests on 'Desert Island discs' are always given a Bible.

The Church of England has always understood just how much religion the English culture can take unlike the Americans who trade votes through their religion. Blair knew that he could not reveal his true faith as the English would have seen this as Popery. Still it would have been useful if he could have allowed his faith to at least put some wisdom into his political judgements.

To lose the Christian culture would mean a replacement for all our fundamental principles that hold the culture together. When Prince Charles, who likes to think of himself as a 'Renaissance Man', stated that he would be 'the defender of all the faiths' he showed his characteristically poor judgement. He vigorously defended the history of architecture but not the history of society? Yet the biggest cultural divide is not between different religions in this nation, but between religions and atheism.

155

Dr Nazir-Ali, claimed the decline of Christianity had led to a collapse of Britishness, and said: "The greatest challenge is that of militant secularism, which is creating a double jeopardy for western cultures. It is losing its Christian discourse at the very time when it needs it most. Let us pray that we are able to recover our Christian nerve in the West and make sure the Gospel is not lost, and that all that is valuable in western culture – much of which comes from its Judeo-Christian background – will survive as a way to enhance cultures in the West and renew them once again."

In the past even the education system saw its role as reinforcing the national culture. Throughout history the role of education was to pass on from one generation to the next the skills, knowledge and wisdom which were important for the survival of the tribe. Education, particularly from Victorian times, was about creating an ordered and harmonious society which shared the same view of life. Values, morality, and national traditions were as important as knowledge and skills because it was them that held society together and made it believe in itself. The 1870 Education Act gave the right to elementary education to all and from then on the state became increasingly involved.

The eleven plus gave any bright and academically talented working-class kids the right to a Grammar School education. Secondary schools were meant to prepare those who had more practical skills for industry and commerce. This was seen by some as discriminatory and damaging but the fact is that this enabled more social mobility than at any other time. The political theory which overturned this system assumed that all children had the same ability and skills. It was based on Marxism. The process of education was taken from the control of the community to the Government. Teachers, like policeman, had been seen as representatives of their own community and they belonged to the local social groups as role models. The Dept of Education sought to take on this power and make teaching a theoretical business. Hence education was taken over by professional theorists who set about changing society through the classroom. The professional educationalist started to implement a range of new theories which largely raged against the traditions and values that had previously united schools.

And so was born a whole new age of educational theories. 'Child centred learning' being a very popular one. This is meant to put children at the centre of the learning process and teachers become facilitators, not directors, of education. OK so possibly this is where it all went horribly wrong, it sounds to me like teachers were not in charge any more.

This led to children becoming the centre of their own universe rather than learning what was passed down from the tribe. This also overturned the importance of the elders of the tribe and the voice of experience. Children were now firmly in control. It was all about them deciding if they could or could not do something; any challenge to this perception by the teacher was seen as authoritarian or even bullying. Adults lost their nerve, teachers lost control and now this irresponsibility has left many children insecure and bereft of any structure to their lives.

The rigour went from state school education. Some areas clung onto their Grammar Schools but they are now largely the preserve of the middle classes who coach their kids into places, and fee paying schools filled the gaps. Competition in school became taboo, as did rigour and challenge. So there was now no need to compete.

The changes in the education system in the 1960s saw the demise of Grammar Schools under the mantle of 'equal opportunities'. After this, all children had the right to have the same state education, the problem is that it was dumbed down rather than up. The new Comprehensive Schools seemed to aspire to the level of the Secondary Moderns rather than the traditional excellence of the Grammar Schools. Excellence could only be a measure if society agreed to what constituted 'excellence', and they no longer did.

So excellence became subjective rather than what it had always been, 'a shared concept'. Once the culture became divided there was no general consensus. So politicians made changes and there was no unity of dissent. The changes in the education system were caused by the politicisation of education. Schools became enforcers of social engineering, which of course, in many ways they always had been, but now the multicultural 'We' brigade were firmly in control of the mass peasants. The culture of equal opportunities led to all children being thrown in together to fulfill the social view that was a vision for the political elite who usually managed to get their children into private education, or if they were really lucky, a church school. Education was now seen as the focus for social justice, after all everyone is equal, it's just that those that could then pay became more equal than others, and if they did not want to pay to go private they could always buy themselves into the best catchment areas.

So an education system which perpetuated the culture by re-enforcing the values that had been passed down through generations was overturned. Schools became centres of socialist engineering and now, especially in the cities, they have become just a form of crowd control. The education system which saw itself as re-enforcing the culture which was characterised by a pride in nationhood, achievement, and ancestry was destroyed. The Secondary Modern system may not have been perfect but it could have been saved. In fact ironically, it is coming back now in different forms. Not all kids are academic, some are more practical. In their weird mixed up vision they felt that giving some kids an education that was less academic was a way of discriminating. They threw away the chances of the clever working-class kids rather than deal with the issues around Secondary Modern education, which were largely around new types of trendy educational theory. Also Technical schools were never fully developed, if they had been fully developed we may have ended up with some tradesmen instead of relying on the much more efficient Eastern European system to fuel our economy. Now we may never again see a working-class Prime Minister, and social mobility is lower than it has even been. So that worked well then.

When Heathcliffe returned from the big city the Brown bounce was flattened by a simple piece of technology called a microphone and Bigotsgate became the reality. But globalisation

158

is useful to politicians as it means that no one government is responsible for anything, everything is linked to global development. Hum very convenient. So the prime minister who as Chancellor presided over the biggest economic bubble, which ultimately burst, was seen by some as so experienced he was the only one who can get us out of this. Presumably because he got us into it. When Alan Johnson resigned as Shadow Chancellor the obvious one to replace him was the person who advised Gordon Brown how to get us into this mess in the first place; Ed Balls-up. Presumable it was felt that two 'Eds' were better than one. Jeremy Clarkson called Gordon a one-eyed, Scottish, idiot. He did apologise for the 'one-eyed' comment, and even the Scottish comment, although I feel that the Scots themselves may be concerned about the inference that being called Scottish is a form of insult. But one thing that no one wanted him to apologise for was calling him an 'idiot'.

The only one with any economic nous is Vince Cable but of course he's far too old and of course bald. For the language of political correctness is overshadowed by an even greater ideology of the last 30 years, 'the Market'. Those folically challenged are not very marketable, hence, William Hague, Ming Campbell, Vince Cable and Ian Duncan-Smith could not be seen as leaders but only followers in the coalition. Winston Churchill and Clement Attlee did not seem to suffer from the same public disdain.

So Teachers are now allowed to search children for cigarettes, drugs and alcohol. If they were paid enough they could get their own. But Nitty Nora has been banned from schools due to child molestation but infestation is presumably OK.

The strength of any nation is dependent upon the national culture. Russia had lost all its self-confidence with the demise of communism, now it is revisiting its cultural roots to get back its pride. In the current Russian society two thirds class themselves as orthodox Christians. They may not all go to church but the orthodoxy is about their cultural heritage. A recent poll in Russia for the most popular historical figure was won by the Tsar, not Lenin or Marx, but the person who epitomised their heritage.

China similarly has rediscovered Confusious and are looking to their own past which Marxism had denied but is now happy to cultivate for its own ends.

The bewilderment of the over 40s is mainly down to the complete cultural shift over the last 30 years. The discipline that was expected, not just in our schools but in our armed services and the health service, is now seen as 'authoritarian'. The sense of individual responsibility and order that was promoted in all ages until the last thirty years made our institutions effective. The NHS relied on Matron. The Sgt Major was one of the most feared men in the army, but often the most respected. He, kept order and harmony amongst the troops. The self-confidence and unity of the culture provided the basis for a stable society. Social stigma that had helped to keep social order has now been banned. The standard moral values that helped keep social harmony were overturned by moral relativists. So no moral judgements are allowed anymore. Anything goes so long as it is within the law. So that's why Mr Blair kept creating so many meaningless laws that were usual unenforceable. So laws multiply and they don't make sense. However, whilst moral judgements are not allowed, except by the Government who make the laws, judgements are being lavished on those who have become our new wave of social outcastes. So smokers, fatties and those who drive Chelsea tractors are the new outcasts

In Wales a painter and decorator was fined by the police for lighting up a cigarette in his van. The police stated that it was his 'place of work'. Another criminal dealt with. Someone else was arrested for throwing a twiglet out of a car. So is feeding the ducks now a crime? Whilst smokers and fatties are social outcasts and blamed for overwhelming the health service, drug users, those with STDs and teenage mums all draw on the health service, but are, of course victims. We should all feel safer in our beds.

So what is the legacy that the 'We brigade' have dumped on the mass culture? They have destroyed the Family and replaced it with the Gang, replaced healthy competition with drugs and alcohol, and replaced the work ethic with three generations of welfarism. So, we are now in a child centred society where it is now estimated that 2/3 children per week die at the hands of their, so called, 'carers'. What they have achieved may have been what they always wanted, the elimination of the mass English culture. The exuberant pleasure with which the mass enjoyed religious activities and festivals had been condemned by the High Church and the Puritans at different points in history. Prior to these high church movements we were quite happy getting pissed, dancing about with bells on our ankles and rolling eggs around. But the church movements were more about calming and controlling than destroying the mass or peasant culture. For they did not loath the mass peasants they just wanted to keep them in check and in many ways the church movements often saved them from themselves, as we saw with the licensing laws and the Temperance movement. They would never have taken away their festivals just given them a different emphasis, and who cared as long as we could sing, dance and be merry, and still roll a few eggs around.

But now the whole mass culture is being destroyed and suddenly we hear murmurs of fear about the alienation of the white working class. So whilst images of Barack Obama and Nelson Mandela are plastered over our schools and institutions as our role models to be held up as some sort of saviours of the British culture, what role models are there for white working-class kids. Lewis Hamilton was also plastered over our schools as some sort of role model but the success of Jenson Button was much less promoted. But why?

In the past the mass culture was fired by pride in its history and tradition and its own role as part of the success of the nation. Those who seemed to epitomise the strength of the mass 'poor but proud' culture were Londoners, who represented the capital of England. When the majority of them were driven out of London in the 1980s the English mass culture was in distress and decline. The capital which seemed to epitomise the strength of the mass culture was now deemed 'multicultural' by the liberal elite. So the caring middle-classes that set out to fight the cause of every threatened tribal group across the planet, are probably looking forward to a time when the English peasants, stripped of their pride and glory, can be safely locked into the past.

The gentle English culture that was represented by The Eagle has now been replaced by the anarchy of Chat and Nuts, so that's what feminism did for the gals. The English culture of the 20th century is one in which the new political elite are dismissive of the mass culture and the only 'right on' response is based on the superior social understanding reached by the 'We' brigade or the chattering classes.

The politics or 'fospel' of personal choice and fulfillment have now taken precedence over individual responsibility. The family is any unit and cohabitation is as good as marriage and one parent as good as two. The new political elite protect their own commandments with the ferocity of a fascist dictatorship. Democracy is seen to be dangerous because it may challenge the elitist views and provide a forum for the mass population who are seen as incapable of making any sensible decisions that the 'We' brigade would accept. Education is then used to indoctrinate them so they can be made to think like the powers that be. It is this moral relativism and the destruction of the mass culture which Orwell feared most, and now 'Big Brother' is in control.

So when you apply your fake tan to keep that young and healthy look, pray that they don't come up with a 'green' alternative. Always take care not to lapse into undisciplined messaging. And when they sew you into your thermal vest for the winter don't forget to contemplate the 'exit from life' strategy that the Government are planning for you. As Woody Allen once said, "I am not afraid of death, I just don't want to be there when it happens. I don't want to achieve immortality through my work. I want to achieve it through not dying."

So you may ask, is it me? Yes it bloody well is!

When we look back at the past we rightly realise that our national culture has been lost. This view of English culture was reflected in the 1940s by George Orwell, we would still recognise this but possibly only in the Shires.

"The gentleness of the English civilisation is perhaps its most marked characteristic. You notice it the instant you set foot on English soil. It is a land where the bus conductors are good-tempered and the policemen carry no revolvers. In no country inhabited by white men is it easier to shove people off the pavement."[37]

And perhaps in our rush to embrace the concept of multiculturalism we forgot the reality of those who live it:

"...my dream is that those lucky enough to be born into a culture of 'ladies first' will let go of the myth that all cultures are equal. Human beings are equal; cultures are not.[38]"

---

[37] George Orwell, England My England'.

[38] Hirsti Ali, Speech for CORE.

THE PEASANTS ARE REVOLTING

"I can't help feeling wary when I hear anything said about the masses. First you take their faces from 'em by calling 'em the masses and then you accuse 'em of not having any faces."[39]

In 1381, and under the leadership of English heroes such as Watt Tyler and Jack Straw, the English peasants marched to London in order to present a petition, 60,000 strong, to the King. The petition called for the abolition of serfdom, tithes and the game laws, as well as the right to freely use the forests. The peasants also demanded that the poll tax be abolished. John Ball, a priest spoke regularly to the people gathered in the marketplace, and expressed the sentiments of the revolt. The rallying cry of the peasants was a rhyme which spread dissension across the South of England:

"When Adam Delved and Eve span who was then the Gentleman?"

So what went wrong with Jack Straw the hero of the English peasants? He seems to have been replaced by Jack Straw the one time Justice Secretary or indeed John Straw the Essex boy who used the diminutive Jack, a generation after everyone else, presumably to create effect. He became Jack Straw and was drafted into Blackburn but not to become the hero of the English but their castigator:

"Beware the English – a nation with the potential for aggression and violence," was the warning from the then Home Secretary Jack Straw, who aired his views on a BBC radio debate about Britishness.

---

[39] J. B. Priestly, *Saturn Over the Water* (1961).

"...The English used their propensity for violence to subjugate the other home nations – before turning their attention to Europe and the British Empire."

So with the help of Jack Straw and the rest of the political class, the English peasants, once so proud and feisty were driven towards the American Dream, which has turned into a nightmare. They became the underclass. They had their belief in nation taken away from them by political correctness. The work ethic, which had sustained their culture, was removed from them and they were given welfare.

When their education system, which was once considered to be the best in the world, was destroyed by 'call me Tony', they were then told they were too poorly skilled and it was easier to bring in immigrant labour. When the credit fuelled 'Blair Boom' arrived they were then told they were too lazy and work shy to do the lower paid jobs, and by this point they probably were. Anyway what was the point, the Government was paying them not to work. The political class said that it was easier and more economically effective to draw in immigrants from poor countries that were only too willing to step up to the mark and would have happily drifted across the sea on a lilo. But was this just stupidity or was it a conspiracy from New Labour, in order to increase the number of their voters through the votes of the immigrant population?

Sir Andrew Green (Chairman of Migration Watch UK) goes for the conspiracy theory.

"So there was indeed a Labour conspiracy to change the nature of our society by mass immigration. New evidence confirms claims made by a Labour political adviser last October which he subsequently tried to Recant. In an article for the Evening Standard, Andrew Neather revealed that 'it didn't just happen: the deliberate policy of ministers from late 2000 until at least February last year... was to open up the UK to mass migration'.

"The huge increases in migrants over the last decade were partly due to a politically motivated attempt by ministers to radically change the country and 'rub the Right's nose in

165

diversity', according to Andrew Neather, a former adviser to Tony Blair, Jack Straw and David Blunkett.

"He said Labour's relaxation of controls was a deliberate plan to 'open up the UK to mass migration' but that ministers were nervous and reluctant to discuss such a move publicly for fear it would alienate its 'core working class vote'.

"As a result, the public argument for immigration concentrated instead on the economic benefits and need for more migrants. Critics said the revelations showed a 'conspiracy' within Government to impose mass immigration for 'cynical' political reasons."

Well how strange that after being defeated in the 2010 election, and after around 13 years of uncontrolled and engineered immigration, Ed Balls-up has now called for a complete re-think on immigration! Well it's a bit late for that Ed!

They took away all the things that had held the Peasants together, all they could give the poor was benefits, extended welfare and a culture of rights not responsibilities. To give them responsibilities would be deemed judgmental, which was non-PC to the liberal elite. But to give the underclass more welfare is like giving heroin addicts more heroin. Oh, they did that as well did they? OK.

But if we look back to our proud heritage how did the Jarrow marchers become the larger louts of our cities. How did the Land Girls become Vicky Pollard or the British Tommy become sperm machines for liberated single mums? And what was wrong when real men drank warm beer rather than fizzy larger, full of piss and wind. And real English ale wasn't just the rallying call of the middle class but the mark of the Englishman. When 'kiss me quick hats', knotted hankies socks and sandals were replaced by velour, vomit and Jeremy Kyle, the English peasants were in danger of extinction.

But we mustn't talk about class. Politicians hate the term and often call it the 'last taboo' with 'race' coming up fast in the inside lane. They hate the word because it has connotations of the old political system where different sectors of society were represented by their own people. When politicians had conviction and a clear agenda right or wrong. The political elite want a classless society but not to make life better for everyone but to stop people identifying with just who they are. It also exposes the politicians themselves, who tend to come from more affluent backgrounds and who have now become a class of their own, 'the political class'.

The political class pretend to work on the creation of a classless society but I fear only because to identify class would impinge on voting patterns and inevitably lead to voters identifying allegiance with a political party. Since the success of the New Labour 'marketing project' politicians have been taught to target scarce resources only on potential voters and the largest groups that you can rely on to actually turn up and vote are, as the Blair project described, 'Mondeo Man' and 'School Gate mums'. So party workers deserted the doorsteps of local constituencies. The Government changed the rules and created around 600 new laws to ensure that, back bench time would be limited and parliamentary democracy was now under threat. So have the political class created the underclass in their own image and likeness?

Well the culture of entitlement is not unique to the underclass; examples show that the political class and some of our top earners also have this attitude. The expenses scandal may lead to future hair shirt parliaments but it demonstrated, not just how politicians lacked accountability to the public, but also how they felt it was their 'right' to do so. They were no different to the underclass. Politicians happily rejected Robin Cooke's calls for reform of the expenses system in 2002 but the Telegraph exposed our politicians and they were both shocked and indignant. They had a right. Bankers also expect bonuses. After all having lost all the retained profits from three centuries of business; they believed they should get a bonus for just recovering this situation. So back to square one. That's like giving someone who has just crashed a train, an aeroplane to fly. So MPs have more fiddles than the London Philharmonic orchestra and Bankers bonuses are enjoyed at the taxpayer's expense. They just don't get it do they.

The description of class is a very complex issue. In the past the upper class despised the middle class because they had pretentions of becoming upper class but never could. They would do frightful things like have doilies on the cake stand. The working class and the upper class always had more in common. Upper class and working class even share some of the same diction, like 'lavatory' and 'pudding', preferring football to rugby. The middle class would possibly say 'toilet' or 'loo' and we may rue the day when they start saying 'Bathroom' but I expect it's inevitable. The upper and working class would say 'pudding' whilst the middle class would use the much more affected word 'dessert', just to show they knew the difference between an arid piece of land and a dish full of calories. The House of Lords, always loathed by the political elite, was usually more in tune with the common people than the career politicians and lawyers that are housed in Westminster Village.

When the English peasants had moral codes the 'We' brigade wanted them to be free of the oppression they had soldiered under and become liberated. They loathed Victorian conformity and structure which had stood firm up until the 1960s. The neo-Marxists yearned for a cultural revolution. But the noble Victorian Quakers like Cadbury's and Rowntree's had a feudalistic attitude towards business and their workers. They felt responsible for their staff. But under Thatcherism, Rowntree's were symbolically eaten up by the Swiss Nestlé and Cadbury's, under Brown, was swallowed up by the Americans. When you have a belief or ethic that is wider than free market forces, then people are communities not commodities but when you lose belief and the market is the only God, people become commodities. As someone once said to me, if business is a rat race you shouldn't be surprised if the rats take over. The Marxists in Russia called them the factors of production and talked about equal shares but they then murdered, probably, more peasants than all the fascists put together.

So as the political class took away the old ideals of the peasants, the 'We' brigade were running for the hills. The problem is that whilst they said they wanted them to throw off the old establishment shackles of Victorian conformity and structure, they actually just wanted them to have THEIR attitudes and morals and to achieve a form of social ethnic cleansing. The result is that now we have the underclass and we are well on our way to the American dream. Charles Murray, an American writer, described what he saw developing in the UK back in 1989 as; a 'nascent underclass', which by 1999 had become one that increasingly resembled, in behaviour and proportional size, the underclass that he believed they have learned to live with in America.

"Before I make that case, let us be clear on terminology. By underclass, I do not mean people who are merely poor, but people at the margins of society, unsocialised and often violent."

The UK Government does indeed understand this, we no longer have a working class, it calls them the 'socially excluded' after having deliberately excluded them through their policies.

"From the mid-nineteenth century through the first three quarters of this century, the United States was seen as a violent unruly society with a lot of personal freedom but not very civilised. During the same period, Britain was seen, rightly, as the most civilised country on earth. Other countries on the continent had low crime rates, but they also had traditions and institutions of authoritarian control. Britain enjoyed extraordinarily low crime and extraordinary freedom. It was a unique, magnificent achievement, proving to the world that liberty and safety were compatible, proving, indeed that a genuinely civil society is possible. But no longer. Britain is just another high-crime industrialised country."

The reality is that the proud working-class English have been largely destroyed. Gone are the working-class heroes, they have been replaced by the Gallaghers, of Shameless. So the aim of the political elite, is to manufacture a liberal Utopia, where we all live 'right and proper' 'hearts and minds'. Where all our kids go to 'Uni' whilst we import foreign labour to do the real jobs. It seemed the decline in education happened when they started to call it 'Uni' rather than University which they probably couldn't spell. The problem is, the new Marxist takeover of the education system was meant to re-educate the masses to think like the 'besot we', but the removal of all social values and the creation of welfarism just meant social chaos. The political class who run our politics and great institutions now, and who lord it over our education system, despise these people, and send them up at every available opportunity. They worry about them being unfit to vote as they may vote BNP, so they want them to be re-educated to be like them. Even Prince Harry was deemed to need re-programming and was sent off to equal opps. training. The state has now become Mummy and Daddy and the Government look like one of those crushingly inadequate parents that appear on Super nanny. The New Labour project was unfortunately very far from its working-class roots and became controlled by self-righteous, middle-class social reactionaries who were consciously driving their own form of morality. They used the term 'appropriate' which is judged by the standards of the left wing elite who believe it is appropriate for the Government to takeover welfare, but not to have a view on personal and sexual morality which they deem not to be an issue for the state. Although the state (or the taxpayer) pays for the outcomes of these activities. Anybody who does not believe that this is 'appropriate' is condemned for 'inappropriate' thinking.

What we now have is what George Orwell feared the most; the development of a political elite that would, disrespect the common people, that would strip them of what had held them together for centuries: faith, family, national pride and the work ethic, all because, in their fascist view, they were absolutely positive that they knew better. Not even the Elizabethans would have been that stupid; they knew the importance of the mass culture and that to respect the English peasants was vital.

"My loving people. We have been persuaded by some that are careful of our safety, to take heed how we commit ourselves to armed multitudes, for fear of treachery; but I assure you I do not desire to live to distrust my faithful and loving people. Let tyrants fear, I have always so behaved myself that, under God, I have placed my chief strength and safeguard in the loyal hearts and goodwill of my subjects; and therefore I am come amongst you, as you see, at this time, not for my recreation and disport, but being resolved, in the midst and heat of the battle, to live and die amongst you all; to lay down for my God, and for my kingdom, and my people, my honour and my blood, even in the dust. I know I have the body but of a weak and feeble woman; but I have the heart and stomach of a king, and of a king of England too."

As the first Elizabeth, the girl Queen gave this speech at Tilbury Essex she proved that the gender verification issue was not a new phenomenon just peculiar to the Olympic athletes but is now, probably, the latest chat up line for behind the bike sheds.

Despite the political class saying that they want to eliminate poverty, whatever that really is, the poor are getting poorer, while the rich are getting richer. But also the North-South divide is getting Wider. The terrible gap between the North and South has now been confirmed as 'the Midlands'. Researchers are now claiming that people living in the South are likely to be better educated and earn more money than their Northern counterparts, a Sheffield University study suggests. Co-author of the report, Professor Daniel Dorling, concluded that the country was being 'split in half'. He said: "To the south is the metropolis of Greater London, to the north and west is the 'archipelago of the provinces' – city islands that appear to be slowly sinking demographically, socially and economically. The UK is looking more and more like a city-state. It is a kingdom united only by history, increasingly divided by its geography."

But it's now not even united by history or its culture. English history is not even taught anymore. Multiculturalism has meant that cities are now being fragmented into ethnic quarters. The cities and the shires are worlds apart. The UK itself has also been torn apart by devolution. I do not believe that the English wanted the breakup of the union, it was, those traditionally known as Taff and Jock. But now that it's happened the English are the forgotten tribe. This was the question raised by the MP Tam Dalyell.

"For how long will English constituencies and English Honourable Members tolerate at least 119 Honourable Members from Scotland, Wales and Northern Ireland exercising an important and probably often decisive, effect on English politics

171

while they themselves have no say in the same matters in Scotland, Wales and Northern Ireland?

This was then termed 'The West Lothian' question. But the West Lothian question has been ignored by successive Governments in the hope that the English would not realise what was going on. This has largely been a successful tactic. With the loss of interest in politics most haven't noticed or are too distracted. If the English had their own parliament, Labour would probably never again be elected. But the disinterest in politics changed briefly at the 2010 campaign. Politicians became panel contestants in the Nick, Gord and Dave show and voters felt they were part of the X factor. But then when they tried to vote they weren't allowed in. But for those that did get in they soon realised that Nick, Dave and Gord were not even on the ballot paper!

Over the last 15 years, many of the great offices of state were held by MPs from Scotland, but whereas the chancellor has responsibility for the United Kingdom economy the English are tiring of Hibernian Anglophobia and the Scottish Raj who hold so much power in England. The announcement made by the Scottish first minister Jack McConnell that he was supporting Trinidad and Tobago against England displayed an undignified chippiness, whilst Alex Salmond signed a card thanking Maradona for the hand of God goal. McConnell needs reminding that his population lives as well as it does thanks to subsidies extorted from English taxpayers. Whilst Scottish students pay no tuition fees, English students could be paying £9,000. Whilst plans may have been laid to sell off the English forest, no such plans were made for the Scottish or Welsh forests. That would have been inconceivable. A travesty of justice.

Now in the capital of England the white underclass lose their own identity and talk in patois. As the pride of their forefathers is wrenched from them, Cockney pride has been destroyed and the indigenous working class, driven into Essex. London has been reconfigured from the safest city in the world, with a united people who defied Hitler's bombers, to a melting pot of multicultural and various tribes with their own national cultures and identity. Whilst our troops die in Afghanistan the major threat

172

to their nation, many believe, comes from within. The indigenous population were driven out by social policies which made it a place they no longer recognised. Part of it became the playground of the rich, the middle-class who commute in from the suburbs and shires and the celebs. The reality is that there are 50 minority ethnic groups in London. The fastest growing group are those of mixed race, who have come to epitomise the 'new' Londoner'. The peasants are now naturally forming into tribal groups. The cockney Londoners that made the Queen Mother so proud during the Blitz have been replaced by the spouters of Street Talk, which is not even English but a mix of Jamaican, Asian and West African who mumble on about Nang, low batties, and nuff crepes. Sadly, multicultural London lacks one thing, the culture of its indigenous population which in future we may see packaged and presented to tourists in a clinical resurrected format. Yet if this was happening on the other side of the world the political class and the middle-class elite would be 'up in arms'.

The closure of Goddard's pie and mash shop which I frequented as a kid, retired to that great pie shop in the sky and was turned into an up-market burger joint. This symbolically left the cockney lying battered and bleeding. Their language has largely disappeared, their markets have been taken over, their traditional family pubs turned into places for 30 something's, and their culture, which once epitomised the English working class, is ignored The thing that was very crucial to the market, like so much in an ordered English society, was that there were rules. Things like every third stall had to sell something different – and that kept a certain order. Let's hear from...

"It's hard to find a pearly king who lives in the old haunts now. The pearly king of Hornsey lives in Shepherd's Bush, the pearly king of King's Cross lives in Arnos Grove, the pearly king of Peckham lives in Epsom and the pearly queen of Newham lives in Jersey!

"It's on the decline simply because of the change in population in London".

The change in inner-London language was first captured back in 1985 in Smiley Culture's single, 'Cockney Translation', which

– while ostensibly about slang – highlighted the fact that young London-born black men and women no longer looked to the cockney for their accent.

> Cockney have name like Terry, Darfu and Del Boy
> We have name like Winston, Lloyd and Leroy
> We bawl out YO!
> Whilst Cockneys say OI!
> What Cockney call a Jackas
> We call a Blue Bwoy
> Cockney have mates
> While we have spar
> Cockney live in a drum
> While we live in a yard
> Say we nyam
> While Cockney got capture
> Cockney say guvanor
> We say Big Bout here
> In a de Cockney translation
> In a dey Cockney translation
> (Smiley's culture)

The very effective political destruction of the working class indigenous Londoners must be a very positive move for the political class. After all they dispersed the London mob, which had always given the politicians a lot of bother. The London mob in Eighteenth century England was dominated, not just by those who rioted, but everyone in the lower classes who were on the streets. This disorderly throng could become so powerful that it would threaten the constitutional process. At a moment's notice the word would go out and a large crowd would congregate and tear London apart until their demands were met.

But the indigenous London population that had stood proud against the Blitz and moulded the traditions and stability of London, now flee from the rising tide of disconnected people who provide cheap labour. The bigger tragedy is the sad and confused fate of older people who look in fear from their windows and do not have the finances to flee to Essex. The dogged and proud old

174

birds, so poignantly portrayed by Joyce Grenfell, are a dying breed. And if they don't die of natural causes the hospitals will finish them off. So as the proud old lady of London herself stumbles on toward becoming the new Mumbai, a good film deal is always possible. A remake of the Road to Morocco could always be shot in the East End of London, with no props. What a bargain!

The English peasants have always been a pain throughout history with their patriotism and sense of national identity. Their arrogance about their nation always being 'the best' had to be knocked out of them, and their attitudes towards Johnny foreigner needed to be cleansed. The middle classes may have a love of all pleasures French but the working classes have never been so smitten by the European culture. All classes in the past have used the French imagery as a way of describing bad behaviour. From French letters to a French Kiss, to swearing which was always, 'pardon my French'. A French Minister hit the nail on the head in 1973 when he explained the difference in attitudes between the classes of the two nations. He said that "the elite tend to admire each other whilst the people tend to despise each other".

The middle-class celebs that railed against Thatcherism foolishly embraced Blairism and took on a cool but new lingo for trendy London. This Estuary English is widely used by many of the middle class in the South and South-East of England particularly among affluent but inherently liberal young in an attempt to mock up a working-class accent. Some people adopt the accent as a means of 'blending in', appearing to be more working class, or in an attempt to appear to be 'a common man' – listen to Ed Balls-up and you can hear this affectation and it is often referred to as 'Mockney'.

Jonathon Ross came to epitomise the London cosmopolitan scene. Ross came from a London working-class background and now seems to personify what the elite would like the working class to be. Ross is a cheeky chappie Max Miller figure that has been hugged and cultivated by the elite. So much so that he could effectively broadcast whatever he liked without any control.

Sometimes his guard slipped and he actually became one of the underclass, when in the company of bad influences. Nevertheless, his views do not travel well, and do not transcend the confines of class and geography, unlike the renegade Jeremy Clarkson who terrifies the elite. His outspoken criticism of Gordon was much ado about nothing as he said: "In fact I was very polite. Jeremy Paxman had called for Ken Livingstone to be burned alive in public. I only called Gordon Brown 'a one-eyed Scottish idiot'."

So let's have a word with a minority ethnic group in London. "Well au revoir garcon, welcome to Nelson Mandela House. It ain't like it used to be, well fings have changed a lot around here especially since mum died, but I've still got Rodders, the Plonker."

Now the dulcet tones of the East End, best demonstrated authentically by Dick Van Dyke, almost as good as John Wayne's, version of a Roman soldier, have been replaced by patois, mockney and 500 other languages.

Yet a cor luvva duck Londoner had a very different culture to the Coronation Street Mancunian. It would have been Ena Sharples "eeh she's no better than she should be" versus Dixon of Dock Green "watch those bikes Andy". Sadly now the existence of either a traditional East End Londoner or a Coronation Street Mancunian is diminishing and often more the vision of middle-class TV producers who like to tussle with the man bags in the Cosmo but soon retire in the evening back to their oasis in the shires, or slip into the cosmo Borough of Hampstead.

The Church of England vicars who once provided spiritual guidance for the poor now toil away as poorly paid social workers mapping their own way to heaven, rather than saving the souls of their parishioners. Well at least until the Pope makes them an offer they can't refuse.

Now we have not 'class' but classes, for everything, not only for parenting, happiness, sex, and how to deal with abusive relationships, but also for Glaswegian, aye, and if only MI5 had this facility many years back 'oh the noo', they would have been able to nail militant union leader Mick McGahey. But the problem was they could 'nee understand de man', especially when he had a wee dram or two. Can't help wondering what they had in mind, certainly not a Glasgow kiss.

But there is something in a voice. The banks filled their pockets with bonuses and then shut down their local services and sent them to places like Bangalore in India. The peasants were not keen on this, not only had they lost their jobs but they were now dealing with phone calls from Indians who they struggled to understand. The way around this was to rename the Indians. Rajest became Ricky and they started to train them, but not in team work, or Health and Safety but the goings on in EastEnders, so that when contacting us they could make the customer feel 'more at home, with them'. How thoughtful.

John Major saw Britishness as an old lady riding to communion on her bike on a Sunday morning. Alex Salmond jumped in and said that was exclusively an English image, but the reality is that it is possibly only an English country image with some town but few city similarities. The industrial revolution changed the nature of the working class but the welfare state change it much more. Working-class women would whiten their doorsteps to within an inch of their lives as a matter of pride and scrub the kitchen floor clean enough from which to eat your dinner. Working-class men would have considered it a matter of pride to show courtesy to those they considered to be further up the social ladder. Ernest Bevin drank wine at functions, despite preferring Scotch, because he wasn't going to have them say that he didn't know how to behave. Tony Blair drank beer in public rather than wine, so he would not seem too posh. Behaviour was always the key to social acceptability at all levels. The main difference is that in Victorian times the working class were enlisted in that project. Even in Elizabethan times they knew that the vitality and culture of the poor was what held the nation together.

Politicians may want to eliminate the use of the term 'class' and move towards some sort of sociological marketing speak about spending patterns psychological messaging and profiling, but the class structure was only a way of explaining how English society had evolved over 2000 years.

Now many of the working class have become the lower middle class, but with a feckless underclass beneath them created from some unforeseen consequences of political engineering. The new middle class has maintained few standards with consumerism its only belief system. The upper-class is usually amoral so nothing's changed there.

A working-class council house kid in the 1960s may have been a bit more rough around the edges but they would not have liked being deemed the 'socially excluded' as we condescendingly now call them, because they certainly were not. When 'call me Tony' said "the class war is over" he actually meant he was going to change the culture of our society so that everyone could be homogenised into a system that meant social restructuring by wealth, rather than by the more subtle distinctions of traditions and culture, and he was in fact emulating an American style society. Nothing very original there then. But what is more terrifying is that he also created the new 'political class', who would be the ones controlling not just our every move but also our 'hearts and minds'. And their main motivator would be not idealism or, political conviction, but just 'staying in power' and keeping their job. What we have now is a fractured society whatever term you use to describe different sectors of society is immaterial, because it is just not joined up. There are no common beliefs or values that hold society together. Beliefs and values were part of the national culture that had to be eliminated. So Tom Finney was replaced by Vinnie Jones and Brief Encounter by Shirley Valentine. The ethos of playing the game as a sportsman and that your personal conduct was more important than winning was replaced by behave like a thug and become a celebrity. Whilst personal sacrifice for your children was more important than running off with a lover, was replaced by sea, sun, sand and sex, whenever you can get it.

The 1966 World Cup footballers represented by the likes of Nobby Stiles and Bobby Moore, who were self-deprecating, honest, but proud of their heritage and to be playing for their nation. They were working-class chaps who were doing what they loved best, playing football. The team of 2010 seemed to be very different. We may want our team to win but the last thing most of them are, is national role models. On 3rd July 2010 when listening to BH on radio 4, I was amazed to hear one of the broadcasters say that the reason England were so poor in the World Cup was because "This thing England is not even a nation, Great Britain is the nation. This England entity does not even exist!" What! I was so angry but then I thought, he could be right. The broadcaster who said it, wanted to believe that England had finally been eliminated and that those who fly the flag were very confused and really just probably a 'bloody nuisance." Too much nationalism. Perhaps the attitude now of our footballers, who would be the underclass if they were not celebrities, is that they have lost the sense of who they are. At the 1966 World Cup final when the game went into extra time and the players were taking a break, Bobby Moore later explained that Alf Ramsay told the England players not to lie down like the Germans. The English psychology had to prove they were of stronger stuff. It was important. The national identity had to be different. In sport someone needs to be superior, there are winners and losers, but most of this comes from individual character and inner strength and belief. It was about attitude and the knowledge of self-identity which has gone from the spoilt stars of our game. Nobby Stiles, when interviewed about his preparation before going on the field stated something like "I put my contacts in, take my teeth out and I'm ready", he was speaking for generations of Englishmen gone before.

The distinction between then and now was not between truth and hypocrisy it was just the way people felt. It certainly wasn't that people were saints. It is thought that during the 1940s the number of affairs was significantly high, especially with doodle bugs and Yanks flouting their stockings, and that was only the men! But the key point was that they knew it was wrong and at the end of the day the family was not to be sacrificed. The difference between the image and the reality became known as hypocrisy but the difference between then and now is absolute disaster.

If you look back to the 17th and 18th century the peasants were a rough lot, and their behaviour often riotous but this was also true of the other classes. The court of the Regency period was full of boozing and whoring and the streets were littered with disorder. The 19th century changed all this out of necessity. The strict Methodism and the philanthropic entrepreneurs set the standards for the Englishman, stopping the moral decay. Good behaviour was the code. Hypolite Taine expressed the difference between a Frenchman and an Englishman.

"The former was elegant, stylish and chivalrous. The latter was a disinterested man of integrity capable of sacrificing himself for those he leads and a man of honour."

Honour and behaviour were also important for all of society in Victorian times, there was a need to be respected. To be called 'common' was the worst insult. Englishmen should be of good character, industrious, honest and sober. The characteristic of an Englishman pervaded all classes. Accounts from the disaster of the Titanic demonstrated this behaviour and, it is now thought that the accounts that lower classes were locked down below decks are unfounded. The belief is that more passengers died on the Titanic because they queued politely for lifeboats. History data shows that in that era Britons were more inclined to be 'gentlemanly' while Americans were more 'individualist'. Social norms such as "women and children first" were very strong in British culture and there were plenty of examples of gentlemanly conduct by British passengers and crew after the Titanic hit an iceberg. It is thought than women with children had a 70% better chance of survival than men. Men would put them in the lifeboats and then have a cigar stand around and be chummy, while basically the boat went down. One gentleman who was rather wealthy went back downstairs after he put his wife on the lifeboat. He put on his tuxedo stating: "if I am going to die, I may as well die as a gentleman and well-dressed." This was, after all, the Edwardian period when to be a gentleman was the peak of society. The captain, Edward John Smith, according to witnesses shouted out: "Be British, boys, be British!" as the cruise liner went down. It was all about self-respect be it rich or poor and of course national identity and character.

This image and ideal was constant until the 1960s when the old order was under threat by upper/middle-class youth who wanted to overturn the old system. But the culture for the working-class peasants of decency honour and integrity really continued in all the English culture until the 1970s when the collectivisation of labour produced its own dictators. The traditional Labour Government was caught up in this moment and lost the ability to reconcile its ideals which led to it losing power for a number of years. So New Labour had to recreate itself and eliminate their working-class image, continuing the Thatcherite agenda to eliminate the working-class. Englishness has gone from the two engines of working-class decency and middle-class rectitude. The working class had to either become lower middle class or be left as the underclass. The Marxist political ideology of cultural homogeneity meant that the old feudalistic class system should be replaced and English culture should be destroyed.

This movement really started in earnest when the lower middle class Mrs Thatcher screeched, and stomped her feet, prior to the voice training of course. After that she was worse. She hand bagged the trade union movement by creating 3 million unemployed and drove out the wets who were traditional Tory gentleman, very upper middle class and not used to such behaviour from ladies of the middle classes. She started the change in the class system in Britain terminally. She did this by changing their values. She wanted to change the working classes, who she saw defined as old Labour voters, and make them Tory voters. She did this by making them feel they needed to 'own' things be it shares or council houses. There was nothing wrong with aspiration, they always had this, but in the past it was based on education.

Social mobility after the wars was at its highest with selective education by ability. Politicians like Nae Bevan and Manny Shinwell may have come from poor families but the value of education and high culture were held in high esteem, as we now see in other less developed nations. If we look back to the 19th century even the poor had probably higher standards of reading than they have now. Thomas Paine's The Rights of Man

181

published in 1803 sold one and a half million copies. William Cobbett's Address to the Journeyman and Labourers sold two hundred thousand copies in only two months. His writings were read on nearly every cottage hearth in the manufacturing districts of South Lancashire. Serialised fictions such as the works of Dickens sold in huge numbers and regular reading of the Bible at home was traditional and widespread. Under Thatcher traditional working-class values were replaced by consumerism.

Blair admired Thatcher and was keen to continue her legacy. He knew she had a formula which would get him into power. As someone once said the only way Labour will get into power again is if they have a leader who looks like a Tory. His use of body language and smarm was something the English had always found obnoxious but everything was changing. For New Labour the policies that won elections appeared to be those which continued the Thatcher project, this 'taking forward' of Thatcherism underlined much of the Blairite rhetoric.

Thatcher removed the majority of traditional working-class industrial jobs from the market, a new 'underclass', below working class emerged. The 'underclass', those unemployed and drawing state benefits as if it was their natural right to do so. They are now firmly at the new bottom of the class system. Or whatever you want to call it. You can still see many aspects of the traditional class system in place in the higher and middling classes if not the working class. Traditionally being upper class is to be educated at public school, use received pronunciation and have ownership of a large number of inherited items such as antique furniture. The upper-class are usually holders of titles, often with substantial inherited wealth. This is a 'closed' club it is nearly impossible to join this class after birth. No wonder Harriet Harman and Peter Hain don't make any reference to their grand background and David Cameron is unhappy that a photo is still available with him riding to hounds and dear stalking.

But, move over guys, we now have the global rich mostly from the Arab states and Russian oligarchs. As the global elite brought out 'brand UK plc', their persona is in stark contrast to the quiet wealth of the old upper classes. Once it was the Kremlin that came begging for cash. Gorbachev and Boris Yeltsin sought bail-out after bail-out from the west, strongly backed by Margaret Thatcher and John Major. Now it is the other way round: Russia sits on a vast pile of resources, and we are basically selling ourselves, our country, our principles and our self-respect. Even before the financial crisis, London was the global leader in the respectability business: offering rich Russians the chance to turn their ill-gotten billions into prestige. Whether you wanted an entree to high society or to popular culture, British go-betweens and highly paid PR barons were willing to provide it. Buy a football team, sponsor a charity, or make a hefty donation to a posh boarding school – and you suddenly gain the right up-market cachet. In exchange for what are, to them, trivial amounts of cash, the numerous oligarchs bought priceless respectability and safety. As fugitives from Russia found, Britain is a safe haven as police and bodyguards work smoothly together; Russian extradition warrants count for little as the UK is up for sale. New Labour, during their extended reign had more in common with these Russians than the old English aristocracy who they have always resented. They quite blatantly spent much time cultivating the oligarchs on board their yachts and at their parties. The political class we know has no moral direction but has it also forgotten that Russia is a national security threat: a point underlined repeatedly and publicly by MI5? On the home front, we seem to have surrendered without any fight at all. Yet the Americans have returned to the old days of yore and excluded 10 immigrants to America who they have identified as Russian spies. Perhaps they know more than we do.

To carry on our class analysis let's get back to the comfort of the English middle class so we don't have to worry about Uranium poisoning or Kalashnikovs. The middle classes usually have a university background and education and are often professionals or business people. They will normally own their own home and earn well above the national average, shop at Marks and Spencer's, have a social conscience but not enough to get down and dirty for a cause, unless of course it involves there own back gardens. Lower/middle-class in the past would do what would be known as a 'white collar' jobs but now probably unable to say 'white collar' so probably a 'lighter collar' job depending on what soap brand you use. The upper/working-classes generally did not hold a university degree but worked in skilled trades or roles such as supervisors, foreman and construction workers or self-employed.

Then came the working class: people who usually had lower educational attainment and worked in semi-skilled, or unskilled clerical work, or in fields such as industrial or construction work. These people were driven by the work ethic. As long as you had a job you had social respectability. These people were poor but proud. The main difference between then and now was that the working classes were driven by the protestant work ethic. They were proud of their nation, their class and their family support system. These people are now almost extinct, pushed out by Poles and cheap foreign labour brought in for that purpose by the political class.

The lower/working-class, either worked in low/minimum wage occupations, such as cleaners, shop assistants, or bar worker. They were often employed in the personal service industry. But these roles in the cities have now been taken by foreigners. The underclass that is now left behind is reliant on state benefits for income. We now have 3 generations with a culture of dependency and a history of expectations. Under New Labour all this became acceptable and social stigma was outlawed. These people were now seen as victims, socially excluded or on the margin of society. These people are now mocked and patronised by the rest of society. Yet the bill to pay for this cultural destruction will be paid for by our own children. When the outgoing New Labour Government left the treasury the message was simple, "We've spent it all."

After World War II social mobility improved greatly with working-class kids gaining access to Grammar Schools but in the last 20 years it has plummeted. The working classes could no longer aspire to a good education, which was now firmly second rate. To have no money meant no self-respect and the prospect of social mobility was gone. There is no morality about where the money comes from, you just need to get the money. No longer would Johnny get a new bike if he worked hard and got into Grammar School, you are all consigned to an education of mediocrity unless you're lucky enough to live in a good area, which you won't cos you're poor. Tough. A new way out of this dire situation is to become a 'celebrity'.

So the political elite then had to tune into this new celebrity culture in order to become one of us plebs so they had to 'hob nob' not just with the global super rich elite, they also had to be tuned into the celebrity culture of Simon or Piers. This worked more easily for Mr Blair, with his teeth and boyish charm but for poor old Gordon, making public statements and updates about Jade Goody's health whilst he had publicly supported her extensive bullying by the media, was painful. Whilst his casual name dropping of Simon Cowell and Piers Morgan in interviews was cringe-worthy. Yes, he was getting regular updates on the health and wellbeing of Subo, and wrote personal letters to X-Factor contestants, giving them a 'bit of a pep talk'. And no doubt some advice about how to be a celebrity. I wonder if they could read the letters, and I hope they didn't arrive 2 years late. I bet they didn't. But 'bigots gate' exposed Gordon's attitude towards the plebs and he got his marching orders although his fingers had to be prized off the door handle of number 10.

But why were the working classes so respected by the other classes up until Thatcherism? The main thing that divided the working class from the other classes during the 1960s era was the collective strength of the trade union movement that became so powerful in the 1970s and consequently so despised by the general public. Earlier battles by the unions had been justified and supported by the people who saw the working class as noble and decent. But the bitter and intense industrial disputes of the autumn and winter of 1978/9 helped change the course of British politics and ultimately the class system.

The Winter of Discontent, as it became known, saw a wave of crippling strikes across the country – and led to the election of

Margaret Thatcher. The situation was explained in the run up to the election by the Tory Manifesto.

"The old Labour Party was driven by an ethos of support for the working classes and indeed was funded largely by the trade union movement, by heaping privilege without responsibility on the trade unions. Their members were also usually either from working-class stock or upper-class Fabians... Labour have given a minority of extremists the power to abuse individual liberties and to thwart Britain's chances of success. One result is that the trade union movement, which sprang from a deep and genuine fellow-feeling for the brotherhood of man, is today more distrusted and feared than ever before. The crippling industrial disruption which hit Britain last winter had several causes: years with no growth in production; rigid pay control; high marginal rates of taxation; and the extension of trade union power and privileges. Between 1974 and 1976, Labour enacted a 'militants' charter' of trade union legislation. It tilted the balance of power in bargaining throughout industry away from responsible management and towards unions, and sometimes towards unofficial groups of workers acting in defiance of their official union leadership.

We propose three changes which must be made at once. Although the Government refused our offer of support to carry them through the House of Commons last January, our proposals command general assent inside and outside the trade union movement.

Picketing Workers involved in a dispute have a right to try peacefully to persuade others to support them by picketing, but we believe that right should be limited to those in dispute picketing at their own place of work. In the last few years some of the picketing we have witnessed has gone much too far. Violence, intimidation and obstruction cannot be tolerated.

The Closed Shop – Labour's strengthening of the closed shop has made picketing a more objectionable weapon. In some disputes, pickets have threatened other workers with the withdrawal of their union cards if they refuse to co-operate. No union card can mean no job. So the law must be changed.

Wider participation – Too often trade unions are dominated by a handful of extremists who do not reflect the common-sense views of most union members. Wider use of secret ballots for decision-making throughout the trade union movement should be given every encouragement. We will therefore provide public funds for postal ballots for union elections and other important issues".

So the romantic notion of the noble peasants once perpetuated by Romantic and Victorian poets was pushed to breaking point when trade union extremists tried to rise to political power. They flexed their muscles and ostracised the general public. The Tories cashed in on this with slogans like 'Labour isn't working'.

The union leaders of the 1970s were every bit as hungry for power as any politician and the ultimate outcome was the betrayal of those who trusted them. Edward Heath had taken the union leaders on much earlier than Thatcher but lost the battle due to his lack of charisma and affinity to the people. Heath was himself from a humble background but had moved on. He disrespected his background and considered himself a European Renaissance man. Aloof and cold he had no time for, or understanding of the peasants. He took us into Europe and then asked us if we wanted to stay. He understood the apathy at the heart of the English and probably understood that we would not retreat out of Europe. He felt threatened by the more able and classically educated Enoch Powell, and in sacking him after his non PC 'rivers of blood' speech, achieved what he wanted which was the total embargo on political debate around this issue. It seemed like Heath saw England and those who loved her as being in the way of what he wanted to create which was a European state. When Powell was sacked by Heath, the Dockers and the London meat traders marched to support Powell and his views on immigration. Left and right were not so clear cut.

At the time of World War One the English governing class was small and intimate, educated in a handful of public schools. In war it took up its customary right and duty to lead the nation. This narrow governing class supplied the bulk of the young junior officers, especially in the early years of the war, and therefore sustained an immensely higher proportionate loss than the nation as a whole.

They included the sons of politicians and poets. The Prime Minister, Mr Asquith: lost his son Raymond and the future Conservative Prime Minister, Bonar Law, lost two of his four sons, Kipling also famously lost his son John.

Anthony Eden, Prime Minister 1955-57 put it in his own words:

"The First World War saw the destruction of the world as I knew it. My eldest brother was killed in the first autumn and my father died a few months later. My other elder brother was interned in Germany, while my uncle, the commander of a squadron in the Royal Flying Corps, was shot down and captured. News reached me when I was in the trenches that my youngest brother, to whom I was closest in age and affection, had been killed at Jutland at the age of sixteen. When a few weeks later I heard, during the battle of the Somme, that my sister's husband had been seriously wounded nearby, it seemed to me that the worst that could happen had happened. Every single male member of the family, with whom I had spent my life before the war, was dead, wounded or captured."

Churchill, commanded an infantry battalion on the Western Front between 1915-16; Clement Attlee, who succeeded him as Prime Minister in 1945, was Regimental Officer at Gallipoli; Harold Macmillan, Guards officer, badly wounded on the Somme in 1916. It is clear that a governing class so painfully affected by the war would be likely to have difficulty in seeing it in perspective but the revulsion at the travesty went far beyond the governing class, which was only a very small fraction of the total population. They were a phenomenon which produced the 'Literature of Disenchantment' in some of our finest poetry.

In 1914 all the armies of the European powers were conscript armies, all subject to a draft of varying degrees of severity. In Britain there was no such precedent there was an intense national self-confidence and belief. Alone among the powers, Britain went to war with a volunteer army, and continued to depend on volunteers for the first two and a half years of war. The response was staggering. Here are some statistics:

298,923 men volunteered for the Army in August, 1914;
462,901 volunteered in September;
136,811 in October;
169,862 in November;
and 117,860 in December.

This makes a total of 1,186,357 volunteers by the end of 1914.

The catastrophe of the First World War wiped out a generation from all classes.

After the war the 1920s homes for heroes were structured for the needs and aspirations of Englishmen. The homes of suburbia were a pure joy, semi-detached homes with neat hedges lawns, and gardens and sheds. All an Englishman would want. The exteriors were clean cut an amalgamation of nature and man in harmony. The occupants were proud of their lifestyle, women were becoming freer from the drudge of Victorian days and the 1950s household epitomised this. Now these smart solid homes are being brought up by Japanese families keen to ape what they believe to be the very best of English culture.

In the 1960s, MacMillan seemed to symbolise the old order and yet he had an affinity to the lower classes that the political elite could never understand. He seemed to care. Possibly an old-fashioned feudalistic approach but he understood as did other upper-class politicians that the working classes were the backbone of the nation. They had experienced, as he had, the horrors of the trenches and witnessed the 'land fit for heroes' become a nation of social injustice and poverty for his fellow survivors. He became one of a select group of MPs on the left of the Conservative Party who argued that more should be done to help the poor, especially during the Great Depression.

He saw the damage mass unemployment could inflict on the fabric of society and this would help shape his economic policy when he became prime minister.

But the Macmillan government was rocked by sex scandals. This seemed to symbolise for the rebellious youth of the 1960s the moral decay of the British establishment. But the reality was just that the Tories were always getting into trouble for trying to get their 'leg over' whilst Labour were usually in trouble for trying to get their 'hand out'.

He was a critic of his successors. In his old age in the House of Lords in the 1980s, he praised the miners then on strike, asserting that they had "beaten the Kaiser's Army" and "beaten Hitler's Army".

In the last month of his life, he mournfully observed "Sixty-three years ago ... the unemployment figure (in Stockton-on-Tees) was then 29%. Last November ... the unemployment (there) is 28%. A rather sad end to one's life".

In the 1950s, working-class kids were proud of their hard working parents and supported by extended families. When Thatcher came to power in 1979 there was a complete change of attitude towards the peasants. The old working-class values had become marred by bullying trade union officials and the battle of power of the winter of discontent was ultimately the beginning of the political elite. Jim Callaghan, Dixon of Dock Green, was replaced by Wurzel Gummidge. Michael Foot represented the end of a Labour era, the idealist, with substance but no image or projection. A new political class was emerging that would only ever be focused on power at all costs. The political class were only interested in one thing, getting and keeping a job. Idealists like Foot and Benn were patronised by the new boys as the left were Left speechless, gagged by hopes of power and political expediency. They sold their souls.

Thatcher was focused on limiting the power of the unions, it was a power battle of epic proportions. Some working-class people managed to pull themselves up by buying council houses or investing in shares, but overall the working classes lost out in the end. Mrs Thatcher may have been a necessary evil but she threw the baby of our manufacturing base out with the bathwater. She always believed she took the peasants with her but they needed to join her class to become truly valued. She had massive battles with Tory wets like Willy Whitelaw and Sir Geoffrey Howe. Yet despite her battles she later said it was clear that "Every prime minister needs a Willy" so that's why Harriet Harman forgot about her in her information leaflet about 'Woman of political power'. She was obviously not considered a feminist, despite becoming one of the most powerful women in the world. Also of course she was never one for political correctness or gesturing unlike the politicians that followed. It was this dogmatic honesty which really made her appealing to the peasants.

She may have wanted to make everyone middle class, but she still represented the attitudes of the English peasants. She was not one of the political elite. She spoke for the people. In one case the UN requested that Britain take 10,000 refugees, but she refused on the grounds that there would be 'riots in the streets' if they were given council housing ahead of 'white citizens'. Mrs Thatcher even bizarrely proposed to the Australian prime minister, Malcolm Fraser, that they jointly buy an Indonesian island to resettle all the boat people. This forerunner of Oliver Letwin's 2003 idea for an 'asylum island' to take all of Britain's asylum seekers was only blocked when Singapore complained that it would set up a rival entrepreneurial city.

On the issue of the Boat People she also said that, "With some exceptions there had been no humanitarian case for accepting 1½ million immigrants from South Asia and elsewhere". She declared, "it was essential to draw the line somewhere". Carrington and Whitelaw were later convinced that public opinion was turning in favour of the Boat People but Mrs Thatcher retorted that those who were pressing the Government to help the Vietnamese boat people "should be invited to accept one into their homes". Very pragmatic.

In the 1970s, the battle was between the old top hats and cloth caps. But, there are now probably more millionaires on Labour's benches than on the Tories'. Especially with funding for peerages. So gone are the Tory toffs with their plumy voices and the 'aye by gum' image of the trade union leaders. The Conservative Party in parliament looks and sounds more like the annual gathering of the Estate Agents' Convention. The good old class symbols needed to be overturned so Cameron poses as a rare site, an Old Etonion out in trainers, and is filmed washing up the dishes on his web cam.

Well, when Britain was poised for the first big television debate from the three main parties, American image creators were called in and Cameron was told by Obama Aides to 'de-posh' himself.

Thatcher started this marketing development, she changed the face of the Tory Party by bringing in the new self-made men. The Wets did not last long in her company, they were gentlemen who could not bear to hear a woman screech and cry, it needed new men for this. They were the new self-made men. The 'get on your bike' more harsher tone of toryism. They had often moved up the class ladder themselves and were, unlike the feudalistic Tories, unforgiving about others who they believed should do the same. Government started to be run just like a business.

Significant changes had also taken place in the Labour ranks; there was a noticeable thinning out of the horny-handed sons of toil. Now, more women, and middle class and wealthy men were thrust upon the benches of Westminster known by some of their more down-to-earth colleagues as "the lily-white fingered lot". But Thatcherism did start the disempowerment of the working classes. In the 1980s, whilst Thatcher still spoke a language that the people understood, New Labour were planning their social coup.

So under Thatcher the working-class had been largely privatised, their values had been disposed of, they had to become individuals striving for wealth and power. Community values, which had supported them and held them together as a major part of their culture, were undermined and devalued as individualism took over. But life did seem more pleasant back then, even with shoulder pads and big hair there was still unity in the culture. Mrs Thatcher still expressed the voice of working-class attitudes, but under Blair the working classes were to be annihilated under a policy of cultural cleansing, as English culture was dismantled.

For the political class to eliminate the English working class this was not about social equality but social engineering. For the English, all the class structure did was categorise the different sections of one homogenous culture. To talk about class irritates the marketing ideologues who would rather look at targeting market segments and leave out class which is much too complex. After all the protectors of the working-class had deserted them. Call me 'Tony' created a new marketing phenomenon. He entered politics with no character until Rory Bremner created one for him. And then, when he knew who he was meant to be, he was the best thespian in the business. He even managed to overturn the old voting patterns. Traditionally, men voted Labour and women tended to vote Tory. Then there was the North-South divide with Labour voters being in the north and Conservatives in the south. But Blair was attractive to women and became acceptable, as he looked like, well a salesman really. He flashed his teeth threw his jacked over his shoulder, rolled up his sleeves and looked like, well a salesmen. He then got rid of any dissent, as Margaret Becket so aptly explained when interviewed about why more ministers did not speak out about going to war with Iraq, she said "We were all comrades". In contrast, "the old Labour MPs and ministers were 'a quarrelsome lot".' Ah so you mean there used to be party democracy Margaret?

Before the 1997 election, John Prescott, then Labour's deputy leader, said: "We are all middle class now."

On a TV documentary, Lord Onslow invited the Prescott's to lunch on his estate. Onslow paid Prescott several undeserved compliments, being well mannered, and the former Deputy PM set about insulting him in his own Manor. He whined on about his mum being the daughter of a Welsh mining family, who had to work in service in the wealthy homes of the Wirral when she wanted to stay with her family in North Wales. He added that Cameron's idea of social mobility is for people to "get on your bike, head down south and take the nanny and servant jobs available in Witney, Oxfordshire.

"You've got a chip on your shoulder," says Onslow. It was hard to disagree, with 'two jags' pouring forth about the plight of the poor and then being part of a Government that destroyed any sort of social mobility, bike or no bike. I think not John, those jobs that your old Ma did are being done largely by illegal immigrants and work for the likes of Baroness Scotland or David Blunkett. Lady Scotland's case had echoes of David Blunkett's resignation as Home Secretary in 2004 after it emerged that he had sought to fast-track the visa application of his lover's Filipina nanny. Bruiser Prescott was a relic of old Labour who knew only rhetoric not action other than his right hook, and of course caused much embarrassment to the new much slicker boys like Alistair Campbell and Peter Mandelson. These guys were not interested in the lower classes, but only those with the power to keep them in Government. You only need to look at the old Soviet Union to see how Marxism really worked and well blow me down this all seems too familiar.

They harboured many characteristics of the current political class. They set up a structure which they manufacture to their own political ends but have no intention of being part of this for their own family. They get their children into the best schools, whilst expecting the plebs to make do with the ones they felt were good for them but not themselves. President Blair wanted to demonstrate his dictatorship by stating that he had eliminated policy by politics and was basing his Government now on 'absolute' facts. He tried to prove this by introducing scientists to his Government so that policy could be based on 'actual facts' rather than just 'politics'. But when scientists started to state the truth as they saw it and it did not fit in with his political agenda they were soon sacked. When Nick Griffin was invited onto Question Time he was relentlessly bullied by the political class, gaining him some sympathy. However, much of a buffoon he is it was clear who the fascists were. Fascism is really only the view that you are the only ones who are 'absolutely right'.

In the past old Labour were about improving the lot of the poorer people. They saw the English peasants as proud, loyal industrious folk who deserved better and would encourage social mobility through their policies. The Victorians led a moral crusade and entrepreneurs like Cadbury's, Rowntree's, and Port sunlight, were feudalistic businesses who had a belief in humanitarian support. Social mobility in the 19th century was stronger than now with many people from poorer backgrounds going on to achieve great things. A good education is now shut down to working-class kids, but the middle classes are seizing every opportunity they can. The working classes had a great respect for high culture and education and always aspired to better themselves. But this was not in a Thatcherist vision of the working-class. She was more interested in them becoming capitalists, home owners and shareholders. Hence Tory voters. The traditional values were destroyed. She hated and feared the old trade union leaders and the muscle they were flexing and they were seen by the English public as bully boys, something the English despise.

The noble peasants we all knew and loved have now become an embarrassment to the political class. They are now the underclass. This new social grouping was created by welfare, the nanny state and the loss of national identity. They became the fodder for successive politicians who wanted to reinvent them in their own image. They took away their pride in who they were, took away their ancestry and their work ethic and worst of all, their culture.

Blair said 'education, education, education'. Our kids wrote education, eduction, edcatone. Get them into universities, by making universities which patronise and insult them. Reportedly you do not even need to be able to speak English at some colleges, to do rather well. The standards were lowered to draw in foreign revenue, whilst the foreigners they drew in never went home.

In 2008 an academic whistleblower, at a world-famous UK university, said: "Postgraduate degrees are awarded to students lacking in the most basic language skills. There are concerns that financial pressures to recruit overseas students for cash rather than quality could threaten the credibility of degrees. More than 60% of higher degree students are now from outside the UK."

With the Coalition Government now trying to resolve the financial chaos left behind by New Labour this situation could get much worse.

The post war project had encouraged the rise of a meritocracy whereby a good education for clever working-class kids, enabled them to compete with rich ones. The post war children were given all the opportunities our kids have lost.

"Indeed let us be frank about it – most of our people have never had it so good. Go around the country, go to the industrial towns, go to the farms and you will see a state of prosperity such as we have never had in my lifetime – nor indeed in the history of this country."

The smart working-class kids that got every opportunity to have the best education went on to achieve great things but what went wrong with those working-class kids? Why did those who were given the social mobility to become leaders, kick the ladder out for those who came behind them? Why did the smart arse kids that went to Grammar School and got all the social mobility they needed, just not lift a finger in objection, when the opportunities for the 'best' education was taken away from the poor but smart kids. The baby boomers just retired to their 50" TV screens. They had it all and their children will pay the price. Well maybe not exactly their children, probably just the children of those who weren't quite so smart or so lucky.

But the New Labour project is now in decline. Beaten at the ballot box in 2010 Brown was in shock. The political party who had created the worst disaster of uncontrolled immigration now argued for immigration to be controlled. Wow that's a turn up for the books! The working class have no affinity to either party and democracy is in ruins.

In the 2010 election New Labour Cabinet ministers were understood to be deeply uncomfortable about someone's decision to target the private schooling and privileged backgrounds of senior Tories. Inevitably the 'playing fields of Eton' smear against David Cameron rebounded as the spotlight was thrown on the privileged upbringing of many Labour ministers and MPs. It is estimated that 11 out of the 27 ministers with regular seats around

196

the Cabinet table had been privately educated. But, Gordon the son of a Presbyterian minister, tried to keep in touch with the common people, and rushed off letters to the contestants on the X factor whilst also making public statements about the health of Jade Goody. Jade was, after all just a Chav who made it to celeb status under the new world order of "yes you can" and "come on down".

Under Blair and Brown democracy was replaced by business managers. Lord Adonis took on Transport and Peter Mandelson made his comeback. Two ministers that never answered questions in the Commons could not be held to account. Senior jobs given to peers not MPs open interesting new debates about the role of ministers. As English society is in tatters and the justice system joins the ranks of the barking mad, we ponder the legacy that Mr Blair gave to us. When there were jobs created by the state we pulled in foreigners to do them and allowed our own people to rot on the dole or do an MA on the Beatles. The economic miracle for which the peasants were meant to be grateful, will now be paid back by their children. The conflict that could arise in the future between the generations could be lethal. Mr Blair achieved the longest period of sustained growth at the blessing of his credit card. Whatever happened to the monthly statistics of the balance of payments, figures that used to be headlines on a monthly basis on the news? They are now so off the scale that no one dare discuss. And there is no point thinking you can go to Iceland to save a few bob. They've lost your money too, so no more partying like a celebrity. The economy now resembles a Greek tragedy with harmony and a script as good as Mama Mia. And whatever happened to that old pillar of society the banks, once a bastion of reliability and respect? Now Captain Mainwaring has been usurped for Wilson the spiv. That old-fashioned slightly crusty institution that has held solid and dependable until the 1990s was taken over by international gamblers. We tragically look back to the days when bankers actually had banking qualifications.

Where did it all go wrong? Was it all down to Dick Van Dyke, yet again? Should we have listened to the advice that it was better to spend tuppence to feed the birds? Was it all Red Ken's fault he just poisoned off the birds and then Gordon sold the banks to us?

In my childhood, borrowing money was always frowned upon and budgetary prudence was vital. Bankers were highly professional and upright characters, known as pillars of society. Yes, 'pillars'. The traditional Bank Manager, knew his customers and made, almost paternalistic, decisions about customers based on knowledge.

"Over to you now Walker..."

Financial prudence in the past was vital to English stability. In a Christian culture the Bible was more about money than sex. Usury, or money lending, was banned, and debt was considered a bad thing. Bankers were meant to be safe professionals steady and trustworthy, you felt safe with Captain Mainwaring in charge and the old bank managers knew their customers and dealt with each on an individual basis. They did professional qualifications at a high standard and were considered to be the most trustworthy members of the community. Now, as it is estimated that 1,000 bankers earn at least £1 million per annum and they are rewarded for cocking up the system with huge bonuses. Apparently our best talent now goes into banking. Well the question is firstly why? We need our best talent in constructive things like manufacturing, and secondly if they are so good why did they fail so badly? The profile of banking was raised under Thatcherism so much so that Goldman Sachs said he was doing 'God's work'. The reality is that all the profit the banks ever earned during the good years of Thatcher and Blair was blown in the banking crisis and in 2010 the sad truth is that around £500 million is paid out by the Government every day, more than they received.

State control in a mixed economy was usually about the control and support of our fundamental industries. In the 1980s Lawson's vision of a share-owning democracy fulfilled three key aims: it meant that costly public services could be hived off; that the sales would raise billions of pounds for the Treasury; and that the privatisations would offer the public a chance to get rich quick and express their gratitude when the next election came around. Mrs Thatcher sold off our state assets. A very sad legacy to a once great industrial nation. And now Dave and Nick plan to sell our forests, but only the English ones of course, not the Welsh and Scottish. The English man will not notice.

Selling off the public sector really began in earnest in 1984, with the flotation of British Telecom. There had been other denationalisations but this was the first aimed at the 'man in the street' and overnight it took the number of shareholders in the UK from four million to five million.

In March the following year, in his budget, the Chancellor went further, promoting the concept of 'popular capitalism' in Britain. Said Lawson:

"Just as we have made Britain a nation of homeowners, it is the long-term ambition of this Government to make the British people a nation of shareholders too; to create a popular capitalism, in which more and more men and women have a direct stake in British industry and business."

Are you having a laugh?

The Victorians understood that production was always the future for survival just like the Germans and Chinese do now. But the benefit system which emerged, created idleness, and often cheating as part of a socially acceptable process. This was endorsed by the new ruling elite who were, of course, happy to do this themselves, strictly within the acceptance of the rules. But if the rules were bent, "sorry, an admin error."

As Britain as a whole became wealthier it has become more welfare dependent, more criminalised, more drugs dependent, more poor and with less social mobility. The Welfare state has roots that go back to the days of Elizabeth the first. In those times the support for the poor was Parish based so it was local, focused and monitored. The only issue was around the old post code lottery between St James and St John's. Workhouses came along much later and were meant to be places where those who said they could not get work, were given work to do. They became dire places and fell into disrepute. The problem with any poor laws throughout history is that they always became abused and were then amended to try and stop the failures in the system. The philosophers and politicians were always aware that people needed support but wanted to achieve this without taking away their work ethic, self-pride and independence. The 19th century review of the poor laws said much that is being said of our current system. The difference is that it all made sense to the politicians, philosophers and historians. They were basically speaking from the same ethos unlike now.

There was always believed to be a link between welfare dependency and crime in 19th century Britain. In 1834 it was said that "Parish aid has a tendency to remove all shame". This may have seemed harsh but the growth in the economy in the late 18th century and the charitable giving of the Victorians reached a new peak that would put Geldoff to shame.

The Times in 1885 recorded that the combined incomes of the London charities was more than the revenue of several European Governments. The average middle-class family gave 10% of their income to charity. The growth of friendly societies and mutuals were booming but eventually destroyed by the Thatcher policies.

So as we destroyed the working class we drew in economic migrants to chase the same dream. A poll in 2009 revealed that more than 7 out of 10 adults want immigration cut by over 80%. Just 1 in 20 adults support the current Level. The You Gov poll, which was commissioned by Migration Watch for the Cross Party Group on balanced migration, found that 79 per cent of people were "concerned" or "very concerned" about the issue of immigration. The 2010 election tried to ignore the voice of the people on immigration. Gordon was indignant at even being asked about it with his demise at Bigotsgate. He was exposed by an innocent Labour supporter who dared to have different views to the political elite. Nick Clegg was also exposed with his policy on an amnesty for illegal immigrants. The problem with the media presidential style campaign was that people were actually unaware of policies, particularly those of the Lib Dems. They were just concerned about whether they looked 'nice'. And that nice man Nick remembered everyone's names in the audience, whilst Gordon only had eyes for Nick, and as for Dave, well having been de-poshed he looked a bit lost.

When the tabloids revealed Lib. Dem. policies Nick was exposed and people change their mind. But somehow he still ended up in power.

The political class opened up England to anyone whilst the peasants invaded Europe for their stag parties. The foreigners who were liberated by the British got a bit of a shock as 'Tommy' returned to just urinate on them by way of drunken stag parties. The working class were once so proud they would clean their floors so you could eat off them. They had aspirations for their children and many great and successful people came from humble working-class backgrounds. They had a healthy respect for education, and the system in place meant they could break through the barriers as social mobility was possible. Now, the 'Land of the rising scum' it may be called by Richard Littlejohn, but who created this catastrophe of three generations of welfarism? Children now have all the rights in the world, but are tortured to death by their own parents in their own home.

It is beyond belief that, in 2008, in a bustling, energetic and modern city like Birmingham, a child of seven was withdrawn from school and thereafter kept in squalid conditions for a period of five months before finally dying of starvation. And now the cruel sport of dog fighting is rife in the Asian community.

Yet other children are so out of control they wreck the lives of others. Fiona Pilkington, was the mother driven by the action of bullies to kill herself and her daughter in a burning car. What made it worse was the utter failure of the police to protect this family despite their pleas for help. The mother contacted her local constabulary more than 20 times over a seven-year period but officers failed to respond because there were "not enough resources". Or the case of the 62 year old Raum Fox tormented to death by youths because of his learning difficulties, with the police powerless to do anything to help.

So people with learning disabilities are treated with less seriousness than those from ethnic minorities. The race hate crime team have no mercy whereas those unable to protect themselves at all are left to the mercy of others. The reality is that we should all be protected from crime equally, with no positive discrimination as this can lead to corruption in itself. Now that we have 'hate' crime do we also have 'love' crime? If some crime is more 'hateful' than others just because it is against a group that someone has deemed as a 'minority' then what about other minorities? Where does this discrimination stop? We then get to the fact that some people have more rights than others. Those with learning difficulties have always suffered from abuse as they are unable to articulate their frustrations and are not in a position of power to do anything about their treatment. Yet those from racial

202

minorities even if they are in positions of power are still given more protection. No one group should have more rights than another.

So how do we decide who has the most rights? How do we protect each group? Is it NOT ok for fatties to be lambasted, if they are genetically that way, but ok if they are just eating too much? Who decides? So whatever happened to the white working class English?

"In Dagenham, where I was brought up, the white working-class electorate, alienated by far-reaching social change and largely ignored by the mainstream parties, could vote for a BNP Member of Parliament. There is a sense of alienation on the part of white working-class people who are saying 'our jobs are being taken by people from abroad'." The former Archbishop of Canterbury.

Endless cases are quoted to support this statement. For example: a Somali woman with children in UK schools is entitled to state benefits, even if she is "a burden on the social assistance system", EU judges ruled yesterday.

"Nimco Hassan Ibrahim, who has four children, was told she must be given a council house because she was once married to a Danish citizen who briefly worked in Britain. A verdict in Luxembourg said parents caring for the children of migrant workers and resident in EU countries are covered under EU rules on freedom of movement – including those who cannot support themselves."

The people seem helpless to do anything against EU laws and a sense of frustration grows. Blunkett was one of the worst offenders as Home security in 2004, he praised the immigrants for the rich culture they gave us, assuming we had a bad one before, when this Island, was at least stable, with a unified culture. So he assumed the indigenous population were presumably work shy and useless. Well who made them that way Dave? Possibly he was thinking of his own household at the time as he was very keen to get an illegal immigrant in to look after his child rather than pay a qualified English nanny. Saved a few bob. So that joke that we need immigrants to work in an aging population slightly

203

mystifies me about what happens when they too get old. Oh dear haven't thought that far forward I don't suppose.

Whatever happened to the English working-class family? That riotous mix of genes and blood with feuds and love. This was particularly true of the cities where family was vital for survival. Melanie Phillips described that "Tony Blair knew that family breakdown was at the heart of the problem with British society and wanted to strengthen the two-parent family. But in a cabinet of feminists, libertines and homosexuals, he lost these argument hands-down. The result was the lame formula subsequently adopted by his Government that it supported marriage and every other type of 'family', too. In other words a relationship free-for-all."

Back to the American experience. "I believe the problems of the underclass are driven by the breakdown in socialisation of the young. Which is in turn driven by the breakdown of the family. But Britain does not have a Government or for that matter an opposition party, that is willing even to say that the family, traditionally defined, is crucially important, let alone act on that premise. There is little point in talking about solutions until the politicians are ready to admit that a problem exists."

New Labour politicians sneered at the image of mothers in 'frilly pinnies' and fathers dressed in shirt and tie for Sunday lunch during the Fifties as 'damaging'. The social stigma which had formed the structure of social cohesion but which discriminated against lone parents and children born outside marriage, was outlawed. The mantra was that marriage could provide stability, but it wasn't for everyone. The focus should not be on marriage, but on the welfare of the child and the quality of the upbringing, and ultimately the rights of the parents. This all went horribly wrong and left social chaos.

The Blair Government responded to this social chaos by forcing some parents on to state parenting courses so that mothers with children by multiple partners could be taught the basics of controlling their offspring. We now have instances when two 3-year-old boys were investigated by police for vandalism. I wonder how they manage to take down their statements. And did you hear about the mum who left her 3 year old alone in a car with another 3-year-old, who tried to beat him to death with a car jack. Taxpayers could pay out £27,000 of hard earned wages for that little dilemma as well. I wonder if the terrible twos are now being replaced by the terrible 3s. When two 10-year-old boys beat two 8-year-olds to within an inch of their lives there were eerie echoes of the James Bulger tragedy. The case and the minds of those involved were so similar that it begged the question again of whether those who are damaged should be allowed to damage others, as if it is their human right to do so. The Bulger case is likely to remain in the psyche of those who were so moved and disturbed by it at the time and the response of Ed Balls and Children's Minister Maggie Atkinson were incredibly naive.

Ed, commented on 15th March 2010 that the Bulger killers 'were not intrinsically evil and deserve a second chance in life'. And Edward Fitzgerald QC, representing Venables, no doubt with the blessing of the taxpayer through legal aid, said his murder conviction had cast "a long shadow over his life".

And now poor John is back inside for owning indecent images of children as young as two and some showed the rape of young girls. Still his new identity paid for by the taxpayer is very reassuring

"Venables claimed to be a 35-year-old married woman called Dawn Smith who abused her 8-year-old daughter, and offered to sell access to the child."

Let's leave the last words to someone who HAS had a permanent long shadow drawn over their life. James' mum told reporters after the comments by Maggie Atkinson:

"This woman owes James and me an apology for her twisted and insensitive comments. Then she should resign, or be sacked...

To say that his killers should not have been tried in an adult court is stupid...

They committed an adult crime – a cold-blooded murder that was planned and premeditated – and they were tried accordingly."

She added: "It is a shock to people like Dr Atkinson that children can be truly evil by 10."

Hence the muddle of family disintegration continues so over to Melanie Philips again:

"One in five cases examined by the Child Support Agency (CSA), no father was registered on the child's birth certificate. Too often the absence of a parent is directly linked to the crime, educational underachievement, drug and drink abuse, mental and physical ill health and other disadvantages that now blight so many of our children's lives and cause so much damage to our society and innocent victims. There are now areas in our country where committed fatherhood is almost entirely unknown and where children are simply abandoned to emotional chaos and blighted life chances. Mr Johnson appears to think the worst thing that can happen is treating people differently and hurting their feelings by criticising their behaviour. But treating everyone the same regardless of how badly they behave is a totally amoral position. It licenses people to behave badly and creates victims out of betrayed spouses or children to whom lasting damage is done. Since Mr Blair was first elected – and found himself facing within Labour's ranks an assortment of radical feminist man-haters, serial adulterers, cohabiting partners who thought marriage was irrelevant and gays – this Government's whole family agenda has been about putting the desires of irresponsible adults first and then crying crocodile tears over the human tragedies left in its wake...

"It has systematically undermined marriage by loading the financial dice heavily against married couples and in favour of lone parents. By doing so, it put a rocket motor under the phenomenon of mass fatherlessness. The result is that more than one in every four babies is now born out of wedlock — a terrifying indicator of social breakdown for which the taxpayer has actually been paying through the nose.

"In the past eight years, the benefits bill for lone parents has, according to maverick Labour MP Frank Field, rung up an astounding £50 billion. This massive sum has been poured into subsidising family breakdown. Has there ever been a society that has put its hands so deeply into its pockets to fund the mechanism for its own disintegration".

Yet middle-class individuals in the UK are endlessly harassed and targeted by mindless bureaucrats. Having recently been on a holiday to a Mediterranean island in a nice up-market holiday complex, I was surprised by the fact that no one confiscated my camera when I took a photo of my kids around the pool, there were no instructions how to wash my hands, no tedious warnings about chicken flu, bird flu or even swine flu.

So while the middle classes are harassed the underclass terrify the bureaucrats because they have no power over them, they just put their fingers up to them and walk away. The sad fact is that if Baby Peter had been middle-class, he probably would have been taken away from his parents and if Kyra Ishra's parents had not been Muslims and black, they would they have been 'pulled' for taking their kids out of school, torturing them and starving Kyra to death. This discrimination is going on endlessly in these Isles and the trouble with the modern UK is that the wrong people are afraid. The middle classes watch over their shoulders for the thought police, or the council for dropping a cheesy wotsit, whilst cruel killers are afraid of nothing, and accurately view the criminal justice system as a feeble joke.

The police, the courts and the social workers are increasingly fearful of the violent, conscience-free underclass, created by years of well-intentioned but disastrous socialism. Whereas the middle class are convenient targets who need to be kept in line, they will obey the law, turn up at meetings and hearings, and take their authority seriously, and off course, pay up.

So just get on with it and pay up. We need £650k to protect Baby Peter's killers as the names of his mother and boyfriend, were revealed by the newspapers. The boyfriend had apparently previously tortured his grandma but that may have been seen as normal behaviour.

With a catastrophic illegitimacy rate of some 40 per cent, not surprisingly family disintegration is causing a new breed of children, who are growing up, and who do not care about the naughty step or the lessons of parenting classes. So the process of concentrating on the child has all gone sadly wrong. Instead of removing children from mothers who were putting their children at risk they just put them back, putting the rights of the mother first. A further tragic outcome of feminism.

At last some people have the dignity to say just how naive they were and how horribly wrong they got it. Over to Martin Nearey from Banardos.

"It was clear that the welfare of the child was the overwhelming consideration of my staff. But, nevertheless, the optimum solution was for natural parents and child to be reunited. The whole direction of statutory and voluntary sector effort, it seemed, was directed at whether the family could be fixed. In time, that would probably involve the children returning to a home which might again descend into inadequacy and neglect. Why would we want to take that risk? Why would we expose a child to the possibility of further neglect? Tasked by Beverley Hughes in 2007 to see whether we might further reduce the numbers in care, and despite being keen to do so, I found it hard to deliver. I was challenged by troubled social workers, who whispered to me in tones which suggested they were struggling with the guilt of heresy, that the best outcomes for many children would often be much speedier separation from inadequate parents followed by early adoption."

And over to you Esther. Esther reflects on what went wrong whilst accompanying a friend to their children's sports day.

"They were forbidden to play any competitive sports. The Head Teacher takes the view that it is morally wrong for children to experience losing. So they played 'silly games' (the boys' description) – which nobody could lose – involving bean bags. The school didn't just over-protect the children; they protected the staff as well, to a lunatic extent. One day my friend was rung up and asked to come to the school urgently with a pair of tweezers. Luckily he was working locally. When he arrived, he found one of his sons had a splinter in his finger. None of the school staff was allowed to remove it because that would be an 'invasive operation'. My friend had brought the tweezers, as asked, and took the splinter out in a few seconds. After that, exasperated, he moved his sons to a different (private) school."

Well lucky him, but not for everyone though.

"Last Friday, I had the pleasure of watching the boys enjoying the drama and suspense of sports day at their new school. The whole event was deeply politically incorrect. There were plenty of races, and loads of winners. My friend told me with amusement that on his sons' first day at the new school, one of them got another splinter, and the matron removed it without a second thought. Why should this kind of common sense be a privilege only available to children whose parents can afford private education? It is pervasive, this over-protective nonsense. I have been a victim of the thought police myself. Not long ago, at an event run by a children's charity, a boy told me he had rung Childline because he was being bullied. 'Did you get through?' I asked with trepidation, since we can only counsel half the number of children who call for help.

'Yes,' he said with a wide grin. 'They were brilliant. I did what they said, and now the bullies are my best friends.' I was filled with delight, and told him so. 'I'm so happy,' I said. 'I'm going to give you a kiss.' And I did, on the top of his head".

Oh dear you were obviously reprimanded for child abuse Esther.

"The irony is that, to an extent, I blame myself for this rubbish. By revealing the extent of child abuse in the BBC TV programme Child Watch in the Eighties, I was part of the revolution in child protection which created these insidious jobsworths."

Well that's Life for you.

Look slick, smile broadly, roll up your sleeves and pretend you are going to do some work. Surround yourself with talentless sycophants, give the people easy credit diverting them from what you are actually doing to their land, and culture and you have the arrival of the leader of the new political class. And you could end up in power for a significant time, living off credit, sell off the nation and import cheap labour to keep businesses happy. Close a lane on the M4 and create your own way into London. Once you are finally kicked out you could be earning millions from the Iraq war and still be charging 150k per speech and 5 million for your memoirs. You could then try and become president of Europe, but oh dear, the luck may have run out by then.

It seems looking back that Mr Blair took over from Thatcher but John Major was in power for a number of years in between. It was almost as if both Blair and Thatcher took power away from him. He was not seen as 'cool' and whilst Mr B was busy creating 'Cool Britannia' Major, was easily mocked by the Blair PR men as reputedly "tucking his shirt into his pants". All this pants stuff was a sign of complete uncoolness unlike Mr B who seemed to epitomise cool, and surrounded himself with the celebrity culture. But Major historically may be redeemed. He may have had a list of things not quite achieved but not cocked up, other than Edwina. Stronger school inspection started, but not the Stalinism of today; privatisation was continued but with more restraint than New Labour, no host of new laws doubling the size of the 600-year-old statute book; none of the consequences of Iraq. But Major lacked the art of self-projection, the Cool Britannia look and art of public relations. He lacked the adventurous spirit for starting an exciting war; his links with the Americans were good but not servile. Major would lose any battle resting upon the cocktail values of the media, but history will recognise the substance, the economic achievement and the wisdom over the Kurds, as it will recognise in Tony Blair a handful of false coins and loads of debt for everyone. The ten year credit fuelled party is followed by one long hangover.

Cool Britannia was no more than the creation of spin merchants and marketing hype to sell the UK to a world audience. And didn't they just sell us off. The phrase was coined during the 1990s to exploit the popularity of various 'Brit Pop' bands, like Oasis, Blur and Pulp and of course The Spice Girls. And it also promoted 'Brit Art'. Various people who were thought to portray the image the Government was keen to promote were invited to 10 Downing Street to be photographed shaking hands with the Prime Minister. Few of them have held on to any long term endorsement of the party though. Noel Gallagher, who was a high-profile visitor to No. 10, said later, in his usual style: "If I could be arsed enough to vote now it would be for the Liberal Democrats."

So Mr Blair you earned all those millions and then expected to be president of Europe? Well so you should, you pushed through the Lisbon treaty which created the job you hoped you would get, but never let the English people have their say. But the Irish got to vote twice. Never mind folks you can have a referendum, but not the one you wanted. You can have one on the electoral system. No, I know you didn't ask for that but Nick did!

The political class rule by deception and disdain for the people. Trotsky's admirers, still see him as some sort of liberal democrat; or, a true champion of the working class. Those big-hearted Old Bolsheviks might have made the Soviet Union some kind of successfully egalitarian society, but when it became clear that the vast crime called the 'collectivisation of agriculture' would involve a massacre of the peasantry, Trotsky's only criticism was that Stalin's campaign was not sufficiently 'militarised'. He meant that the peasants weren't being massacred fast enough. And so this is true in England, but in England the massacre was a cultural one which mainly disenfranchised the working classes leaving them in the wilderness and their nation on its knees.

State Education is, as all Marxists know, a great tool by which to manipulate society. It is the supreme method of social and cultural engineering. You can take away history, rewrite it and promote your own agenda. It also allows the children of the rich, who live in the best catchment areas, to avoid its worst examples and they can get a proper education. Some of the New Labour elite, when in power, made religious conversions which were out of sync with their secularist liberalist beliefs just to ensure their children were not exposed to the state fiasco sausage factory they imposed on everyone else. Now we have an Equal Opportunities Minister but no equality of opportunities.

A damning report on income inequality by Professor Hills in January 2010 demonstrated that the richest 10% are now 100 times better off than the poorest. It makes extremely uncomfortable reading for anyone who wants a more equal society. The results are very sobering. One measure indicates that by 2008, Britain had reached the highest level of income inequality since soon after the Second World War. The richest 10% are now 100 times better off than the poorest, with individuals in the top 1% of the population each possessing total household wealth of £2.6 million or more. This is a wake-up call.

You could understand why the Tories would not mind the top quality Grammar Schools being eliminated, they could find sanctuary by moving into the best catchments areas, and no longer would their kids have to compete with smart arse council estate kids for entry to the old Grammar Schools. Much more egalitarian. It is more difficult to understand why the so called 'party of the working classes' would have wanted to deprive working-class kids of the same standard of education as those who could pay for the privilege. The reality is that the Marxists and cultural revolutionaries wanted to use schools as the great Marxist cultural reform. And indeed if you listen to those that push the policy of university for everyone nonsense, they argue that this is largely for 'cultural education'. It is the first time I have heard of getting pissed every night, waking up in strange places, and living on cans of beans, described as a 'Cultural education'. It was always just 'class surfing' for the kids of the well-off.

Now the top universities have had to start setting their own exams to sort the 'wheat from the chaff'. So what hope for the peasants who are stuck with the education system of mediocrity and have no way out via the Grammar Schools? Well the political elite never partake of that which they deem 'right and proper' for the peasants. But playwright Alan Bennett, came from a working-class background and decided to give all his scripts to the Bodleian Library, saying he was making the gift to repay the free education he received. He said of the endowment:

"I see this gift as an obligation repaid. I say with some pride that I had a state education. school, university – none of it cost my parents a penny. It's a situation young people today can only dream of and this is wrong."

212

Having told our kids to get in debt, leave the family and go to rubbish colleges where some offer only 5 hours tuition per week, this ludicrous system is now being undermined by the credit crunch. In 2010, 6,000 places are being cut, so you better get used to it kids. Tony got it all wrong.

So back to Harry Harperson being described by Peter Hitchen in 'A Class Apart':

"Harriet Harman, a fierce upper-class radical married to leftist union official Jack Dormer, managed to get one child (supposedly on the grounds of his religion) into the oratory, a Roman Catholic secondary that is a grammar schools in all but name. Soon afterwards, she got her second child into St Olave's an openly selective Grammar Schools (but not catholic) far from home. On this occasion faith seemed to matter less.

"Mr Blair himself, thanks to the catholic faith of his wife, was able to escape bad local comprehensives and get his children into the Oratory. To hope for a place at Camden School for girls; you must dwell almost within sight of its gates… once again, it just so happens that, discontented with the state schooling available for their daughters elsewhere in London, the Blairite pollster Philip Gould and his fashionable publisher wife Gail Roebuck moved to a property close to this excellent school – which is officially a non-selective comprehensive but has most of the features of an old style girls' Grammar School. Nearby also lives former Health Secretary, Patricia Hewitt, and her husband, the one time communist, now a judge, Bill Birtles. Their daughter also attended Camden girls. Another prominent Labour MP, Jon Ruddas, was recently found to have used his parliamentary allowance to buy a second home in Notting Hill, which just so happens to be in the catchment area of the super – and exceptional – Cardinal Vaughan Roman Catholic state school.

So Peter, quite rightly compares the liberal elite to the communist elite.

"In communist Moscow, those with red power, much more useful there than money, used it to get their young into the famous school number one, a great deal less equal than most Moscow comprehensives, but officially just the same. The Lenin High

School in Havana is for the sons and daughters of Fidel Castro's relational elite. In Pyongyang, North Korea's capital, the Mangyongdau Revolutional School is at least as exclusive as Eton."

The political class have no code of honour only rules that must be followed to enforce their agenda. The compliance culture is nowhere more clear cut than in parliament. The Legg report on the expenses scandal noted that 'a culture of deference had developed in Westminster' and also that there was a need to 'instill a more code where none existed...' Tony Blair famously said that the New Labour project would only be complete when the Labour Party learned to love Peter Mandelson, and this eventually happened, after Mandelson's return to Government in 2008. His sheer swagger won over the Parliamentary Labour Party immediately. But by 2010 he was on his way out again. Andy Burnham, reportedly said: "Peter loves the spotlight but it's time to leave the stage." When the Dark Lord published his book, Tony Blair, is alleged to have made a series of angry phone calls to try to halt publication of what he deemed a 'salacious' autobiography probably because he feared it would overshadow his own book.

But the political class always look for political opportunism never a point of honour. And when they were exposed by the Telegraph for the expenses scandals they were not only shocked by public reaction, they were positively indignant. Why would the taxpayer care about them spending our money, it was expected? And furthermore when any political scandal is finally exposed just bring on the 'enquiry'. An enquiry is a device which enables the politicians to do unforgivable things which they then apologise for, look shocked when it all goes wrong and initiate an enquiry which they feel vindicates them. This then enables them to employ very rich ex-civil servants and give them loads more money to spend months coming up with some meaningless statement. Chilcot said he was 'puzzled' by some of the processes he had come across during his enquiry. What he meant was he didn't believe a word, a bit like the Copenhagen summit on climate change. This was when politicians jetted from all over the

214

world, ate huge lunches and dinners, talked endlessly and then came to no agreement.

So let's celebrate 'sisterhood' with the Blair Babes, at the taxpayer's expense, of course. Harry Harperson, via the Equal Opportunities Office, produced a memorable pamphlet about the impact of females in power but forgot to mention the first female British Prime Minister. Poor Harriet was forced to apologise, yet again, very sincerely of course, for being stupid. This 'Women in power' fact sheet was produced mainly for schools, so no wonder it was inaccurate biased and only politically correct from a Marxist perspective. So Harriett did what her Government was unashamedly doing all the time, rewriting history to suit her political objectives. So who do we have in this document that was pushed into our schools to indoctrinate our children. It supposedly charts the most famous women in power. Well Mrs Thatcher is missing but there is the ex-major of slough, never heard of her. Oddly enough Shirley Williams, who would be considered a traitor by Harriet is also missed out but don't worry the first black woman MP is in their, as if anyone would care who that was, and no doubt Baroness Scotland figures somewhere. Look out for parked cars Harriet and just because you can get away quickly without leaving your details, what would you say about the underclass who do that in Peckham "Oh contraire, you plonker".

So are the political class responsible for the destruction of the English heritage and our working-class heroes? Blair's ideological position was that he was critical of Labour's dependence on the working-class vote. He wanted Labour to cultivate middle-class liberals. He believed Thatcher had changed the face of British society and New Labour should pick up the mantle. New Labour rejected the working-class voters as now just too small to worry about and now talk in disdain about their move towards the BNP. Labour's 'modernisation' depended on appealing to 'Middle England', and they believed that increasing numbers of people were moving away from the Tories and rejecting their policies. Labour was now embracing privatisation, low taxation and the free market. As Mr Mandelson famously commented: "We are intensely relaxed about people getting filthy rich." A far cry from Keir Hardie, Mandy.

In 1995, a new strategic document from adviser Philip Gould, called for a new 'command structure' involving 'less but better people, a new culture and a new building', with the leader as the 'sole ultimate source of authority'. Hence the move to Millbank, the establishment of the 'rapid rebuttal unit', the clique around Blair and the attacks on party democracy outlined in the 'Labour Into Power' document. The voice of the peasant was lost and the New Labour marketing project was so successful that the Tories could only attempt to replicate the formula rather than fight against it.

The modernisers' obsession with the media and its power to win or lose elections for Labour led to them actively cultivating the tabloids. Blair met with News International executives prior to the election, and in the minds of the Blairites such moves bore fruit when The Sun declared for Labour in the election. In the spirit of 'you scratch my back I'll scratch yours', Labour dropped both its proposed ban on cross-media ownership and any talk of taking Rupert Murdoch before a Monopolies and Mergers Commission inquiry. In 1997 the wind of change was strong enough to re-configure a Beverly Hills facelift.

New Labour were convinced that the key job of Government was to stay in power. They now understood that it was 'Middle England' who voted and mattered. The old image of the staunch Labour voters had gone and now they believed these people were unlikely to get out of their welfare padded sofas to vote. So they were replaced as Mandelson put it, by 'school gate mums and Mondeo men'. Political correctness also reigned and in 2003 a white paper was produced by Sir David King on energy use but nuclear power was not even mentioned. The old guard either just kept quiet or joined the party and set about feathering their own nest. Neil and Gladys were estimated to have earned over 10 million in pay expenses and pension over their 10 years in the EU in Brussels. Now back at the centre of British politics Lady Kinnock is in the House of Lords and Neil gave advice to Gordon. No wonder he had problems. The European parliament's secrecy over expenses means we cannot find out how much Gladys received in the daily attendance allowances but figures suspected are very high. Well not bad for a primary school teacher. At least the minority British parties are trying to be honest and get rid of the whole gravy train, whilst building up their political power, quite rightly through the funding.

A major problem with the political class is that the rules never apply to them only those they want to rule. Baroness Scotland is a prime example, her comments about taking on an illegal immigrant was that it was no worse than 'forgetting to pay the congestion charge'. This has the same ring as those MPs who dabbled in cannabis whilst at university, quite normal really it's just those peasants who we need to keep in line. For us it's just class cruising, goes along with sleeping in tatty flats and eating lots of baked beans on toast, shows we've seen life and of course, culture. We now have a class of political automatons and being economical with the truth is a must. Honesty in politics is now banned, since the New Labour project proved so successful at fooling the British voters. Why overturn a winning formula. So Alan Johnson who was indignant at getting caught out on the expenses fiasco spoke out about how he felt and was made to apologise for saying what he believed to be true. It is understood that 80 MPs objected to the castigations they got during the expenses row, so feeling was riding high. There is now potential for another new film 'Swindlers List'. Yet the politics of 'gesture' honesty is now big business. The Tories used this in the 2010 election campaign with their "We are the honest ones" approach. Whilst New Labour continued to say sorry, very sincerely, for almost everything.

So Gordon tried to tell us we were on the 'Road to Recovery', well Dorothy Lamour is dead so who will be his co-star, Harriet Harperson? His team kept trying to tell us he was a 'towering figure' on the world stage, well at 6'2" he probably was, especially when compared to the vertically challenged Nicholas Sarkozy and Silvio Berlusconi.

For the English peasant money must now be found at all costs, so they sell their bits on e bay. It is cited around a dozen kidneys have been on offer on e bay, whilst it was also reported that Peter Mandelson announced he was willing to 'serve his country', for a fee, no doubt. Well possibly we could send him to Afghanistan. Or perhaps laying table at the Whippit Inn would be more appropriate, still now he's got one over on Tony with his book, and the BBC gave so much time to promoting this, he may not be looking for a job anymore

The political expenses scandal in 2009 was a catastrophe and exposed their complete disconnection between the representatives of the people and the electorate. Yet MPs seemed baffled by public outcry, they'd got away with everything else hadn't they? In 2010 Gordon was gob smacked by the impact of Bigotsgate. He actually said what he meant, and we heard it. So the Dave and Nick double act, wobbles on and Dave cannot be allowed to forget during the 2010 election campaign, when asked ,what is your favourite joke and he replied, 'Nick Clegg'. You're not laughing now Dave!

In order to divert the populace from the dire economic crisis, the New Labour Government fueled the fears of the worried well, with swine flu and bird flu and then we were left with billions of pounds worth of vaccine. Whilst obesity is costing the health service £1 million per day we are told that large thighs protect you from heart attacks. Good.

Politicians are now even more divorced from their electorate and grassroots politics. Councillors are more complacent and don't do doorstep campaigning but are given 'self-promoting' funds. Our democracy is in tatters and not just because of the expenses scandal, that was just the final nail in the coffin, it is about the fact that career politicians have no connection with the people, despite the 10k per year allowance they get for 'bigging themselves up' to the electorate. Never mind, one MP felt the way forward would be to double their pay, and that would restore public confidence!! As the professional class of politicians' increases, there is now a crisis of funding as volunteers desert local parties. To increase funding, a new system of 'tithing' has been put in place by both major parties. In 2006 Sunderland council imposed a levy of 3% and a councilor who objected to this had to leave the party. Now New Labour and Liberals rely on tithing. The Conservatives are not obliged to donate funds but feel they really ought to do so. This is really state funding of political parties by the back door. But do the local taxpayers know? I think not. Not to mention the fact that councillors vote for their own remuneration. This also happened with MEPs who often feel no links to their political party other than the fees they need to pay them from the expenses they get from the EU. This tithing has helped the smaller parties, in fact UKIP quite honestly explain that they have grown threefold at the expense of the EU funding, and the BNP and Greens will do the same.

When the trade union extremists got rid of Uncle Jim Callaghan, the new breed of politicians would take no chances. Conviction politics was at an end and only power mattered for both parties. You see everyone needed to be as Mandy would say 'On message'.

But why do the politicians despise the common people and what happened to our democracy? After all MPs were meant to represent the people.

New Labour created a party that deserted the working classes and the middle-class political elite made up of Trotskyites and Marxists seized control but under a new disguise of cultural Marxism. Supported by much of middle England under the control of Blair they tried to create society in their own image and likeness and anyone who tried to go against this were termed to be 'politically incorrect'.

Now the police are under investigation as two female officers are put under surveillance by their local Council. Did they put people in a cell? Did they restrain them with handcuffs? Did they sneak up behind them and say "hello hello hello what's going on here then." No, they looked after each other's kids.

And surveillance is a vital weapon in the fight against, no not gang warfare, knife crime or drug barons, but parents who dare to break the rules and try to get their kids into decent schools. It may be wrong to try and get the best schools for your kids by hook or by crook but don't they deserve a good education? Just provide them with one can't you!

219

The old working-class Marxists at least understood the people and were honest about their agenda. Even the upper/middle-class politicians like Michael Foot and Wedgewood Benn were at least honest and genuine about the people and their aims. Yet when Michael turned up for remembrance Sunday in a donkey jacket, he was cast aside by the new boys. The old Labour Fabians like Foot and Benn loved the peasants in a kind of patronising way. The Gordon Brown who wrote a biography of the Scottish socialist politician James Maxton would probably not have been electable as British prime minister if he hadn't re-modelled himself. The transformation of Brown and Blair, made the socialist workers wince. There were individuals in Blair and Brown's cabinet who hated many policies but who stayed silent to save their jobs.

So let's explore the working-class credentials of the 'people's party'. "The defence secretary Bob Ainsworth attended Marxist meetings. Mandelson was a member of the communist league". Ralph Milliband, a well know Marxist writer has two sons, the Milliboys, who have done very well. So New Labour kept in check the working-class members who spoke out of turn as the political elite made their plans to eliminate the working classes and become a political ruling class.

The peasants often live in places in England where a dire shortage of state housing has become the most controversial political issue of our time. The statistics are stark. One in 12 council homes in England are now lived in by migrants, while the list of people waiting for social housing has doubled during Labour's time in power to 1.7 million.

So the answer is not to deal with the problems of immigration, broken marriages or fatherless children which is the prime cause of the demand for more housing, just build more houses. In any other context the logical approach would be to look at demand and supply side issues. With regard to housing the issues of the type of demand is never looked at, only ever plans for increasing supply. What about demand? So let's cover this green and pleasant land with more concrete housing jungles.

With the NHS the demand on the service is ever increasing but the Government has not the nerve to discuss a new service, yet the Americans use our NHS as an example of 'really bad practice'! It's no wonder really, the hospitals in London are now so congested that they are giving ambulance teams £38.50 bonus for everyone they actually manage to stop going to hospital.

The voice of the white working-class is barely allowed to intrude into British politics or culture. In metropolitan circles, where sneering at any minority ethnic group would be regarded as an outrage, white working-class opinion is all too often treated with suspicion or contempt as 'white trash'. The word 'chav', for instance, is now often accepted as a way of marking the behaviour of the working class, even though any similarly abusive description of ethnic minorities would lead to police inquiries. What is particularly bizarre about this approach is that, until recently, the white peasants were seen as an integral and respected part of our national life. Working-class heroes, like Michael Caine or George Best, were celebrated as national icons, their strong accents and easy self-confidence adored by the public. Working-class life was realistically portrayed in novels, films and dramas. Working-class culture was the driving force in popular music, comedy and sport. It was harsh, vibrant, often troubled but always cohesive.

Things have now got so bad for the working-class in our cities that a Sunday Times article on the subject of the disadvantaged doesn't dare mention race or ethnicity, but the images shown are all young white youths. No doubt some people covered by the official definition of 'Not in Education, Employment or Training' must be from ethnic minorities, but simply on numerical grounds it must be a predominantly white group. According to the ST, there are 1.1 million Neets aged 16-24. In the 2001 Census data there are only in *total* about 120,000 'blacks' in this age group. (Of course there are also South Asians, Chinese, etc, but no one will imagine that they are significant in the Neet phenomenon.) As to young 'blacks', they have a slightly higher unemployment rate than whites, but they also have a higher rate of continuing in full-time education or training. The only significance of blacks that I see in the Neet phenomenon is that young white uneducated kids have a tendency to ape the worst aspects of black urban culture: gangster rap, crack, petty crime, and general insolence. In London, especially, white yobbos often speak with a touch of Jamaican patois, which sounds really comical.

So white youths are now causing major concerns and the issue needs to be resolved. The drunkenness in Oldham got so bad that the Government tried to deal with it by blaming the sellers of alcohol not the drinkers. To blame the drinkers would be very judgemental, so just which seller are we to blame? The pre-load from Tesco, the girl's handbag that hoards the surreptitious booze, the first bar or the last bar? One location can't be responsible for the violence that arrives at its door. And with a stabbing every week in Oldham, a solution has now been found. You make them form a post office style queue for the bar. So the Government has managed to destroy the post offices in our villages, and reinvented this orderly structure in the bars of Oldham. So as the bouncers call customers up one at a time, they now have to count how many drinks they have. When interviewed customers just replied, we'll have to go somewhere else then, we're not queuing here all night! Another bizarre solution to a self-inflicted problem.

So let's leave the white trash in their post office queues, let them now become fodder for middle-class derision.

Traditionally the white working class also had strong political opinions and could be heard pouring forth political views in many of the working-class social centres. Pub politicians and philosophers were the norm. Johnny Speight said of his character Alf Garnett: "I didn't create him I just grassed him up. I get most of the material for Alf standing around in pubs, all I really am is a recorder."

Johnny Speight created Alf Garnet as part of his own Marxist views, but instead of despising him the English peasants loved him. The spoutings of the bigoted Alf was the humour which Speight himself felt was the best way to puncture prejudice. But what do you do when the peasant audience do not see your socialist views? Johnny Speight may have had working-class roots but his politics came in line with much of the middle class left wing. This was the culture the Marxists and the liberals wanted to destroy. Benny Hill was a simple gentle soul who came to epitomise peasant culture, but he was removed from his BBC slot, despite the fact that he was at the top of his career with his shows being sold all over the world. From the late 90s onwards free speech was censored in public places and views were sterilised until they became outlawed. The working-class people were intensely political and cared about their nation and the institutions that held them together. In the 90s political correctness stopped open debate and the peasants were emasculated. The Garnets were ultimately replaced by the Royal Family.

The music halls had been the roots of English comedy and were enjoyed by all classes who identified with the performers. Later on comedians like Morecambe and Wise learnt their art in just such forums. Humour had not been very multicultural but epitomised traditional English culture. The entertainment producers like Billy Cotton, came from working-class roots and probably would have been appalled at the current elitism at the BBC.

Now the humour from the middle-class derides what is now sees as the underclass. Vicky Pollard of Little Britain is a chav, the latest object of middle-class derision. But the sneering reveals more about the detractors than the chavs. There is at least some honesty coming from Chav princess Cheryl Cole who said: "If we weren't doing this, we'd be on the checkout at Tesco."

This candidness is unlikely to be echoed by the likes of the Geldoffs or the Jaggers, just names born to be famous.

So comedy has also been re-configured, and it's really not funny. Comedian Jim Bowen echoed the fears of many when defending his friend, the late Bernard Manning.

"Who is to say that a man dressed up as a woman who goes around urinating everywhere is not offensive, but Bernard Manning's jokes are?" Bowen has a point.

He felt the condemnation of this undeniably popular working-class icon, smacked of hypocrisy.

"Make no mistake," he said. "Bernard Manning's great 'crime' was not that he was a comedian who told offensive jokes, but that he was a working-class comedian who told offensive jokes."

One of the Idle-class comic Jimmy Carr (Royal Grammar School, High Wycombe; Caius College, Cambridge), in contrast to Manning, Carr is a regular fixture on our television screens and on the airwaves. But a more recent gaff about the troops in Afghanistan, saying that we will have more talent in our Paralympics team, may have gone too far.

Then there's the sneering, offensive humour of Little Britain, brought to us by Matt Lucas (Haberdashers' Aske's, Bristol University) and David Walliams (Reigate Grammar School, Bristol University). Targets of the show include single parents, disabled people, the incontinent and people with mental health problems – but of course it's all perfectly acceptable, because Lucas and Walliams, unlike Bernard Manning, are good middle-class chaps who went to university when university had some currency.

The reason why such non-working-class comics dominate today is that commissioning/production positions in television and radio are now monopolised by middle-class (and mainly Oxbridge) graduates. Thirty years ago, when Billy Cotton Jr was head of light entertainment at the BBC, working-class, non-university educated writers like Jimmy Perry, Eric Chappell, Galton and Simpson, Dick Clement and Ian le Frenais were responsible for much of the comedy output. Because they knew their territory and had a genuine empathy for the class they came from, the comedy they produced laughed with the peasants and not at them.

To answer Jim Bowen's question, it's the middle-class, Oxbridge-educated television and radio supremos who decide that Manning is off limits, but the equally unsavoury humour of Lucas and Walliams, Carr and Baron Cohen is not. Sachs being Jewish and very exclusively middle-class relieves him of sanctions, as he is just too intelligent, or Lenny Henry's ridicule of working-class black people is allowed because he's black. If only Bernard

Manning had gone to the 'right' school and made it to Cambridge, who knows – he might even have ended up being nominated for an award.

One of the best portrayals of the way the social structure operated in England is through the gentle humour of Dad's Army. It's timeless success represents a continuing reproach to its 'I'm going to be as shocking as I can to create effects", successors. From the 1980s onwards, 'comedy' series have mainly sought to shock and revolt viewers rather than amuse them. They provoke the laughter of embarrassment rather than appreciation. From the conflict of interests between the blustering, blimpish, middle-class Captain Mainwaring, superior in rank only to the laid back, public school-educated, Sergeant Wilson, and the continual battle between the Home Guard and the ARP wardens, led by the town greengrocer, Hodges, over who got to use the church hall as their base of operations. Dad's Army revealed how such an upheaval affects social standing.

For all the mockery, rivalry and human frailties, the platoon and its members are ultimately portrayed as heroic. Captain Mainwaring is pompous but basically decent, patriotic and of course brave. When he occasionally loses command, things rather fall apart and his worth is understood. He is also kind and patient and gives time to the indulgent storytelling of Corporal Jones recognising his value despite his advanced years. He is also understanding of Godfrey's weak bladder. He also does not bear malice even sharing the base accommodation with the much more disagreeable Air Raid Warden Hodges. For the millions of people around the world who have seen the series, as well as the pure comedy, it also demonstrates the essence of, we need to say, the British character, as if I leave out Frazer I'm doomed. The problem is that the working class of England today have no vision of society beyond the acquisitive – no version of themselves or their habits as anything other than transitional, on their way up or on their way out. The working class are now not proud to be such but being working class is, at best, a waiting room for people who aim to become middle-class if possible.

So why aren't the peasants revolting?

The working classes were broken by Thatcher, fooled by Blair and ignored by Brown. Mrs T was surprised by the ease with which England surrendered. People were willing to see their society lose the unions and its nationalised industries – even the status as a society. The English working-class had been docile and careless for years. The people were so quiescent, so demoralised, so drunk, so fearful of outsiders, so drawn to fantasy and spite and so lacking in purpose as a social group.

"By the late 1990s, the working class were no longer a working-class – their traditions, habits, and jobs, even in some places their speech, and were given over to new forms of transcendence offered by celebrity culture and credit cards and the bogus life of the fantasy rich. Depression among the children of the poor, many of them third-generation unemployed, has been recorded as being the worst in Europe. And yet, weren't their lives supposed to be better? The leisured poor were Blair's gift to Britain, people who craved not values but designer labels and satellite dishes."

The loss of social values of the English underclass has left them in a poor state. The political class are nervously aware and lack respect and affection for them. They have no values and no common belief system to hold them together. Their depression is of epic proportions. The sense of community and traditions which held those people together has been dismantled by people who had a grand political scheme and what is left is cultural disorientation. The pride in nationhood and traditions was removed by those who could not identify with this and wanted to destroy the old world order. They were the powerful ones, the political class. They held the money and the political power. Others who should have acted were silent, too obsessed by their own lives trapped in their own bubble. The political elite held all the cards, and these people were an embarrassment. A people who lose touch with their culture, lose touch with themselves.

"Since the English working class became the underclass any energy is driven towards criminal activity not political reform. The London mob were dismantled by the political classes and moved to Essex. They now lack the revolutionary urge – but today the tendency has become nearly sociopathic. The radicalism of Cobbett Hazlitt, Orwell and the programme of Robert Owen – these writers were all there, spry with their times, but we see almost nothing of their influence on the English today. No one is prepared to oppose the exploitative relationships that define their lives? No one. There is no objection. There was no real objection during the premier years of fat cattery, still with us despite the crunch, when bosses were taking salaries 75 times higher than their average employee. The working class of England take their deracination completely for granted. Disenchantment is the happy code that informs every byway of the underclass: service jobs, celebrity dreams, Lotto wins, leisured poverty on pre-crunch credit cards, it's all there, part of the story of an English people whose grandparents never had it so good. The younger ones laugh in the face of diminishment. Or they turn to drugs. They now speak easily of the decline that they inherited. They say 'it's just life'. They should rightly blame us." The baby boomers had it all.

We do not talk now of pride, of battles great, we don't celebrate Agincourt just Bonfire night and now some bizarre American festival of Halloween. The English working class are far ahead of every other European lower class in the sheer energy of their indifference.

The hunger for distraction among the English working class is nothing new, but what is new is the need to find a sense of national belonging in that distraction rather than in their own cultural history which the political class have put in a waste bin for us. Since the loss of national identity supporting the English team is all the peasants have left to focus on. Fans are moved to paint their faces red and white not on election day, not even on Armistice Day, but on holiday in Majorca or at international fixtures where 22 men will struggle to score goals. The statistics show that English fans abroad will still turn to violence in this situation faster, and more regularly, than any other football fans in the world.

Fans identify nationally, with their own history and seem to see themselves as warriors. Whilst at home patriotism is banned. So as the footballers pathetically let us down, where can we turn for our inspiration. We used to have patriotic songs, beliefs and of course our narrative history, which showed we were one of the most powerful countries in the world, yet just a small island. Robert Burns was in no way a simple nationalist and a wild patriot – he died in the employ of the British Excise – but his work nevertheless captures the essence of Scottish working folk on the brink of the industrial revolution.

Orwell's view of his England relied on a notion of self-respect for the English working class. He believed in the transcendent ability of the English to be their gentle selves in the face of adversity. Perhaps he would have been disbelieving to see how the English poor have themselves become conjoined to their own adversity, distanced from their own collective powers and distracted from their best traditions of non-acceptance, dreaming of goods and fame as being great and lasting values. Or maybe he always knew it and wondered why no one was saying it. At the close of Homage to Catalonia, as he arrives back in England, we find this sentence:

"And then England – southern England, probably the sleekest landscape in the world. It is difficult when you pass that way, especially when you are peacefully recovering from sea-sickness with the plush cushions of a boat-train carriage under your bum, to believe that anything is really happening anywhere."

But now they may have tried to eliminate it and say it doesn't exist but "class is back – but no longer just working class, but with an added distinction 'white working class'. If class inequality is making its way back onto the political agenda, this is because there are legitimate issues and grievances to be discussed and debated. Classism and scorn for poor white people and their perceived 'culture' is rampant and deemed to be socially acceptable, with 'chavs', NEETs (Not in Education, Employment or Training) and hoodies publicly reviled and ridiculed. It's an issue that few in education are willing to acknowledge, but white working-class girls and boys are the worst performing groups in secondary education

Unlike the working-class heroes of the 1960s who came out of the Grammar Schools, the social mobility of the poor has been removed and they are now second class citizens. It may have been a plot to remove their social mobility, and it certainly proved effective. The children of the lower classes now have to attend schools which feed them a diet of PC, sociological twoddle rather than academic excellence. Academic rigour is not something the lower classes have a right to, unlike in days of old, this is only for the middle-class kids. The lack of respect for authority, which has been encouraged, has also led to 'student power' with kids being asked to be on the panel for teacher selection. Now the Teaching Unions are complaining that teachers are being humiliated by students. One student had reportedly called a candidate humpty dumpty, well it's not racist, and so I suppose that's OK. And other pupils stopped teachers getting promotion as they had given them detention in the past. One teaching candidate was even asked to sing when he was being interviewed for a job by a pupil!

Now there is a fear that a debate on class seen through the lens of race could be counterproductive and harmful. Well perhaps they should not have engineered the situation we are now left with.

So the white working class are the losers in the struggle for scarce resources, while minority ethnic groups are the winners. In these terms, the white working class has been left behind by multiculturalism, or indeed because of it.

If New Labour were to succeed in their attempt to make England multicultural then the culture of the English had to be destroyed. In their rise to power the so called party of the people, so disregarded the peasants whose pride in Englishness had held them together. The Marxist political elite's dream was coming true. So they need to legislate to keep them under control, and take away all their values and morality which had been given to them by their ancestors and cultural heritage. Free speech was eliminated and the surveillance state was introduced just in case things got completely out of hand. The Scarman report said that "Positive discrimination to tackle racial disadvantage was a price worth paying" but for who, certainly not him.

So whatever your educational needs, the UK can meet them. Let's sell our kids chance at university and get people in from abroad to pay. Is this really us?

"There are more than 3,000 educational institutions that welcome international students in the UK. You can choose from a variety of routes through the education and training system. It has an exciting, fun culture. The UK is a cosmopolitan place to live. Many thousands of families from around the world have made the UK their home, creating a richly diverse, open-minded, multicultural society. There are also more than a quarter of a million international students in the UK at any one time.

You've probably come across the UK's vibrant popular culture through its music, television and films. Now you can find out what it's like to be a real part of it. This is after all the home of Robbie Williams, Coldplay, Radiohead, Michael Owen, David Beckham, Jude Law, Ewan McGregor and Kate Winslet. UK people like to get together and enjoy themselves. Theatres, concerts and art galleries can be found in all large towns and cities; big sports events take place every weekend; pubs and restaurants are everywhere." So come on over. But wait a minute be cautious folks. Remember what was said by that academic 'whistleblower'.

"The academic, at a world-famous UK university, says postgraduate degrees are awarded to students lacking in the most basic language skills.

There are concerns that financial pressures to recruit overseas students for cash rather than quality could threaten the credibility of degrees.

But Universities UK says there are "rigorous" checks on standards.

The number of overseas students taking higher degree courses, such as masters and doctorates, has soared – rising more than eightfold since the mid-1990s.

More than 60% of higher degree students are now from outside the UK.

Overseas students have been seen as a lucrative source of revenue – with the Higher Education Policy Institute calculating payments to universities of almost £1.5 billion per year in fees plus £2.2 billion in living costs".

And this was in 2009 before the coalition took over and exposed the money spent on higher education. The money promised for our kids is just not there now so it is likely that more foreign students will be needed, and more student protests will take place.

Is it any wonder that overwhelmingly, the BNP's most fertile territory is in the white working class. So how did the mainstream parties manage to lose these voters?

It would appear that the efforts of the political class to embrace different communities and reduce discrimination against minority ethnic and immigrant groups may accidentally have sent a signal to some poor white voters that their needs are being ignored.

The kicking out of Red Ken and the massive vote for Boris Johnson in many outer boroughs in the 2008 mayoral election almost certainly resulted from voters in boroughs such as Bexley, Bromley and Havering feeling "left out" of Ken's London.

In areas where migrants have settled, councils have had to deal with the complex issues raised by the sudden change in their population. Because England is a very centralised country, the Government's resource allocation mechanisms cannot accurately provide sufficient resources to match the needs of areas with large migrant populations.

The Government tried to justify the flood of immigrants by saying that they would boost the economy and increase overall output. So they put our kids out of work and told them to get into huge debt and go to college, not to do the lower paid jobs that their families had been proud to do for generations. They had already eliminated many of the jobs but those that were left were filled by immigrant labour and our kids were taught that they were too good to do these jobs, everyone had to go to university. What a joke!

The 1960s seem light years away, from the days when actors such as Albert Finney and Michael Caine built careers on working-class chutzpah. Today, the left is often suspicious of such people, seeing them as a threatening, racist 'underclass'.

Why does Orwell always get it so right. Here is Orwell on the working-class culture.

"The genuinely popular culture of England is something that goes on beneath the surface, unofficially and more or less frowned on by the authorities. One thing one notices if one looks directly at the common people, especially in the big towns, is that they are not puritanical. They are inveterate gamblers, drink as much beer as their wages will permit, are devoted to bawdy jokes, and use probably the foulest language in the world. They have to satisfy these tastes in the face of astonishing, hypocritical laws (licensing laws, lottery acts, etc, etc.), which are designed to interfere with everybody but in practice allow everything to happen. Also, the common people are without definite religious belief, and have been so for centuries. The Anglican Church never had a real hold on them, it was simply a preserve of the landed gentry, and the nonconformist sects only influenced minorities. And yet they have retained a deep tinge of Christian feeling, while almost forgetting the name of Christ. The power-worship which is the new religion of Europe, and which has infected the English intelligentsia, has never touched the common people. They have never caught up with power politics. The 'realism' which is preached in Japanese and Italian newspapers would horrify them. One can learn a good deal about the spirit of England from the comic coloured postcards that you see in the windows of cheap stationers' shops. These things are a sort of diary upon which the English people have unconsciously recorded themselves. Their old-fashioned outlook, their graded snobberies, their mixture of bawdiness and hypocrisy, their extreme gentleness."

And that is it, the Victorian laws were put in to control the mass population but still allowed them to function in a way that they kept the dignity and respect of the other classes.

The English working class have had everything they held dear ripped from them. Their faith has been undermined, along with

232

their noble aspirations and values. They have been taken into state control and live in riotous estates where they smoke crack, joyride cars and have their senses dulled by mindless computer games and cable TV and social mobility is now one of the worst in the developed world. The English working class are all but gone, to their middle-class aspirations. Big Brother says we are all global now and hence nothing in their politics is any longer about the peasants, or indeed any people, it's about a few marginal constituencies. So don't expect anyone out on your doorstep unless you're a marginal swinger. And you peasants, well forget the high ideals of your forefathers, the work ethic, and any spiritual belief you may have had, just get on Big Brother.

So the English peasants have had the sage and onion stuffing knocked right out of them and the curry and chips of the 1970s has been replaced by pure curry. They seem to have been over run in their own manor. The ruling political class see no problem with this. They get better restaurants, cheaper labour for their builders and nannies, but they live in the nicer areas, and get their kids into the better schools. The middle class just got much better at seizing their opportunities.

The sad thing is that the working-class kids who had the benefit of Grammar School education are the baby boomers who now just return to their homes and hope something will change. The peasants did have a political view but they were destroyed by PC and state fascism. They did have beliefs, which were protestant Christian, and they were destroyed by secularists. They did have a pride in who they were but this was eliminated by multiculturalism and the destruction of English heritage.

The peasants may have been poor but they had their pride. In 'It's a long way from Penny Apples', the author Bill Cullen now a multimillionaire asked his mother why despite being poor she gave money to the nuns?

"To help the poor," she said.

"But aren't we poor," he asked.

"Not at all son, you're not poor haven't you a roof over your head, clothes on yar back. Gumboots on yar feet. Good food every day. As healthy and strong as a young bull, you are. With a

233

mammy and daddy, who minds ya and loves ya. No son, we're not poor. We're very rich."

The irony is that the Accrington PALS who were mercilessly wiped out by a war that used the peasants for political points, are much like our boys currently in Afghanistan. Our troops are sent out to Afghanistan to fight the Taliban. The problem is there are two brands of the Taliban, one lot who are blowing up innocent bystanders in Pakistan and which the Pakistani Government are trying to stop. But the Afghanistan Taliban are the ones the Pakistani Government were supporting when they were in Government in Afghanistan and they would still support them just in case they get back into Government in Afghanistan as they don't want them as an enemy on their borders. Never mind the complex issues of getting supplies into the land-locked country. It has now been sorted. You see the troops have been struggling to get supplies through so they have brought in security companies to protect the supplies. The security companies find the easiest way to do this is to pay protection to the Taliban. The Taliban don't squander their money on foreign holidays or bling, they just buy more guns to shoot our troops. Hence in the best form of Greenist Government it's all sort of re-cycled. It's a shocking and sobering thought that during the first war in 1839 the Foreign Office made a statement that said to the effect that "no foreign power could ever hold Afghanistan".

Our troops are still proud of who they are, they are proud to be British and Jock, Taff and Paddy jog along just like they did pre-devolution. But much of this identity is about what is still held dear in the forces, because it is understood that without the unity of identity it would all fall to bits. But generally our proud working-class people have changed and you have to ask what would Jade Goody have epitomised as one of the peasants if she had been born 20 years earlier? She has been pretty slagged off by much of the media and has gone from saint to sinner in quick succession, back and forth, just for the circulation figures. She was a victim of the social engineering project successive Governments have felt was so successful. She was brought up on a sink estate, as a child came to know both drugs and crime, and was barely educated. She then lived the dream which became a nightmare when she was projected to celebrity by Big Brother and from that point on became a media chattel to be manipulated and exploited till the day she died.

There was her ex-crack addict mum, Jackie, demanding "privacy" before selling her grief in a world exclusive magazine deal and Jade's cheque book death-bed wedding to Jack Tweed. Ridiculed for being thick, vilified for being racist, and finally sanctified in death. It was a resounding comeback for the Bermondsey kid. The ultimate testament to the reality TV era where all that matters is fame, money and taking an "incredible journey". She was after all just an Essex girl.

Comedians and writers shamelessly promote the stereotype of the young women from Essex. The view is that they usually apply significant amounts of fake tan, giving them a glowing, orange, appearance, while they are also known for their bleached blonde hair with jokes like: "Why do Essex girls wear so much hair spray? So they can catch all the things going over their heads." These young females could appear typically in the big towns in England. Long-blonde hair, flashing their knickers, showing their boobs, with a bottle in one hand, low-cut tops and a short skirt, complemented with white stilettos they can often be seen dancing around a handbag at a club with their friends, usually enjoying alcohol. But the attitude and disdain for these people is about their loss of all dignity. These girls would have been the factory girls who worked hard all day and went to the palaise in the evening. They courted 'nice young men' and got married supported by the extended family and mostly lived happily ever after, content with their lot and proud of who and what they were. Another favourite joke is: "What do a bowling ball and an Essex girl have in common? Chances are they'll both end up in the gutter." Sad how things change.

The current social landscape is one of the quiet, invisible business of the people being walked over, and saying nothing, and thinking that's just the way it is. The disdain for the people of England that is shown by our politicians is demeaning and short sighted. Poor old Gordon as Prime Minister was caught out saying what he actually thought and believed in:

"Visiting Rochdale earlier today, Prime Minister Gordon Brown met briefly with 66-year Gillian Duffy, who briefly discussed with him her concerns over the national debt, tuition fees, welfare policy and immigration.

Surrounded by a scrum of photographers and journalists, Brown listened intently, did his serious face, then did his smiley face, and declared it "was very nice to see you, take care".

And then he got into his car and drove away where, unfortunately for Brown and Labour, the following conservation was recorded:

Gordon Brown to aide: "That was a disaster... You should never have put me with that woman. Whose idea was that?"

Aide to Gordon Brown: "*What did she say?*"

Gordon Brown to aide: "Everything. She's just a bigoted woman, said she used to be a Labour voter. It's ridiculous."

It is, absolutely ridiculous Gordon. What was the woman on about. You don't need people like this. Normal, hard working, working-class people they are a thing of the past and should be consigned to the litter bin.

In patronising these people Gordon you revealed your own vanity and other politicians seem to think they are also removed from the peasants. But our leaders of the past inspired us and we were a people at one with each other and the rest of the social structure. George Orwell reflected on this as the bombs flew over during the Blitz of 1941.

"Looked at from the outsider even the cockney and the Yorkshireman have a strong family resemblance... and even the distinction between rich and poor dwindles somewhat when one regards the nation from the outside. There is no question about the inequality of wealth in England. It is grosser than in any European country, and you have only to look down the nearest street to see it. Economically, England is certainly two nations, if not three or four. But at the same time the vast majority of the people feel themselves to be a single nation and are conscious of resembling one another more than they resemble foreigners. Patriotism is

236

usually stronger than class-hatred, and always stronger than any kind of internationalism".

But, downtrodden, our kids just shrug and say "Whatever". But is this real, have our kids really given up on what was so important to their ancestors?

At the moment when it seemed likely that England might be invaded, Anthony Eden appealed over the radio for Local Defence Volunteers. He got a quarter of a million men in the first twenty-four hours, and another million in the subsequent month. One has only to compare these figures with, for instance, the number of conscientious objectors to see how vast is the strength of traditional loyalties compared with new ones.

"The intellectuals who hope to see it Russianised or Germanised will be disappointed. The gentleness, the hypocrisy the thoughtlessness, the reverence for law and the hatred of uniforms will remain, along with the suet puddings and the misty skies. It needs some very great disaster, such as prolonged subjugation by a foreign enemy, to destroy a national culture. The unity of the people of England has been developed by the slow alchemy of centuries of unbroken culture."[40]

So is it too late for the peasants to redeem themselves, were they important or even necessary? Has the destruction of English culture, resulted in the end of the proud peasants of England?

"They have given us into the hands of the new unhappy lords,
Lords without anger and honour, who dare not carry their swords.
They fight by shuffling papers; they have bright dead alien eyes;
They look at our labour and laughter as a tired man looks at flies.
And the load of their loveless pity is worse than the ancient wrongs,
Their doors are shut in the evenings; and they know no songs.
We hear men speaking for us of new laws strong and sweet,

---

[40] George Orwell, 'England My England'.

Yet is there no man speaketh as we speak in the street.
It may be we shall rise the last as Frenchmen rose the first,
Our wrath come after Russia's wrath and our wrath be the worst.
It may be we are meant to mark with our riot and our rest
God's scorn for all men governing. It may be beer is best.
But we are the people of England; and we have not spoken yet.
Smile at us, pay us, pass us. But do not quite forget.

For we are the people of England, and we have not spoken yet.[41]

---

[41] G.K. CHESTERTON The Secret People

THE END?

So what really did happen to the English? Were they just too tolerant? The political elite are always speaking for us telling us what we think, and what we are. They explain and describe us as what they would really like us to be. But is this tolerance they bleat on about really an English characteristic? Jack Straw described us as 'dangerous'. Was the veneer slipping and was he saying what he actually thought about us rather than just what he wanted us to be?

The English were definitely arrogant about their country, but the tolerance came from this arrogance because they always knew they were the best and they just tolerated everyone else. So we need to ponder, is God still an Englishman?

I think this silent and lofty disinterest of the English was abused by the political elite who wanted to destroy the national identity which had historically always put a damper on any ideological, political and social revolution. This unified culture was, for the social revolutionaries, just a 'bloody nuisance'. So they created a political revolution without even having the decency to tell us.

As part of the New Labour revolution, those on Planet Politics had to marginalise the indigenous culture and take control of their history by removing its narrative story. They had to take over the education system and out great institutions like the BBC. They had to create new institutions and loads and loads of quangos. They had to expand the public sector and create their own rules of engagement and fill them with mindless bureaucrats whose main ideology was anti-nationhood. They had to create laws which silenced free speech and debate.

The peasants, who had always historically dealt with politicians in their own inimitable way, needed to be eliminated. The foot soldiers and the English archers needed to be broken up. It was they who were the real danger. But 'our boys' were still needed for Iraq and Afghanistan and continue losing their lives for an ideal that the politician had written off, but which keeps them fighting; Patriotism and a belief in the sanctity of their own culture.

So the peasant were put on the dole and immigrants were brought in to do the jobs created by the Blair boom. They took over their houses and schools, especially in the cities, and the peasants were driven out. Education was taken over by those who wanted to change the world and create a social liberal utopia and everyone then had access to equally bad education; unless, of course, you could afford to pay for it or move into the best catchment areas. When we talk about the political class, we talk about everyone involved in this political engineering.

When England was taken away from the English, the middle-classes were so busy using their credit cards to understand what they were losing. The peasants were silenced by political correctness and welfarism. When the credit bubble burst, reality struck. Bigotsgate may have just been the final epitaph to a troubled Prime Minister, but it was significant in that it symbolised the extreme contempt with which people were treated, and whilst Blair may have been able to sneer his way through this, Brown was a different kettle of fish.

As the spin men and lawyers took over, our once proud nation was sold off. New laws were then put in place to keep us under control. The equality laws were put in place so employers can be sued for cases of 'unwanted conduct'. This means that if someone says a comment or joke in the workplace and it is heard by a third person who is offended by it, they can sue the employer. These laws are to protect minority or disadvantaged groups. Well, who are they, and what about us? At a time when businesses are struggling for survival, the British Chamber of Commerce estimates the cost of just interpreting the legislation to be £190 million. Never mind more jobs for lawyers. This law is 'barking mad'. I suppose the only one who is going to be 'offended' by that comment is dogs. Are they protected under the legislation as a disadvantaged group?

Our salvation as a nation was our unity. In the past, the moral code was clear, if you were a criminal you were put in jail and Sergeant Dixon felt your collar. Good and evil, right and wrong, were understood by everyone, it was the culture. Now the victim is arrested and the criminals are set free. Their human rights to commit murder must not be infringed. A crazed Iraqi immigrant who stabbed two doctors to death, won the right to say in Britain because he would be a threat to the public if deported to his homeland and this would also breach his human rights. So are the people of England less valued or just stupid?

I'm not blaming those affectionately termed Taff, Jock or Paddy. They had a right to their own identity and as a minority culture, they were positively encouraged to do so. They were not to blame for the demise of the English, but they will be pleased to dance at their wake. The people who needed to eliminate the English were the middle class liberal elite who despised the history of English domination and wanted a global future. When Mr Heath hooked us up to Europe and silenced the debate on immigration, the whole process had begun.

Now the Coalition Government jogs along quite nicely, because the very useful thing with the political elite is that they are all the same type of people, so a coalition is 'no probs'. They all come from the same background. When Nick Clegg is reported to have asked Rory Bremner, "Do you do me?" He is said to have replied, "Do YOU do you." Well, now Nick actually does Dave. So why on earth would Dave and Nick not get on? And, of course, as power is the main motivator they score on both points. The problem is, of course, the rank and file members are like the feuding families at this marriage of convenience. The outcome of all this political manipulation and control is that our institutions are now further from the people than they ever were. The BBC of Lord Reith was firmly at one with its people. Now, the politicians and the institutions live in another world and blindly say what the country is, feels and wants. There is constant reference to 'our country' without actually even understanding what they mean by 'our country'. Now people are angry and frustrated.

But political satire had always been perfected by the English, and Churchill, for one, had great fun doing this and was also wise enough to understand that this was a vital part of democracy. After all, he'd fought against those who took politics too seriously. Now we have those very people in Government. The jollity that used to follow on from political trips with sing songs between the media and the politicians like Mrs Thatcher were soon stopped by the New Labour spin doctors, who did not want their mask to slip for one minute. This good humour and satire showed that politicians were not infallible and that sending each other up was fine. When Mrs Thatcher was said to have invited a left wing correspondent to lunch, he reportedly stated that he would not attend because he did 'not like her policies'. She is said to have replied, 'Yes, but does it spoil your appetite?' It all proved ultimately that the world and history could not eliminate the English but the political class possibly could.

'The danger is not always violence and force. Those we have withstood before and can again. The peril can also be indifference and humbug, which might squander the accumulated wealth, of tradition and devalue our sacred symbolism. To achieve some cheap compromise or some evanescent purpose'.

With all this political gesturing the need for satire and humour has never been greater. It has been said that satire died when Henry Kissinger got the Nobel Peace Prize. English humour died when PC took over and eliminated free speech. The historical basis for liberalism must be the Enlightenment when God was challenged and Man became supreme. The irony is that the tenant of the enlightenment was free speech or as Voltaire explained: "I may not agree with what you say, but I will defend to the death your right to say it." No one ever thought that Voltaire's position on the Enlightenment could have ever been overturned by the 'thought police'. You can burn books in America but not in England. It seems the English have been silenced and their jokes are inevitably racist.

But when Andy Murray said he would "rather support anyone than England in the 2010 World Cup", and Alex Salmond, who was asked if it was an error that he signed a card thanking Diego Maradona for scoring the 'Hand of God' goal that knocked England out of the 1986 World Cup – intimated that it was "just a wee joke. Where's your English sense of humour?" Sorry Alex, it was taken away from us by the Scottish Raj. So as the Scottish promote their 'wee land amid the mists and midges of the highlands' a number of famous Scots have come out of the heather to do this. As anthem Caledonia whined on, Sir Sean Connery, Lulu, Amy Macdonald, Sandi Thom, Eddy Reader, Brian Cox, golfer Sam Torrance, triple Olympic champion Chris Hoy, and international rugby players Thom Evans and Kelly Brown, combined to present the anthem Caledonia against the background of iconic Scottish scenery. I wonder how many of these celebs actually wanted to stay and live in Scotland. Hum. Only joking, Alex.

The English character was always different, and understood internationally to be so. We were not demonstrative like continentals but understated. George Santayana, American philosopher in 1922, observed 'The Englishman... is disciplined, skillful and calm – in eating, in sport, in public gatherings, in hardship... he is the ideal comrade in a tight place; he knows how to be... well-dressed without show, and pleasure-loving without loudness... What ferocious Anglophobe... is not immensely flattered if you pretend to have mistaken him for an Englishman'. This stereotype may not have been the reality, but it was the aspiration of every Englishman. Good behaviour came from national pride, the work ethic and a sense of responsibility to the family and the community.

Well, Dave and Nick now have their own problems. Crime is reported to be most common in England and Wales and the 2010 'Stop the Rot report' rebukes our police forces for giving up the streets to yobs. I don't see Dave hugging many hoodies now, but then, he's got a few other problems too. NHS standards are now 19th in the world, just before Turkey and the criminal neglect of children continues to rise, whilst revolting students ransack the Tory HQ.

The unity of English culture had developed over 2000 years. Everyone understood the rules of behaviour. By taking away the structure of the culture, the Government now has to create legislation to control not only behaviour, but actual beliefs. Our current society has too much choice but no basis from which to make our selection. A big shop where we can have all we want but what we need is so fundamental to our existence, and we can't buy it, we can only earn it or believe in it.

Edmund Burke warned of this political arrogance when the French Revolution took place and we should heed his words as political dogma takes over, we are in danger of slipping into complacency. By denying our culture and heritage, we are denying our history and ancestry, things that have been learned over generations.

"To deny the voice of past generations and to discount their views and attitudes is arrogance beyond belief, because a person's moral estimation is limited, people are better off drawing from the general bank and capital of nations and of ages than from their own intellects".

Our roots, which we encourage every other culture in our Island to visit, are about our history, our heritage and our ancestry. It's about being inspired by the Wiltshire Hills or a Churchill speech. It's your culture, its been passed down to you through the ages from generation to generation. It's the narrative or your history how you came from where you were to who you are. It's the views that inspire you and the stories that you will never forget. It's the words that are repeated through generations, and the songs that are sung. The playground games that are played out and the tales that made you proud. The baby boomers grabbed it all and shut their doors. They just prayed their children could be saved.

So beware the politicians whose objectives are certainly not nationalism, but their own political ideology, which is fine, if it is supported by the People of the Nation. As Edward Abbey, an

American essayist wrote, 'A patriot must always be prepared to defend his country against his Government'.

So let's get back to the days when Raymond le Blanc spoke English and Des O'Connor was white. We need to get back to the days when footballers stubbed out a Woodbine before running onto the football pitch having bump-started their lungs first thing in the morning. So here we are, where we are, and it's not a happy place. English common sense that evolved over centuries has been replaced by verbal diarrhea. Is God still an Englishman? Well, Alistair Campbell said quite firmly, "We don't do God". They obviously didn't.

So get those bells attached to your legs and get out your knotted hanky. Roll a few eggs around and go wild and use your conkers without protective clothing. Take no heed of the thought police and be not afraid. As Churchill once said: "If you're going through hell, just keep going..." But more importantly tell your kids, how good it was. Your culture is something you need to pass on to your kids. Culture is not the preserve of the hoighty toighty, but the sum character of a nation. The soul of England cannot be destroyed by the Milliboys, the EU, New Labour, or the Nick and Dave show.

But always beware of words for they can be manipulated to destroy you. When Tiger Woods told his wife he was just going out to 'play a round', it was a misunderstanding anyone could make. It was also just a little slip when Cameron said we were 'junior partners to America in 1940', Churchill would have turned in his grave. So when in battle an English commander sent a message to his foreign ally stating that 'Things are getting a bit sticky', no one came to support our boys. What the Englishman meant was, "We're being slaughtered". Anyone watching a 1940s film, would have understood, but not a foreigner.

"The Stock Exchange will be pulled down, the horse plough will give way to the tractor, the country houses will be turned into children's holiday camps, the Eton and Harrow match will be forgotten, but England will still be England, an everlasting animal stretching into the future and the past and, like all living things, having the power to change out of recognition and yet remain the same".

Can we really allow them to destroy us and eliminate what we had that was so precious?

So back to George Orwell:

"Talk to foreigners, read foreign books or newspapers, and you are brought back to the same thought. Yes, there *is* something distinctive and recognisable in English civilisation... It is somehow bound up with solid breakfasts and gloomy Sundays, smoky towns and winding roads, green fields and red pillar-boxes. It has a flavour of its own. Moreover, it is continuous, it stretches into the future and the past, and there is something in it that persists, as in a living creature. What can the England of 1940 have in common with the England of 1840? But then, what have you in common with the child of five, whose photograph your mother keeps on the mantelpiece? Nothing, except that you happen to be the same person."

To go into a tourist shop in London and ask for an England flag and be given the Union Jack by an English youth, who then proceeded to tell me that he did have the 'red and white one' but it was not the English flag, it was the football flag. The English flag was the red, white and blue one, made me sad.

When we speak of England, we are not talking about a football team, or even just talking about a national ideal or stereotype, but a civilisation that stretches across who we are and who we ever wanted to be.

"Above all, it is YOUR civilisation , it is you. However much you hate it or laugh at it, you will never be happy away from it for any length of time. The suet puddings and the red pillar-boxes have entered into your soul. Good or evil, it is yours, you belong to it and this side of the grave you will never get away from the marks it has given you..." (Orwell, The Lion and the Unicorn)

When we look at England now we see a repressed nation, that once proud identity denied by those who would plot to destroy its existence. So don't let them tell you that you don't exist. You do, but only if you insist you do. And don't deny your past; we are all sinners and few are saints, that's just the human condition. Our culture may not have been perfect, of course it wasn't, but it was certainly held up by other nations as an example of something that definitely worked. So be proud and embrace your past and don't let them destroy your future. The present must be in a permanent dialogue with the past in order to shape the future. As Mr Churchill said, "A nation which has forgotten its past, can have no future."

But let's not be glum, let's begin our end on an inspirational note:

"This royal throne of kings, this sceptred isle,
This earth of majesty, this seat of Mars,
This other Eden, demi-paradise,
This fortress built by Nature for herself
Against infection and the hand of war,
This happy breed of men, this little world,
This precious stone set in the silver sea,
Which serves it in the office of a wall
Or as a moat defensive to a house,
Against the envy of less happier hands –
This blessed plot,
       this earth,
           this realm,
               this England".[42]

---

[42] William Shakespeare. *Richard II*, Act II, Scene I.

Bibliography

Ali, Hirsti. Speech for CORE (January 2007).

Ali, Nazir (The Times, 2nd February 2008).

Ali, Nazir (Telegraph 24th June 2008).

Bagley, Katie (The Sun, 3rd October 2008).

BBC Mobile news. Public policy group Reform (2nd September 2008).

BBC Trust. Impartiality, Fact or Fiction (Seminar, 22nd September 2006).

Bentham, J. Anarchical Fallacies (published 1816).

Betjeman, John. Collected Poems.

Bigotsgate (Sky News, April 2010).

Bowcott and Travis. The Thatcher Papers Quotes (Guardian 30th December 2009).

Bowen, Jim/ Manning, Bernard quotes – Neil Clarke (Guardian.co.uk, 19th June 2007).

Bulger, James. (BBC New Mobile 14th March 2010).

Burke, Edmund. 'Reflection on the Revolution in France'.

Campaign for an English parliament.

Chadwick, A. Heffernan, R. *.Labour Phenomenon.*

Chesterton, GK. 'We are the people of England –The Secret People'.

Churchill, Winston. Speech 4th June 1940.

Cooke, Peter (Observer, 8th July 1962).

Coe, Seb. On the Olympics.

Coughlan, Sean. 'Whistleblower on Degrees' (BBC News education reporter, 17th June 2008).

Churchill, Winston. Speech to Parliament (4th June 1940).

Cullen, Bill. Mammy and the poor – ' In praise of penny apples'.

Cunningham, Mr (The Sun, 17th October 2008).

Daily Telegraph, 6th September 2007.

Dalyell, Tam. Speech (14th November 1977).

Dorling, Professor Daniel. Sheffield University Report.

Eden, Anthony. Letters about First World War.

Eliot, T.S. 'Notes Towards the Definition of Culture'.

Elizabeth I. Speech at Tilbury.

Ellian, Afshin (2002).

Elliott, Francis (Sunday Times, 5th November 2007).

Gorer, Geoffrey. People Newspaper 1951 Reader survey conclusion.

Green, Sir Andrew. Migration Watch (Daily Mail, 10th February 2010).

Green, Sir Andrew (Migration Watch, 4th November 2007).

Gould, Philip. On New Labour command structure – *The New*

Guardian Education (19th August 2010).

Hitchens, Peter (Daily Mail 15th November 2008).

Hitchens, Peter. *The Broken Compass: How British Politics Lost its Way*.

Ishra, Kyra (Guardian 30th December 2009).

James, Clive. 'Pointless Changes' (Radio 4, 16th and 18th February 2007).

Johnson, Paul. 'Off short Islander p62'.

L'Angleterre, Sur. 'Hippolyte Taine Notes'.

Littlejohn, R. (Daily Mail, 21st December 2007).

Littlejohn, Richard (Daily Mail, 8th January 2008).

MacMillan, Harold. about the profumo affair.

MacMillan. 'Never had it so good speech' (20th July 1957).

Major, John. On politicians.

Manning. B. Obituary (Daily mail, 20th August 2007).

McKeever, Paul (metro.co.uk).

Mulholland, H., Gentleman, A. Income Equality Professor Hills (Guardian, 27th January 2010).

Murray, Charles (Civitas in association with the Sunday times 2001).

Murray, Charles. 'The Underclass'.

Nearey, Martin (GMT, 24th January 2009).

NEETS (Telegraph, 19th June 2008).

Parfitt, Andy (Controller of Radio 1 Statement).

Phillips, Melanie. 'Why Labour Despises the Family' (Daily Mail, 27th July 2006).

Phillips, Melanie (Daily Mail, 10th March 2008).

Posse, Saxon. Smiley Culture Cockney Translation 1984.

Powell, E. 'Rivers of Blood' (20th April 1968).

Powell, E. St. Georges' Day Speech (23 April 1961).

Priestley, JB (Broadcast 5th June 1940).

Priestly, JB. *Saturn Over the Water* (1961).

SAMA 82, Report.

Sentamu, John. Sermon (November 2005).

Sentamu, John. Sermon (22nd March 2007).

Sentamu, John (19th October 2010).

Shakespeare, William. *Henry V*.

Shakespeare, William. *Henry IV*.

Shakespeare, William. *Richard II*.

Singh, Amar (Evening Standard, 10 January 2007).

Sunday Times 2nd April 2008

Straw, Jack. The Brits (Radio 4, 10th January 2000).

Swift, Jonathan. 'A Modest Proposal'.

The Guardian, 25th August 2006

The Myth of St. Bob (The Independent, 17th June 2005).

The Observer, 5th December 2004

Titanic (Daily Telegraph 9th Aprl 1998).

Tory Party Manifesto 1979.

Tweedy, Neil. On Baby P (Daily Telepgraph,15th November 2008).

Tweedie, Colin. Interview (Radio 4).

Observer, 3rd August 2008.

Orwell, George. *1984*.

Orwell, G. 'England my England'.

Orwell, George. 'The Lion and the Unicorn'.

Orwell, George. 'Essay on the English Language'.

Orwell, George. 'Working Class' (Lecture: F. Mount, 26th November 2010.

Osborne, John. By John Raymond New statesman 1957.

Transworld Education home page. 'Come and study in the UK'. Voltaire

Wake up to Wogan listener (Radio 2).

Watts, Peter. Pearly Kings – Death of the Cockney (Time Out, 2nd July 2007).

Wells, Norman. Family Education Trust, 'too much too soon'.

West, Ed (World New, 8th July 2010).

Wikepedia reports on the charge of the light brigade.

Wise, Sara. *The Blackest Streets: The Life and Death of a Victorian Slum.*

YOUGOV Poll. Stats on public perception of immigration (Daily Telegraph).